Ethico-Religious (

# Ethico-Religious Concepts in the Qur'ān

*Toshihiko Izutsu*

McGill-Queen's University Press
Montreal & Kingston · London · Ithaca

© McGill-Queen's University Press 2002
ISBN 978-0-7735-2426-2 (cloth)
ISBN 978-0-7735-2427-9 (paper)
ISBN 978-0-7735-7051-1 (ePDF)

Legal deposit third quarter 2002
Bibliothèque nationale du Québec

Printed in Canada on acid-free paper that is 100% ancient forest
free (100% post-consumer recycled), processed chlorine free
Reprinted 2007, 2010, 2015

This book was first published in cooperation with the
McGill University Institute of Islamic Studies as no. 1
in the McGill Islamic Studies Series.

McGill-Queen's University Press acknowledges the support of the
Canada Council for the Arts for our publishing program. We also
acknowledge the financial support of the Government of Canada
through the Canada Book Fund for our publishing activities.

**Library and Archives Canada Cataloguing
in Publication Data**

Izutsu, Toshihiko, 1914–
Ethico-religious concepts in the Qur'ān
First published in 1959 under title: The structure of the
ethical terms in the Koran.
Includes bibliographical references and index.
ISBN 978-0-7735-2426-2 (cloth)
ISBN 978-0-7735-2427-9 (paper)
ISBN 978-0-7735-7051-1 (ePDF)
1. Koran – Ethics. I. Title.
BP134.E819 2002    297.5    C2002-900228-1

This book was typeset by Dynagram Inc.
in 10/12 Times.

# CONTENTS

# FOREWORD

THE REPUBLICATION OF THIS BOOK IS A CAUSE FOR MUCH PLEASURE. IT HAS been out of print and out of circulation far too long. At the time of its original publication in 1966 it was one of the finest, if not, indeed, the very best study of the Qur'ānic world view ever to have appeared in a Western language, and it has lost none of its significance with the passing of time. The Qur'ān is the Scripture of the Muslim community, which now numbers one-fifth to one-quarter of the world's population. It is a keystone of the great Islamic enterprise of the past and a continuing source of guidance for the Muslim community in our time. As such, it has been among the most influential writings of all human history. It has, however, been little understood outside Muslim circles and still less appreciated. For many years there was a paucity of serious Qur'ānic studies in Western tongues. Material setting forth the Qur'ānic message objectively, in detail, and clearly was simply not to be had. The situation reflected a broad disinterest in Islamic matters among Western scholars and even more among the Western public. Izutsu's work went far toward remedying this lack, though at the time of its publication it did not receive the attention that it merited. His masterful and lucid analysis offers an exposition of the Qur'ān's teachings that was unequalled at the time and is still among the best we have available.

In the interval between the first appearance of this book and the present, much has happened to evoke a greater interest in all matters Islamic, including the teachings of the Qur'ān. Both developments in communication and technology that have drawn the world closer together as well as specific events have contributed to a burgeoning desire among the Western public for knowledge of Islām and the Muslim peoples. Happenings in faraway regions of the Muslim world have affected the lives of people elsewhere directly and powerfully. Places that many people could not have found on a map a decade ago are now household words that appear in the headlines of our daily newspapers. The Iranian Revolution of 1979, which brought to power a government claiming an Islamic base and putting control in the hands of the clerical class, not only resulted in important international realignments in the Middle East but had repercussions in other places as well, including Canada. One result has been an expanding interest and curiosity about Islam. An unintentional but important by-product has been a veritable explosion of literature about Iran, Islām generally, and, in particular, the Shi'i branch of Islam. Where before there was little information to be had on many aspects of these subjects, now there is such an abundance – growing with every passing day – that it is all but impossible to come to terms with it.

The Gulf War but especially the terrorist attacks on the United States, culminating in those of 11 September 2001, have reinforced the awareness of Islām and the desire to understand the principles and convictions that it represents. These events have also, in their turn, stimulated the growing flood of literature relative to Islām. Although Professor Izutsu's studies did not have contemporary political or military events in mind and do not directly address the problems that arise from them, they are nevertheless timely and of immediate relevance to our present situation. They offer a brilliantly conceived, carefully crafted, and insightful analysis of the Islamic world view to which statesmen and diplomats, as well as scholars and the general public, should pay serious attention.

There are two aspects of this important book that are, perhaps, of more interest to scholars and specialists in Islamic Studies than to others. One is the masterful way in which the author contrasts the Qur'ānic world view with the outlook of pre-Islamic Arabia. Using the poetry of the pre-Islamic Arabs as well as statements in the Qur'ān itself, Izutsu has analysed the attitudes and values characteristic of the people among whom the Prophet Muḥammad appeared and to whom he preached his message. He has shown both how the Qur'ānic world view diverges sharply from that of pre-Islamic Arabia and, at the same time, how it incorporates elements of the old pagan Arab perspective, modifying them to fit within its own scheme of things. The study thus shows the rise of Islām to have involved both continuity and change in Arab life. This approach has two important consequences. One is to bring great clarity to the Qur'ānic message. The other is to locate the Qur'ān firmly in the cultural and historical context in which it appeared. In consequence the Muslim Scripture, which is otherwise often difficult, becomes much more readily understandable and its impact easier to grasp.

The other aspect of Izutsu's study that deserves particular notice is the innovative method he employed to describe the concepts in which he was interested. He proceeds by a process of semantic analysis that determines the semantic field of each of the ethico-religious terms studied. Every term in the text is surrounded by other words that constitute its field or its structure. The meaning of a term, he argues, is to be understood through its relation with the words that surround and accompany it. In effect, the method allows the Qur'ān to interpret itself. His method and the way in which it is to be employed are presented at length in the first section of the work. It is important not only for the light it throws on the Qur'ān but is applicable and useful for the exposition of other texts as well.

The Muslim community looks upon the Qur'ān as the literal word of God delivered to the Prophet by an angel. Along with the example of the Prophet, the Qur'ān provides the guidance necessary for human beings to lead lives pleasing to God in this world and to gain the reward of Paradise hereafter. Nothing is of more importance for understanding Islam than an understanding of its Scripture. Izutsu's work is a fundamental resource for study of the Qur'ān, one that was pioneering in its time and whose merit and significance have not diminished.

Charles J. Adams

# PREFACE

THIS BOOK IS A REVISED EDITION OF MY EARLIER WORK PUBLISHED IN 1959 by Keio University in Tokyo, under the title, *The Structure of the Ethical Terms in the Koran.* Judged by the yardstick of my current thinking, the book stood much in need of improvement as a whole and of drastic revision in not a few places. In undertaking the revision, I have tried to make it a more satisfactory expression of my present views. Thus important additions have been made, many points which I now consider unnecessary have been dropped, and a number of passages have been completely rewritten. So much has it been altered that the book may very well be regarded as a new one, although the material used remains largely the same.

The title itself has been changed, lest the reader be misled into thinking that the book deals with all the ethical terms that appear in the Qurʾān. Such is not the case. The Qurʾanic terms of ethical and moral implication may be roughly divided into two major groups. One consists of those terms that concern the ethical life of the Muslims in the Islamic community (*ummah*), the other of those that are of an ethico-religious nature. The concepts in the second category go deep into the essential nature of man as *homo religiosus.* They reflect the spiritual characteristics which, according to the Qurʾanic understanding of human nature, man as a religious being should disclose. And, in an essentially 'ethical' religion like Islām, these human characteristics must necessarily be religious *and* ethical at the same time, there being no real distinction between the two in this particular context.

The book deals systematically only with this second group of ethical terms. Those of the first class stand outside its interest, apart from a few exceptional cases.

It remains to say a word about the theoretical part of this book. In the original edition, considerable space was given to abstract speculations regarding current theories of ethical language; methodological observations were scattered throughout the book. In the new edition, an abstract theory of ethical language has been replaced by a more fundamental theory of the linguistic or semantic world-view which underlies the entire analytic work, and the methodological principles which regulate the analysis have been gathered together in an introduction.

The present study consists of three parts: an exposition of the methodological principles of semantic analysis; the relation, positive and negative, that exists between the pre-Islamic tribal moral code and the Islamic—in our particular case, Qurʾanic—ethics; and an analysis, by a consistent application of the methodological rules explained in the first section, of the major ethico-religious concepts in the Qurʾān.

The system of transliteration employed is that of the Library of Congress, with these exceptions: *alif maqṣūrah* is rendered here by *á*; *tanwīn* is transliterated only in adverbial expressions. Qurʾanic verses are cited in terms of both the Flügel and Modern Egyptian systems. Where these differ, the Flügel numeration is set down first, followed by an oblique mark and the Egyptian verse number. Except in a very few cases, I have always tried to give my own interpretation of the Arabic in quoting from the Qurʾān and other literary works, though in the case of the Qurʾān I am, needless to say, heavily indebted to some of the earlier renderings by such scholars as Rodwell, Sale, Pickthall, and Arberry.

This revision was undertaken at the suggestion of Dr. Charles J. Adams, Director of the Institute of Islamic Studies at McGill University. He has shown a lively interest in the work from beginning to end; and without his constant assistance, sympathy, and encouragement the book would not have assumed its present shape. I take this opportunity to express my sincere gratitude for all his help.

The names of two other persons must be mentioned in this connection with an equally deep sense of gratitude. One is Mr. William J. Watson, then chief librarian of the Institute, who was kind enough to read the manuscript when it was completed and who made helpful suggestions regarding even the minutest details of expression. The other is Miss Margery Simpson of the McGill University Press, who edited the text. I have changed not a few passages following her reasonable and very constructive advice. I am most grateful to Mr.

David Ede for his help in proof-reading and in preparing the index.

Finally, it is my most pleasant duty to thank Professor Nobuhiro Matsumoto, Director of the Institute of Cultural and Linguistic Studies at Keio University, for generously giving me permission to have this work published in this revised form. The original edition was written and published under his sponsorship in Japan.

TOSHIHIKO IZUTSU

# PRINCIPLES OF SEMANTIC ANALYSIS

# INTRODUCTION Language and Culture

WE MAY APPROACH THE SUBJECT OF ETHICO-RELIGIOUS CONCEPTS IN the Qur'ān in a number of different ways. We may start from the elaborate systems of Islamic law which, in later ages, came to regulate all phases of human conduct to the minutest details, and find that we are led back to the Qur'ān as the original source of all these commands and prohibitions. Or we may start from the no less elaborate systems of theology, which we will discover to be nothing but a theoretic treatment of the basic problem of what a 'true believer' should believe in, what kind of attitude he should take towards God, and how he should act according to the dictates of his belief. Or again, we may set to work picking up more or less systematically various teachings and opinions on morals contained in the Qur'ān, put them in order, and write a book called 'The Ethics of the Qur'ān'.

My concern in this book is of an entirely different nature from these and similar undertakings. The difference lies mainly in the analytic method I am going to apply to the Qur'anic data, which is to make the Qur'ān interpret its own concepts and speak for itself. In other words, what is central to my inquiry is not so much the material as the method of linguistic analysis applied to that material, the specific point of view from which it attempts to analyze the semantic structure of the value words of the Qurʾān in the field of conduct and character.

I should like to begin by laying special emphasis on what may appear at first glance almost a truism, the importance of not placing any reliance at all on the indirect evidence furnished by translated texts. Translated words and sentences are partial equivalents at the very most. They may serve as rough-and-ready guides to our fumbling first steps, but in many cases they are quite inadequate and even misleading. And in any case they can never afford a reliable basis for discussion of the structure of the ethical world-view of a people. This, as I have just said, may seem too commonplace a point to be emphasized specifically. The real importance of this principle, and the grave danger in not paying constant attention to it, will be brought home, however, if we are but reminded that even when we are actually reading a text in the original we tend almost unconsciously to read into it our own concepts fostered by our mother tongue, and thus to transmute many, if not all, of its key terms into equivalent terms obtainable in our native language.[1] But if we do this, we are, in reality, doing nothing more than understanding the original text in a translation; we are, in other words, manipulating translated concepts without being aware of it. Baneful effects of this kind of unconscious 'transmutation' are making themselves felt in contemporary ethical literature, particularly in the sphere relating to comparative studies of different systems of moral ideas. And this tendency has been greatly fostered by the amazing development of cultural anthropology in recent times.

The growth of cultural anthropology is too remarkable to be ignored by anyone seriously interested in problems of culture and human facts. So most contemporary writers on ethics are forced willy-nilly to pay some attention at least to the existence of moral codes far different from those found in their own cultural sphere. Thus something assuming a superficial resemblance to comparative ethics is now in vogue. Not infrequently we meet with such 'comparative' consideration even in the works of those who would hold that there is no real pluralism in ethical matters, that the essence of man's morality is one and the same in the world, irrespective of time and place.

In the great majority of such cases, however, sweeping conclusions are drawn from 'comparative' consideration of ethical terms based on the unconscious manipulation of 'transmuted concepts'. Professor Morris Cohen in his *Preface to Logic*[2] points out the danger

[1] This point will be made clear theoretically in the next chapter.
[2] Morris R. Cohen, *A Preface to Logic* (London, 1946), p. 16.

of relying on the too easy equivalence of the Greek word *areté* with 'virtue' in discussing Aristotle's view of the 'virtuous' man. He remarks that the English word 'virtue', which is used almost exclusively as the equivalent of *areté*, is very misleading; *areté* would be more accurately rendered as 'excellence', the object of admiration. Whether or not his view is right is a question I must leave to one side for the moment. Let us, for convenience of exposition, take it as proved by closer examination of all relevant passages in which the word *areté* occurs. Suppose now that someone, setting out to write a paper on the conception of virtue among the ancient Greeks, gathers his data from English translations of Plato and Aristotle in which *areté* is invariably rendered as 'virtue'; or, as often happens, that he makes such a conceptual transmutation every time he comes across the word *areté* in the original text. The danger of his attempt is patent. Taking the wrong equivalence, *areté*=virtue, and without stopping a moment to question the validity of this formula, he might be led into futile discussions about the nature of the Greek 'virtue' or about the divergences of opinion between the English and Greek peoples on the essence of 'virtue'. The semantic content of the English word 'virtue' would in this way be read gratuitously and unconsciously into a Greek word which has, in fact, nothing in common with it except perhaps some vague connotations of personal excellence and admirableness.

Unfortunately mistakes of this kind are encountered very frequently in contemporary writings on ethics. This will become obvious when, for example, we examine carefully the writings of some Western scholars who have availed themselves of English translations only in forming their views on the ideas of righteousness and justice in Japanese Shintoism or Chinese Confucianism. There are in Japanese and Chinese a number of words which correspond to a varying degree with 'righteousness' and 'justice'; but whether we are justified in founding a comparative ethics on such vague equivalences is extremely doubtful. The same is true of the Arabic word *ṣāliḥ*, whose semantic structure will be subjected to rigorous analysis in a later passage. This word is generally translated in English as 'righteous', and I shall show how little it has in common with the English adjective in its semantic constituents.

Far be it from me to assert that all attempts of the kind just described are entirely useless and meaningless. That would be another piece of sweeping assertion. All I want to emphasize is the grave danger of being led unconsciously into erroneous theories about the nature of morality by manipulating translated concepts and not trying to analyze scientifically and rigorously the original concepts themselves. I am not an extreme historical relativist. 'The more we study moral codes,' writes Nowell-Smith, 'the more we find that they do not differ on major points of principle and that the divergencies that exist are due to different opinions about empirical facts. . . . Thus all codes agree that we have a duty to requite good with good; but obedience to this rule will involve behaving in ways that will differ according to the view that a society takes of what it is to do good to someone.'[3] He seems to be quite right here, and perhaps no objection can be raised against him as long as he speaks of moral codes in terms of such abstract principles, away from all divergencies of opinion coming from concrete facts. Perhaps at this high level of abstraction human nature is the same the world over, and I do not deny the possibility of establishing in this way a number of very general rules of morality which will be common to all human beings *qua* human beings.

The more fundamental issues of morals arise, in my view, rather in the much lower realm of empirical facts and practical experience. It is here, in the midst of the concrete reality of human life in society, that the semantic content of every ethical term is formed. If the view of what it is 'to do good' varies from society to society, then the semantic structure of the word 'good' itself must of necessity be different in each case. But even this already presumes the existence in every language of a word that will correspond more or less adequately both in meaning and use to the English word 'good', admittedly one of the vaguest and fuzziest in the language. In any event, it is safer not to make such unwarranted assumptions if we are to avoid projecting the structural characteristics of our own language upon the semantic contents of the vocabularies of other peoples.

These considerations have, I think, explained a good deal about the position I am going to take concerning the semantic aspects of language. It will be my basic attitude throughout this work to maintain a strict objectivity in dealing with observed facts, and to decline to take sides between the conflicting theories on this subject. But on the topic of the interconnection between language and culture I am going to take up a very definite position. And this will unavoidably give a marked personal coloring to my outlook on the problem of ethical terms. I shall strongly incline to a pluralistic theory which holds that people's views of what is good and bad, or right and wrong, differ from place to place and from time to time, and differ fundamentally, not as trivial details to be explained away as degrees in the scale of a unitary cultural development, but as more basic cultural divergencies having their roots deep down in the language habits of each individual community.

[3] P. H. Nowell-Smith, *Ethics* (London: Pelican Books, 1954), Chapter I, Section 2.

The theory of meaning which underlies the whole structure of the present work is not in any way my original contribution. It is based on a particular type of semantics which has been developed and elaborated in West Germany by Professor Leo Weisgerber and which he calls 'sprachliche Weltanschauungslehre'.[4] His theory coincides very largely in its major arguments with what is generally known today as 'ethnolinguistics', a theory of interrelations between linguistic patterns and cultural patterns which was originated by Edward Sapir in his later years in the United States. Each of these two schools has its peculiar characteristics, but since it is impossible to discuss them in minute detail I will, in what follows, unite the two, giving only those main points of their argument which are of immediate concern to us.

Instead of describing the theory in abstract form, we shall begin by considering some concrete examples. Take, for instance, the English word 'weed'. One dictionary defines this word as 'wild herb springing where it is not wanted', in short, an undesirable, unwanted herb. Now in the world of objective reality, that is, in the realm of nature, there is no such thing as an 'undesirable' herb; such a thing can exist only in the sight of man, who looks at the infinite complexity of natural objects, puts them in order, and evaluates them in accordance with his various purposes. The concept of 'weed' is the result of such a process of ordering, sorting out, evaluating, and categorizing. It embodies, in this sense, a particular point of view, a particular subjective attitude of the human mind.

The common-sense view simply and naively assumes the existence of a direct relationship between words and reality. Objects are there in the first place, then different names are attached to them as labels. In this view, the word 'table' *means* directly this concrete thing which exists before our eyes. But the example of the word 'weed' clearly shows that this is not the case; it shows that between the word and the thing there intervenes a peculiar process of subjective elaboration of reality. Our minds not only passively reflect the structure of reality, but more positively look at reality from a particular point of view, a particular angle; and it is this mental activity, which the Germans call *Geist*, that makes the thing really exist for us. There is a certain act of creativity, an elaboration of the given material in a certain direction, between reality and language. And that precisely is the proper domain of Meaning. In modern terminology, this may be expressed by saying that each word represents a particular linguistic categorization of nonlinguistic reality. But

[4] See for example his book *Vom Weltbild der deutschen Sprache* (Düsseldorf, 1950).

categorization necessarily implies the mental process of gathering many different things into a unity, and this is only possible on a certain principle. This principle is the particular angle from which man approaches reality, and it is conditioned culturally and historically.

The example of 'weed' is an extremely clear, but not in any way an exceptional, case; all the words we use are essentially more or less of this nature. Benjamin Whorf,[5] by a detailed and systematic comparison of the most representative Indo-European languages such as English, French, and German, on the one hand, and some of the American Indian languages on the other, has brought to light the astonishing fact that these two groups of people live in, and experience, the world in two totally different ways. They cut up the world of reality and classify it into totally different categories, on entirely different principles.

The point may be elucidated by the English word 'table'. Let us suppose that we have before us two tables, one round and the other square. The word 'table' is applicable to both. In other words, we classify both the round table and the square as 'table'. A table is a table whether it be round or square. Such is our common-sense view. But this common-sense view comes from the fact, often ignored, that we have a concept of table in which form plays no decisive role. Only because of this peculiarity in our concept of table do we classify two individually different things as 'one thing'. In reality the round table and the square table before our eyes are two different entities, but in our mind they are essentially one and the same thing. I say 'essentially': this essence is supplied by our basic mental attitude.

Benjamin Whorf found, to his amazement, that there exist in non-Indo-European parts of the world peoples who classify and categorize things in terms of their basic forms: round, square, rectangular, cubic, solid, liquid, etc. For them the criterion of form or shape is decisive in determining whether a thing belongs in this category or that. In the eyes of these peoples, a round table and a square table are two entirely different things and must be designated by two different names. From their point of view, there is absurdity, something quite arbitrary, illogical, and incompatible with the structure of reality itself, in the Western way of categorization, in which such different things as a square object and a round object are lumped together indiscriminately in one and the same category.

By this simple example we can perceive clearly that there is no

[5] See Benjamin Lee Whorf, *Language, Thought, and Reality* (Cambridge, Mass., 1956). See also Paul Henle (ed.), *Language, Thought, and Culture* (Ann Arbor, 1958), for a clear and concise exposition of the contemporary situation of this branch of linguistics.

*[handwritten margin notes:]* 'weed' another for 'square' category and 'square' category for one language What is the criteria of classification? How are diff. things categorized. A table may be in 'table' category for

solidly objective, simple, one-to-one correspondence between a thing and its name. Between them there always comes a peculiar mental activity, the creative act of seeing subjectively the thing as thing, a particular perspective. Thus, in our case of 'table', the particular perspective we adopt is that of pragmatic utilitarianism. We ignore the criteria of round and square and classify them both as 'table' simply because both are objects fabricated to serve the same purpose. Here the formal difference naturally recedes into the background. While for some other peoples, it is precisely the shape of the object that is decisive, because they look at the world in terms of shape, not in terms of purpose.

And if this is the case with such a simple word as 'table', how much more should it be the case with less common objects and with higher abstractions. All who have tried to translate from one language to another know how embarrassingly difficult it is sometimes to render adequately a very common word by a corresponding word or phrase in another language. Very often we simply give up hope and say, 'it is absolutely untranslatable', as Dr. Faust does in the beginning part of Goethe's work, while grappling with the problem of translating the Greek word 'logos' into German.[6]

All this is ultimately due to the fact that each of these untranslatable words embodies a very particular mental attitude peculiar to the community to which the language belongs. But these are merely some of the special cases in which the intervention of a particular perspective underlying the word-meaning comes out with utmost and unusual clarity. To tell the truth, this is more or less the case with any word in any language. The difference between 'table' and 'logos' in this respect is not so great as would appear at first sight.

Each one of our words represents a particular perspective in which we see the word, and what is called a 'concept' is nothing but the crystallization of such a subjective perspective; that is to say, it is a more or less stable form assumed by the perspective. Of course the perspective here in question is not subjective in the sense that it is individual; it is not individual but social, for it is the common possession of a whole community, handed down from preceding ages by historical tradition. And yet it is subjective in the sense that it brings in something of the positive human interest which makes our conceptual representation of the world not an exact duplicate of objective reality. And semantics is an analytical study of such perspectives crystallized into words.

[6] All the key terms of the Qur'ān are examples in point of this fact. Take, for instance, the word *kufr*. Suppose we translate it 'disbelief'. What a difference! The whole mental attitude that underlies the conceptual structure of *kufr* is lost the moment we begin to understand it in terms of the English concept of 'disbelief'.

Our immediate experience of reality is in itself an undifferentiated whole, as Henri Bergson has said. The Ancients called this *hulé* or 'materia prima' (the *hayūlá* of the Arabs), and quite recently the French existentialists saw in it a chaotic, amorphous mass, where all things lose their definite contour, and the world transforms itself into an obscene, nude, blind mass of paste or dough which only causes nausea. The human mind has carved out of this undifferentiated whole a number of separate and individualized forms. The number and nature of these forms varies from people to people, and, in the history of one people, from age to age. A rich vocabulary like that of Arabic indicates that the people who use the language have isolated more independent units out of the whole of reality than a people with a poor vocabulary. What is important, however, is that each people has gone its own way in determining what *is* to be isolated, and from what point of view. That is to say, the process of carving out separate forms is always dependent upon and directed by the subjective interest of each particular community; it is determined not so much by the objective similarity among things as by the subjective perspective in which they are viewed. Whatever aspect of reality appears significant for our hope and anxiety, or our desire and will, or our acting and doing, that only is taken out as an independent segment and receives the stamp of a name, thereby becoming a 'concept'. Only what is related to the focus of subjective personal concern, only what is felt to be essential to the whole scheme of life, is selected from the ever-changing flux of impressions, and becomes fixed with a special linguistic accent, which is nothing other than what we generally call a 'name'.

Thus, upon the originally formless mass of existence, the human mind has drawn an infinite number of lines, and made divisions and segments, large and small; and the world of reality has in this way received the imprints of linguistic and conceptual formulation; and an order has been brought into the original chaos.

The words, and the concepts they stand for, constitute a complex system with many articulations. This organized whole behaves somewhat like an intermediary screen between the human mind and pre-conceptual reality, which reaches it modified, reflected, and even distorted by the particular articulation of the screen.

Usually we are so accustomed to this middle screen, and it is something so natural, so transparent, that we are not even aware of its existence. We naively believe that we are experiencing directly and without any intermediary the objective world as it naturally is. According to this common-sense view, the natural, objective world is already there before our eyes from the very beginning, with its own articulations and divisions, well-ordered and fully organized. We think that we simply perceive this organized world, form in our minds as many concepts as there are natural divisions, name them, and so make up our vocabulary.

Such a common-sense view ignores the fact that any given aspect of reality, to say nothing of the whole of reality which the Greeks called Chaos, is properly speaking capable of being divided up into as many segments as you like, in whatever way you like, and from whatever angle you prefer. And without the mental act of dividing the raw materials of immediate experience into a number of independent units—the act of 'articulation' as it is called in semantics—the world would be completely meaningless and absurd, as the existentialist philosophers say. We need not effect this articulation by ourselves, for a ready-made system in the form of vocabulary is always there as a cultural inheritance from our forefathers; and we assimilate it when, as children, we learn our mother tongue.

Thus the immediate reality of existence, whatever it is, is not presented to our ideation as it originally and naturally is, but rather through the prism of symbols registered in our vocabulary. This prism of symbols is not a mere imitation, a mere duplicate of the original reality, and the symbols do not correspond exactly to the forms of reality; they are rather ideational forms, by the sole agency of which anything becomes a real object for our intellectual apprehension.

What is most important to remark in this respect is not only that each community has its particular way of isolating the segments and units, which are therefore peculiar to itself, but that these segments and units form among themselves a system. They are not simply there without any order; on the contrary, they constitute a very complex, highly organized whole. And the way they are combined and put in relation with each other is no less peculiar to the community than the nature of the segments themselves. This organized whole, peculiar to each community, is what is called vocabulary.[7]

Vocabulary—or, more generally, language with its web of connotative patterns—is primarily a system of 'articulatory' forms, in accordance with which we dissect the perpetual flux of nature into a certain number of entities and events. In Benjamin Whorf's pertinent words, each language is 'a provisional analysis of reality', since 'language dissects nature differently'. Even the same kind of ordinary experience is usually segmented by different languages in different ways. Out of one and the same situation, different languages tend to isolate different categories of essentials; and each language has its own peculiar way of grouping the units thus isolated into a

[7] On the structure of 'vocabulary' as an organized system of conceptual network, see my *God and Man in the Koran*, Chapter I, Section 4, 'Vocabulary and Weltanschauung'.

certain number of higher systems, which again are put together into a comprehensive network of concepts. And that is vocabulary.

Each vocabulary, or connotative system, represents and embodies a particular world-view (Weltanschauung) which transforms the raw material of experience into a meaningful, 'interpreted' world. Vocabulary in this sense is not a single-stratum structure. It comprises a number of sub-vocabularies, existing side by side with—usually—overlapping areas between. And the conceptual network formed by ethical terms is one of such relatively independent sub-vocabularies, consisting of a number of relatively independent conceptual sectors, each with its own world-view.

Semantically a moral code is a sector of this meaningfully 'interpreted' world. Such a statement may at once remind the reader of Dr. John Ladd's contention in his remarkable book, *The Structure of a Moral Code*,[8] that a moral code is part of an ideology. There are in fact many points of resemblance between my standpoint and his; and these may be due in the last analysis to the fact that in establishing my own theory I owe much to his penetrating insights into the nature of moral discourse. There is, however, one basic difference between us. It is that he has carried out his investigation of Navaho ethics on the evidence of ethical 'statements' as distinguished from 'sentences'. In more concrete terms, he has relied on translated information as his primary evidence. At the beginning of his work, we find him trying to justify his position by drawing a clear-cut distinction between a *sentence* and a *statement*. The sentences 'Das Haus ist weiss', 'La maison est blanche', and 'The house is white', he argues, are different sentences, but all make the same statement. In a 'statement' one does not have to specify what words are actually employed to communicate it, nor does it matter at all what language it is couched in. He goes on to say that this particular characteristic of the 'statement' was especially valuable in reporting his interviews with his native informant because, since he did not understand the Navaho language, he could not know what sentences the informant used.[9]

Now this, as I have suggested earlier, is exactly contrary to what I am about to do in my work. From my standpoint, what matters most is the uttered *sentences* of an informant, not his *statements*, which are said to remain the same in whatever language they may be clothed. The very existence of some such thing as 'statement', common to many different languages, seems to me highly questionable. If, as Professor Roger Brown[10] suggests, even such commonplace

[8] John Ladd, *The Structure of a Moral Code* (Cambridge, Mass., 1957).

[9] *Ibid.*, p. 21.

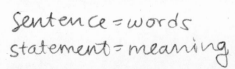

[10] Roger Brown, 'Language and Categories', published as an appendix to *A Study of Thinking* by J. S. Brunner, J. J. Goodnow, and G. A. Austin (New York,

words as *mère* and 'mother' are not strictly identical and the French word *amie* differs in an important way from both German *Freundin* and English 'lady friend', it is quite unlikely that a sentence used to communicate a moral judgment in one language should be precisely duplicated in other languages.

Edward Sapir has repeatedly remarked that even comparatively simple acts of perception are controlled in large measure by the social patterns of connotation, and are therefore culturally relative.[11] If this is so, how much more should this be true of valuational acts in the field of human conduct and character. Every culture has a number of traditional patterns of moral evaluation which have become crystallized historically in the body of its ethical terms, and these conversely furnish the speakers of the language with a complete set of channels through which to categorize all moral phenomena. By using the semantic patterns of their native language, the members of a community can easily analyze, report, and evaluate any human action or character. But this involves a commitment to living in strict conformity with the norms of evaluation that are codified in the ethical terms of that language.

How are we to devise a scientifically reliable method of analyzing the fundamental structure of such a semantic field? How is it possible to explore the semantic categories of a given language in a way that will fulfill the requirements of a scientific investigation? By 'scientific' I mean primarily empirical or inductive, and, in the specific context of the present inquiry, an analytic study of ethical terms that will be as little prejudiced as possible by any theoretical position of moral philosophy.

The best way to proceed, in my opinion, is to try to describe the semantic category of a word in terms of the conditions in which it is used. What features of the environment are necessary if the word is to be used properly to designate a given event? Only by attempting to answer such a question can we arrive at the correct meaning of a given word.

The choice of this method is based on my conviction that language, in its connotative aspect, is first and foremost an important manifestation of that tendency to categorize so characteristic of the human mind.[12]

---

1956), which is, to my knowledge, by far the best treatise ever written on this subject. See particularly p. 311.

[11] See, for example, his 'The Status of Linguistics as a Science', *Selected Writings* (Los Angeles, 1951), pp. 160 ff.

[12] For a detailed scientific account of the process of categorization in general and its importance in the structure of the human mind, I would refer to the previously cited work *A Study of Thinking*, by Brunner, Goodnow, and Austin.



if translating human to human
* language is so difficult + meaning can't
exactly match, what about translating
God to human - seems even more impossible

The ethico-religious terms of a given language form a particular system of categories which is comprised within the larger connotative system of the language in question. The central problem for the investigator is to seek the defining attributes for each term, by virtue of which an illimitable number of discriminably different persons or acts are categorized into a class and thus receive a common name. By examining analytically the key ethico-religious terms in a language, the investigator may gradually come to know the basic structure of the system through which all events involving moral judgment are filtered before appearing in an accessible form to the members of that language community.

The process just described is precisely the process of language-learning in children. And in this type of inquiry the investigator deliberately places himself in the awkward position of an infant beginning to speak its mother tongue, or that of an anthropological linguist faced with an entirely unknown language. The child learns the use of the word 'apple' by observing the behavior of his parent-tutor in naming it, and so establishes a denotive relationship between the word and the familiar kind of fruit. By repeating this process many times, he comes to group new instances into the class APPLE by means of such perceived properties as size, color, and shape. In just the same way the child learns the use of moral vocabulary. The way in which he learns to apply a particular ethical term to a particular type of situation does not differ in any essential point from the way in which he learns to apply the word 'apple' to a certain sort of object.

Perhaps we may profitably remind ourselves at this juncture of the Original Word Game referred to by Roger Brown.[13] In this game the player, by carefully observing his tutor's use of the 'original' word, tries to relate it with a particular nonlinguistic category. In order to succeed, the player must first of all isolate correctly the criterial features of the nonlinguistic category. In other words, he must discover what particular kind of stimulus has elicited just that kind of verbal response from his tutor.

The task is indeed no easy one. In most cases a whole process of trial and error has to be gone through before the player grasps as he

---

According to the authors of this book, categorization may best be defined as the cognitive operation by which organisms code the events of their environment into a certain number of classes. For anything or any event to be classified in this way, it must possess a certain number of defining attributes, by virtue of which such categorial differentiation becomes at all possible. The evidence for the existence of a category is the occurence of common response to an array of objects or events on the part of the organisms concerned. A category once formed, the individual begins to show a marked tendency to respond to an array of objects and events in terms of their class membership rather than their uniqueness (Chapter I, pp. 1–24).

13 Brown, pp. 284–285.

should the tutor's use of words. And so it is, essentially, with our investigator. He sets out to observe minutely all the available instances of the actual use of ethico-religious terms, analyzes carefully the situational contexts, constructs hypotheses, which in turn he must check against further evidence and revise if necessary, and hopes in this way to arrive at a satisfactory solution to his problem.

This is, in outline, what we are going to do with the ethico-religious terms of the Qurʾān. But of course we are not so severely handicapped as the infant who as yet possesses no language, or even as the anthropological linguist. For classical Arabic is one of the best-known languages in the world, explored to the minutest details of both grammar and vocabulary. We have good dictionaries; much philological work has been done; and, in the domain of Qurʾanic exegesis in particular, we are provided with many authoritative old commentaries. For theoretical reasons, however, our methodological principle forbids us to rely too heavily on these secondary sources. They are to be used at the very most as valuable auxiliaries; we must not forget that they may prove more misleading than enlightening, unless we are very cautious in availing ourselves of the evidence they afford.

All this may give the impression that I am making the problem needlessly difficult, when the object of inquiry is a well-explored language. That this is not the case will, I hope, gradually be made clear in the course of this book. Here I want only to draw attention to one important point. This seemingly tedious, roundabout procedure has a very obvious advantage over all others as a practical method of dealing with ethical terms. It enables us to analyze words of moral evaluation by the same process as we use for words of other kinds. Viewed from the standpoint of this method, ethical terms—particularly those belonging to the primary level of ethical language—stand quite on a par with ordinary name-words such as 'table', 'apple', 'eat', 'walk', or 'red'. For the underlying process of learning is essentially the same in all types of words.

# I. The Scope and Focus of the Study

ISLĀM, WHICH AROSE IN THE SEVENTH CENTURY IN ARABIA, UNdoubtedly represents one of the most radical religious reforms that have ever appeared in the East; and the Qur'ān, the earliest authentic record of this great event, describes in vividly concrete terms how in this period of crisis the time-honored tribal norms came into bloody conflict with new ideals of life, began to totter, and, after desperate and futile efforts to resist, finally yielded the hegemony to the rising power. The Arabia of this epoch, from the pre-Islamic time of heathendom to the earliest days of Islām, is of particular importance to anyone interested in the problems of ethical thinking, in that it provides excellent case material for studying the birth and growth of a moral code.

In the so-called Age of Ignorance (Jāhilīyah), the pagan period prior to the advent of Islām, strange customs and ideas connected with idolatrous beliefs were rampant among the nomadic Arabs. Most of these Islām rejected positively as essentially incompatible with divine revelation; but a considerable number of them it adopted, with modifications in form and substance, and succeeded in making out of them high moral ideas to be incorporated into the new code of Islamic ethics. By following carefully the semantic transformations which the principal ethical terms in the Arabic language underwent during this most critical period of its history, I hope not only to reveal the guiding spirit of the Islamic moral code, but also to throw fresh light on the more general theoretical problems of ethical discourse and the role it plays in human culture.

The very nature of Qurʾanic thought makes it necessary for us to distinguish between three layers of moral discourse. There are, in other words, three different categories of ethical concepts in the Qurʾān: those that refer to and describe the ethical nature of God; those that describe the various aspects of the fundamental attitude of man towards God, his Creator; and those that refer to the principles and rules of conduct regulating the ethical relations among individuals who belong to, and live within, the religious community of Islām.

The first group is composed of the so-called Names of God: words such as 'Merciful', 'Benevolent', 'Forgiving', 'Just', or 'Majestic', describing this or that particular aspect of God, Who is conceived in the Qurʾān, as in all Semitic religions, as being of an essentially ethical nature. This group of concepts, which was later to be developed by the theologians into a theory of divine attributes and which may aptly be described as Divine Ethics, lies outside the scope of this book.

Over against this Divine Ethics may be put Human Ethics, comprising the two remaining groups of concepts. The second group concerns the basic ethical relationship of man to God. The very fact that, according to the Qurʾanic conception, God is of an ethical nature and acts upon man in an ethical way[1] carries the grave implication that man, on his part, is expected to respond in an ethical way. And man's ethical response to God's actions is, in the Qurʾanic view, religion itself. It is, in other words, at the same time both ethics and religion. For to say that a man should take up such and such an attitude to God in response to His initial attitude to mankind, and that man should act in such and such a way in accordance with God's commands and prohibitions, is both ethical and religious teaching. In this sense, all the concepts belonging to this second class may be described as ethico-religious concepts. And it is this particular class of ethico-religious concepts in the Qurʾān that will constitute the proper subject of study in this book.

The third group relates to the basic ethical attitude of a man to his brethren living in the same community. The social life of the individual is ruled and regulated by a certain set of moral principles with

[1] On this particular problem see Izutsu, *God and Man in the Koran* (Tokyo, 1964), Chapter IX.

*ethico-religious vs judicial rules/*
*expectation/practice      regulations*

all their derivatives. These regulations constitute what we may call the system of social ethics, soon to be developed in the post-Qur'anic period into the grand-scale system of Islamic jurisprudence. Properly speaking, this also lies outside the scope of the present study, although reference will often be made to it, especially in the first part of the book, which attempts to distinguish between the ethical principles of the Qur'ān and those of Jāhilīyah.

It must be borne in mind, of course, that these three groups do not in any way stand aloof from one another, but are most closely related. And this comes from the basic fact that the Qur'ānic worldview is essentially theocentric. The image of God pervades the whole of it, and nothing escapes His knowledge and providence. Semantically this means that, in general, no major concept in the Qur'ān exists quite independently of the concept of God and that in the sphere of human ethics each one of its key concepts is but a pale reflection —or a very imperfect imitation—of the divine nature itself, or refers to a particular response elicited by divine actions.

*trust + fear*

It is significant that the second class of ethico-religious terms is ultimately reducible to two most basic concepts in striking contrast to each other: absolute trust in God and pious fear of Him.[2] This polarity is nothing but a reflection in the believing mind of man of the very polarity which is observable in the nature of God Himself: His infinite goodness, benevolence, mercy, and loving care, on the one hand; and His wrath, spirit of vengeance, and ruthless chastisement of those who disobey, on the other. Human ethics, the ethico-religious attitude of man towards God, is in this sense a reflection of divine ethics.

Fundamentally the same holds true of the third group of concepts which expresses the various aspects of the ethical relationship among members of the Muslim community. Man should act with justice and righteousness towards his brethren because God's actions are always absolutely just and right. Man should never do wrong (*zulm*) to others because God Himself never does wrong to anybody. Everywhere in the Qur'ān man is admonished not to wrong others or himself in his human relations. And this is but a reflection of the nature of God, Who repeats that He will never do wrong 'even by the weight of an ant' or 'by a single date-thread', and declares in one passage:

I do absolutely no wrong to My servants [i.e. the believers]![3]
(L, 28/29)

2 The former is expressed in the Qur'ān by the key words *islām* and *īmān*, and the latter by *taqwā*.
3 More literally, 'I am not a wrong-doer (*zallām* an emphatic form of *zālim* meaning "he who wrongs others".'

The Qurʾān also teaches that one should treat one's parents with kindness out of mercy when they attain old age:

> Thy Lord has decreed that you should serve none save Him, and that you should be kind to parents. If one or both of them attain old age with thee, say not 'Fie!' unto them nor chide them, but speak unto them respectful words and lower unto them the wing of humbleness out of mercy (*raḥmah*), and say, 'My Lord, have mercy (*irḥam*) upon them, just as they raised me up when I was a small child.' (XVII, 24–25/23–24)

It is worth observing that here the connecting link between God's nature and human ethics is furnished by the key concept of 'mercy' (*raḥmah*), which is common to both orders of being. And, if we remember that the Qurʾān never tires of emphasizing God's mercy and compassion, it will be easy to see that, in the Qurʾanic conception, the human *raḥmah* is but an imitation on the part of man of the divine *raḥmah* itself.

This basic dependence of human ethics on divine ethics comes out in a more definite form in the following verse, which clearly states that one should try to pardon and forgive others because God Himself is always ready to forgive and be compassionate.

> And let not those of you who possess plenty and ease swear not to give to kinsmen and the poor and the emigrants in the way of God. Let them forgive and show indulgence (even if the latter do not satisfy them in every respect). Do you not wish that God should forgive you? God is Forgiving (*ghafūr*), Merciful (*raḥīm*). (XXIV, 22)

This much is, I think, enough to show how the three groups of ethical concepts are closely related to each other. In analyzing any of the major Qurʾanic concepts relating to human ethics, we should never lose sight of their fundamental relationship to the ethical nature of God Himself.

It is characteristic of contemporary ethical literature that philosophers, when they discuss the nature and structure of ethical language, are mostly concerned with words of the secondary level of moral discourse, such as 'good' and 'bad'. Indeed, 'good' is their favorite word. They tend to engage in endless discussions of such problems as 'What do we mean when we utter the sentence "X is good"?', 'Are there such things as "good-making properties" in the world?', or 'Does "good" describe something or is it simply an expression of emotion?' I do not in any way deny the importance of these problems, but it is also true that by so doing the moral philosophers overlook the very significant fact that in actual life our moral evaluations are mainly made on the primary level of discourse. In ordinary circumstances we pass a moral judgment on other people by saying, for example, 'So-and-So is a very pious man', or 'So-and-So is a hypocrite'. 'Pious' and 'hypocrite', like 'humble', 'generous', or 'stingy', are ethical terms of the primary level. And the system of these and similar words determines the true characteristics of the moral code of a community.

Now words of the primary level are essentially descriptive, whilst secondary-level ethical words are essentially evaluative. The word 'generous' is first and foremost a genuine descriptive word; although, insofar as it evaluates the quality of generosity as praiseworthy, it is more than mere description. It is, then, primarily descriptive and secondarily evaluative.

Primary-level ethical terms are ordinary descriptive words that are normally used with more or less serious ethical implications. The main function of the secondary-level terms is classificatory; they are chiefly employed to classify various descriptive properties, such as 'humility' or 'generosity', into a recognized category of moral values. When, for example, we call a man 'good' because he has a set of properties generally designated as 'humble', we are thereby ranging humility in the class of praiseworthy qualities. In this sense, secondary ethical terms may justly be called ethical metalanguage, and the distinction between primary and secondary level would roughly answer to the logician's distinction between object-words and logical words.

Ethical words of the primary level are, then, descriptive words charged with an ethical or evaluative force. It is important to keep in mind, when trying to analyze the ethical language of any given community, that the main body of a moral code is, linguistically, always composed of words of this category. And this is, of course, true of the Qur᾽anic moral code.

It has often been said that, at the time of the Revelation, the Arab did not yet possess an abstract concept of good and bad. This is simply a different way of saying that the real mechanism of the Qur᾽anic moral code works on the level of primary ethical terms. The point will become much clearer if we cast a cursory glance at the so-called five categories of acts (*aḥkām*) which were developed by the *fiqh* scholars of later ages, and which represent genuine secondary ethical terms.

1. *wājib*, 'obligatory', duties prescribed by God as absolutely necessary, neglect of which is punishable by law.
2. *mandūb*, 'recommended',[4] duties recommended but not obligatory,

[4] Also called *masnūn*.



scale of acts ranging
required to ~~prohibited~~
(good) prohibited (bad)

fulfilment of which is rewarded, but neglect of which is not necessarily punishable.

3. *jā'iz*, 'indifferent',[5] actions that may or may not be done, entailing neither punishment nor reward either way.
4. *makrūh*, 'disapproved', actions disapproved but not forbidden, not-doing of which is rewarded, but doing of which is not punishable.
5. *maḥẓūr*, 'prohibited',[6] actions forbidden by God, and therefore punishable by law.

These five terms for the categories of the believers' acts represent an elaborate system of metalanguage in which any act has its proper place and is evaluated with reference to a fixed standard of good and bad. The role of these terms is not to describe concrete properties; it consists in classing all deeds as belonging to one or other of the five categories of ethical value. Such a system of well-developed secondary ethical terms is not to be found in the Qur'ān itself. It is but a superstructure, and the real basis of the ethical life of the Muslim is a far more intricate network of moral values expressed by innumerable ethical terms belonging to the primary level of discourse.

Not that Qur'anic ethics has no words of the level of metalanguage. There are in the Qur'ān words that must be regarded as more evaluative than descriptive. Most, if not all, of the terms that will be treated in Chapter XI, under 'Good and Bad', do behave, at least in some of their uses, as genuine secondary terms. Words like *khayr* and *sharr* for 'good' and 'bad', or words meaning 'sin', such as *dhanb* and *ithm*, are classificatory rather than descriptive in both nature and function. The important point to note, however, is that by themselves they do not form a whole system of moral ideas. The system of moral ideas actually at work in the Qur'ān is based almost exclusively on primary-level value-words.

The difference between the two levels will be made clear by a consideration of a few concrete cases. Take, for example, the word *kufr*, which is one of the most important value-words in the Qur'ān. The word means the attitude of ungratefulness towards favors and benefits received. As such, it is a genuine descriptive word with a concrete factual content. At the same time, it is clear that the word is invested with an evaluative aura which makes it more than mere description. And it is this evaluative aura or halo, which surrounds the descriptive core of its meaning, that makes *kufr* an authentic ethical term on the primary level. A comparison of this word with one like *dhanb*, belonging rather to the level of metalanguage, will at once confirm this view.

[5] Also called *mubāḥ* 'allowed'.
[6] Also called *ḥarām*.

*Dhanb*, as I shall show presently, denotes in most cases in the Qurʾān the same thing as *kufr*. Both may refer ultimately to the same state of affairs, but they refer to the same thing in two characteristically different ways. While *kufr* conveys, primarily, factual information about a case of ungratefulness or disbelief and only secondarily suggests that it is bad, *dhanb* first of all condemns it as belonging in the class of negative or reprehensible properties. In the former, the evaluative force is but an aura, in the latter it is evaluation itself that constitutes the semantic core of the word.

Thus, in the semantic behavior of the primary ethical terms, we have to isolate two different layers: descriptive and evaluative. True, as a matter of actual fact, these two layers of meaning are fused together into a semantic whole, but it is theoretically possible and even necessary to draw a dividing line between them. Thus, in the essentially nonreligious context of Jāhilīyah, 'humility' and 'self-surrender' were considered something disgraceful, a manifestation of weak and ignoble character, whilst 'haughtiness' and 'refusal to obey' were, in the eyes of pre-Islamic Arabs, marks of noble nature. With the advent of Islām, the balance was completely overturned. Now, in the purely monotheistic context of Islām, 'humility' in the presence of God and total 'self-surrender' to Him became the highest virtues, and 'haughtiness' and 'refusal to obey' the marks of irreligiousness. In other words, the terms denoting these personal properties completely changed their value. While the descriptive layer of their meaning remained the same, their evaluative force changed from negative to positive or from positive to negative.

It may be argued that, in ethical matters, the levels of object-language and metalanguage are not separated by a clear line of demarcation, that it is extremely doubtful whether the two, if they do exist, are really so fundamentally different. To a certain degree, such an objection is well-founded. We have to admit that, as far as natural language is concerned, everything begins at the primary level. Even what I have called here the 'secondary' ethical terms must, in accordance with the universal rule of language growth, originate in the sphere of ordinary descriptive words, to develop from there through a number of stages towards the ideal type of 'pure' value-words. So, in a sense, all differences between the two levels of ethical speech may be reduced ultimately to one of 'more or less'. But here, as elsewhere, difference of degree, when it goes beyond a certain limit, changes into a difference of kind. Thus, even such a representative ethical term of the secondary level as the English word 'good' has still a descriptive aspect. Only this descriptive element in 'good' is so trivial and insignificant as compared with its evaluative aspect that we can safely consider it an authentic member of the ethical metalanguage.

'Pure' value-words of the type of 'good' are very few and far between in the Qurʾān. The Qurʾanic moral code as a linguistic structure is mainly composed of primary ethical terms in the sense just explained, with a few secondary terms scattered here and there. The formation of a systematic ethical metalanguage in Islām is the work of jurisprudence in its first centuries. And it is the former class of words that plays the leading role in structuring the Qurʾanic moral consciousness.

# II. The Method of Analysis and Its Application

THERE ARE A VARIETY OF WAYS IN WHICH ONE GETS TO KNOW THE meaning of a foreign word. The simplest and commonest—but unfortunately the least reliable—is by being told an equivalent word in one's own language: the German word *Gatte*, for example, means the same as the English 'husband'. In this way the Arabic *kāfir* might be explained as meaning the same as 'misbeliever', *ẓālim* as 'evil-doer', *dhanb* as 'sin', and so on. There can be no question that there is recognizably some sort of semantic equivalence in each case; on the other hand, anyone acquainted with the Arabic language will have to admit on reflection that these apparently nearest equivalents are far from being able to do justice to the original words. A *ẓālim*, for example, is not exactly an 'evil-doer'; between *kāfir* and 'misbeliever' there is a difference too important to be ignored.

In my Introduction I pointed out the danger of drawing hasty conclusions from such equivalences. In point of fact, translation turns out to be far more frequently misleading than enlightening. Nor is this hard to account for. As Professor Richard Robinson has rightly seen,[1] every word-word definition, of the *Gatte*-means-husband type, implies a word-thing definition to those who already

[1] Richard Robinson, *Definition* (Oxford, 1950), Chapter II, Section 2.

know what 'husband' means in English. In exactly the same way, if the equivalence *ẓālim* = evil-doer is given to hearers or readers who know only the meaning of 'evil-doer', they have no other way of learning the meaning of *ẓālim* than by putting it into the semantic category of 'evil-doer'. They understand it, if they understand at all, not directly but only by analogy with the connotation of 'evil-doer'. By going through the semantic category of another word formed in the tradition of an alien culture, the meaning of the word is in danger of distortion. To avoid this danger, measures should be taken to transform the word-word definition, *ẓālim* = evil-doer, not into such an indirect word-thing definition but into a direct one, correlating the word immediately to a definite piece of nonlinguistic reality.

To translate *ẓālim* by 'evil-doer' or 'wrong-doer' may be a simple expedient for getting to know the meaning of the word, and presumably no one will deny the advantage of this expedient as a practical first step in language-learning. But it is just a first step. If we wish to grasp the semantic category of the word itself, we must inquire what sort of man, what type of character, what kind of acts are actually designated by this name in Old Arabic—in our specific case, in the Qurʾān. Even a single example, provided that it is well-selected and relevant, may prove extremely illuminating:

> The curse of God is on the *ẓālimīn* [pl. of *ẓālim*] who try to debar men from God's path, desire to have it crooked, and would never believe in the next world. (VII, 42–43/44–45)

Does this not constitute in itself a kind of verbal definition of *ẓālim*?

And we have in the Qurʾān a huge number of similar examples of the use of the same word. By gathering them in one place, comparing them, checking them against one another, may we not reasonably hope to get an original word-thing definition of this Arabic word? That this is possible will be shown on many occasions in the course of this book.

Turning now to the equivalence *kāfir* = misbeliever (or 'disbeliever' or 'unbeliever'), we may observe at once the essential difference of the outer structure itself. Unlike the equivalence *murūwah* = manliness, to be discussed later, the two halves of this equivalence show no correspondence in word structure. The Arabic word *kāfir*, to begin with, is an independent unit of structure which cannot be further analyzed into component elements. Whichever English equivalent we may choose clearly consists of two parts: an element implying a negative (mis-, dis-, un-) and another element representing what may be called the material side of the meaning. This material part is, in each case, 'believer'. That is to say that the semantic categories of the English equivalents of *kāfir* are all based on the fundamental concept of belief.

There is, to be sure, no denying that the semantic category of the Arabic word *kāfir* itself contains an important element of 'belief'. But, it must be remembered, this is not the only basic semantic constituent of the word, nor is it the original one. An examination of pre-Islamic literature discloses that the real core of its semantic structure was by no means 'un-belief', but rather 'ingratitude' or 'unthankfulness'. The word *kāfir* was originally the contrary of *shākir*, 'one who is thankful'.

In Islām, as we shall see later on, one of the keynotes of belief is gratitude, thankfulness. And this is the counterpart of the Qurʾanic conception of God as the gracious, merciful Lord of men and all beings. In fact the Qurʾān never tires of emphasizing the purely gratuitous act of benevolence on the part of Almighty God, which He bestows upon all beings. In return, man owes Him the duty of being thankful for His grace and goodness. *Kāfir* is a man who does not, would not show any sign of gratitude in his conduct.

The word *kāfir* comes to acquire in the Qurʾān the secondary meaning of 'one who does not believe in God' because it occurs very frequently in contrast to the word *muʾmin*, which means 'one who considers something absolutely true' or 'one who believes', and to the word *muslim*, meaning 'one who has completely surrendered himself to the will of God'. More generally speaking, the semantic category of a word tends to be very strongly influenced by the neighboring words belonging to the same meaning field. And when the nature of a word is such that it comes to be used with remarkable frequency in specific contexts alongside its antonym, it must of necessity acquire a noticeable semantic value from this frequent combination. Thus one and the same word, *kāfir*, comes to mean a different thing according to its use as the contrary of *shākir*, 'one who thanks', or as the contrary of *muʾmin*, 'one who believes'. In the first case it means an 'ingrate', and in the second 'unbeliever'. The first important semantic element—and it is the original one—is completely lost the moment we begin to interpret the word *kāfir* solely in terms of 'belief'.

The semantic discrepancy between words and their foreign 'equivalents' naturally increases as we turn to those regions of existence where unique modes of vision tend to dominate and where language is charged with the task of reflecting and expressing the truly ethnic features of a people's life. Indeed we might lay down as a general rule that the more a word is expressive of a deep-rooted ethnic feature of a given culture, the harder it becomes to transpose it properly into another language. There are in every language a certain number of words that are notoriously untranslatable. Such is for instance English 'humor', French 'esprit', or German 'Gemüt'.

Such also are words like *ḥamāsah*, *murūwah*, and *jahl* in Old Arabic, which are all typical of the life and manners of pagan nomadic Arabia in contrast to the Islamic ethical culture. The first word, *ḥamāsah*, is explained by Professor R. A. Nicholson[2] as denoting a peculiar combination of bravery in battle, patience in misfortune, persistence in seeking blood revenge, protection of the weak, and defiance of the strong. As we shall see later, this is but a very rough-and-ready sort of approximation. But even this much cannot properly be conveyed by 'courage' or 'bravery', which is usually given as its English equivalent.

Now if we take a further step and add to this complex of noble qualities two more important elements, that lavish generosity so characteristic of the desert Arabs, so well typified by the semi-legendary figure of Ḥātim Ṭā'ī, and the unswerving loyalty to tribal interests which is no less characteristic, then we have another virtue called *murūwah*.

The *murūwah* represents the highest idea of morality among the Bedouin, the virtue of virtues, or better still, all the ideal virtues of the desert combined in one. The word *murūwah*, as far as concerns the outward form, seems to correspond admirably well with 'man-ness', being composed of a radical with the meaning of 'man' (as opposed to 'woman') and a formator which confers on all radicals to which it is annexed an abstract sense of quality or property. So the word means etymologically something like 'the property of being a man', and one may feel amply justified in using the English word 'manliness' as an exact equivalent of *murūwah*. As a matter of fact, this may do in contexts where no need arises for semantic precision. But it must always be borne in mind that the equivalence between the two is limited to the purely formal side of the word structure. And it is precisely where the purely formal ends that semantic problems of real import begin. For the content of *man*-li-ness itself must of necessity vary according to the set of features of *man* chosen as the keynote of the semantic category. And the number of characteristic features of man is practically limitless. Even supposing that all languages agreed on the point of considering the quality-of-being-a-man sufficiently relevant to social life to give it an independent linguistic expression, each language would have its own peculiar way of selecting a certain number of features from among many, and its own peculiar way of combining the elements thus selected into a particular semantic category. So it is with the Arabic *murūwah*. Its

[2] R. A. Nicholson, *A Literary History of the Arabs* (Cambridge, 1953), p. 79.

meaning, as a semantic category, has behind it a long history of nomadic life in the Arabian waste; it is so deeply immersed in the atmosphere of desert life, that only copious notes about the latter can make it understandable in its true peculiarity.

The third of the words mentioned above, *jahl*, has a story of a somewhat different kind to offer. Since a consideration of this word is of direct relevance to the immediate subject of my book, I shall here describe in some detail the basic structure of its semantic category. I shall try to avoid as far as possible the needless repetition of what Ignaz Goldziher established a good many years ago in his famous study.[3]

Before Goldziher published his paper and showed in a conclusive manner how one should properly understand this word, *jahl* had long been thought, even among Arab philologists, to be the exact opposite of *ʿilm*, 'knowledge', with, consequently, the basic meaning of 'ignorance'. So it came about quite naturally that the most important derivative of this word, *jāhilīyah*, by means of which the Muslims used to denote the state of affairs before the rise of Islām, was generally understood, and translated, as the 'Age of Ignorance'. Now the method which Goldziher adopted in his attempt to elucidate the original meaning of the word coincides in all essential points with what I call in this book the method of semantic analysis. He collected a large number of important examples of the actual use of the root *JHL* in pre-Islamic poetry, subjected them to a careful analysis, and reached the remarkable conclusion that the usual traditional opinion about *jāhilīyah* was fundamentally erroneous. *Jahl*, according to his conclusion, is not the opposite of *ʿilm*; in its primary sense, it stands opposed to *ḥilm*, which denotes 'the moral reasonableness of a civilized man' (Nicholson), including roughly speaking such characteristics as forbearance, patience, clemency, and freedom from blind passion. If we add to these another important element, 'power', the subject's clear consciousness of his power and superiority, the picture is complete. In later usage, and sometimes even in pre-Islamic poetry, we find *jahl* used as the real antithesis of *ʿilm*, but only in a secondary and derivative sense; its primary semantic function is to refer to the implacable, reckless temper of the pagan Arabs.

Let us now turn to the problem: How did the Prophet himself conceive of the state of *jāhilīyah*? What did the word mean to Muḥammad and his contemporaries? In the *Sīrat al-Nabī* (The Life of the Prophet) by Ibn Isḥāq there is an interesting story told of an old pagan named Shās ibn Qays. The event occurred not very long

[3] Ignaz Goldziher, *Muhammedanische Studien* (Halle, 1888), I, 319 ff. For a more detailed and more systematic analysis of the word, see my *God and Man in the Koran*, Chapter VIII.

after the Prophet's Hijrah to Medina. This 'enemy of God' was an old man, most stubborn in offering resistance to the new religion and showing a bitter hostility to the followers of Muḥammad. One day he passed by a group of Anṣārs from Aws and Khazraj, two important Medinite tribes, once implacable enemies, but now tied together by a newly formed bond of friendship under the leadership of the Prophet, and fighting for a common cause. When he saw them talking together in a happy and friendly fashion, he was suddenly filled with envy and rage. He secretly instigated a Jewish youth to sit with them and recite verses composed by poets of both tribes to remind them of a series of blood feuds and ferocities that had happened in pagan times.

Things went as he wished. A violent quarrel arose among the people. And at the provocative words of one of them, 'Do you desire to recommence it? We are ready!' all went out to a volcanic tract near by, crying 'To arms! To arms!'

When the news reached the Prophet he hurried to the spot and said to them, 'O believers, how dare you forget God? Are you again tempted by the call of the Jāhilīyah (*bi-daᶜwa al-jāhilīyah*), when I am here among you, when God has guided you to Islām, honored you, and cut off thereby the bond of Jāhilīyah from you (*qaṭaᶜa bihi ᶜankum amr al-jāhilīyah*) delivered you from disbelief, and made you friends of each other?' Upon this they realized that all this was due to Satan's instigation, and wept embracing one another.[4]

This passage brings out two important points concerning the word in question. First, that the *jāhilīyah* was conceived by Muḥammad and his companions not as a period of time that had now passed away, but rather as something dynamic, a certain psychological state apparently driven away by the new force of Islām, but surviving secretly even in the minds of the believers, ready to break in at any moment upon their consciousness; and that this was felt by the Prophet to be a standing menace to the new religion. Secondly, that the *jāhilīyah* had practically nothing to do with 'ignorance'; that it meant in reality the keenest sense of tribal honor, the unyielding spirit of rivalry and arrogance, and all the rough and rude practices coming from an extremely passionate temper.

It is precisely here, if anywhere, that the true significance of the Islamic movement as a great work of moral reformation must be sought. In brief, the rise of Islām on its ethical side may very well be represented as a daring attempt to fight to the last extremity with the spirit of *jāhilīyah*, to abolish it completely, and to replace it once and for all by the spirit of *ḥilm*. Ibn Isḥāq has preserved for us another

[4] Ibn Isḥāq—Ibn Hishām: *Sīrat al-Nabī*, ed. F. Wüstenfeld (Göttingen, 1859–1860), I, 385–386.

piece of interesting tradition which throws much light on this aspect of *jāhilīyah.*

Immediately after the occupation of Mecca in A.H. 8, Muḥammad sent out troops into the regions surrounding the town. It was a work of pure missionary zeal; he ordered them to invite people to Islām only in friendly terms. Among those sent out as missionaries was the valiant Khālid ibn al-Walīd, known by the nickname of the 'Sword of Allāh', and he came to a tribe called Banū Jadhīmah. When the people saw him, they seized their weapons to fight. Khālid assured them of his peaceful intention and ordered them to lay down their weapons, for, he said, all other people had already accepted Islām; war was now over and everybody was safe.

But when they laid down their arms, notwithstanding the sincere warnings of a man of the tribe, Khālid tied their hands behind their backs and began to behead them. The news reached Muḥammad in Mecca. Thereupon he is said to have raised his arms so high that 'his armpits could be seen' and cried three times, 'O God, I am innocent before Thee of what Khālid has done!' Then he ordered his son-in-law ᶜAlī saying, 'Go at once to the people, examine thoroughly the affair, and trample down the custom of Jāhilīyah (*Ijᶜal amr al-jāhilīyah taḥta qadamayka*).' ᶜAlī hurried to the district with great sums of money and paid for all the blood and property.[5] It may be worth remarking that a little further on in the same passage, we find a certain person commenting on this behavior of Khālid with the words: 'You have done an act of Jāhilīyah (*ᶜAmilta bi-amr al-jāhilīyah*) in the midst of Islām.'

Those two incidents give us an important hint as to what was meant by the word *jāhilīyah* at the time of Muḥammad. They allow us also to get a real insight into the ethical motives that underlie the movement of Islām. It will be clear that what Islām was aiming at in the sphere of morality was a complete reformation of life, based on the abolishment of the *jāhilī* practices and their replacement by certain types of conduct arising from the spirit of *ḥilm.*

In the Arabic dictionary, *Tāj al-ᶜArūs* by al-Zabīdī,[6] the word *ḥilm* is defined as 'the act of reining one's soul and holding back one's nature from the violent emotion of anger' and in *Muḥīṭ al-Muḥīṭ* by al-Bustānī[7] as 'the state of the soul remaining tranquil, so that anger cannot move it easily; and its being unperturbed by any calamity that occurs', 'the state of calm tranquility notwithstanding the attack of anger', and 'being slow in requiting the wrong-doer'. It should be noticed that *ḥilm* was no new discovery of Muḥammad.

5 *Ibid.*, II, 834–835.
6 al-Zabīdī, *Tāj al-ᶜArūs* (Cairo, A.H. 1306–1307), VIII, under ḤLM, 355–358.
7 al-Bustānī, *Muḥīṭ* (Beirut, 1867–1870), 443–444.

On the contrary, it was one of the most highly esteemed virtues among the old pagan Arabs. Only it lacked a firm ground. The genuine Arabs of the desert have always been notoriously passionate people who may be moved to any extremes on the smallest provocation. Tranquility of the soul, the 'ataraxia' of the Greeks, is for them the most difficult thing to achieve, and, if achieved, to maintain for long. In order, therefore, that *ḥilm* may become the real pivot of all moral life, it must be given first of all a firm basis. This was furnished by the sincere belief in Allāh, the sole Creator of the whole world. It is to this *ḥilm* firmly grounded in monotheistic belief, the moral reasonableness of a religiously cultured man, that *jāhilīyah* stands diametrically opposed. Let us now turn to the Qurʾān itself to see whether or not the examples it offers confirm this interpretation of the word.

There are in the Qurʾān a number of verses in which various derivatives from the root *JHL* occur. The form *jāhilīyah* appears four times, in Sūrah III, 148/154, V, 55/50, XXXIII, 33, and XLVIII, 26, of which the last is perhaps the most important for our purpose. It runs as follows:

> When in the hearts of those who persist in unbelief arose the characteristic arrogance, the arrogance of *jāhilīyah*, then God sent down His peace of soul upon His Messenger and upon the believers, and imposed upon them the formula of self-restraint, for that was most befitting to them and they were most suited for that.

What I have translated here by the 'arrogance of *jāhilīyah*' (*ḥamīyat al-jāhilīyah*) refers to that overbearing haughtiness of a tribal man, the staunch pride so characteristic of the old pagan Arabs, the spirit of stubborn resistance against all that shows the slightest sign of injuring their sense of honor and destroying the traditional way of life. It is to be remarked that this spirit of passionate resistance is here made to contrast sharply with the calmness of soul sent down from Heaven upon the believers, and their disposition to maintain control over themselves in critical situations, to conquer their own passions, and to remain tranquil and forbearing in the name of religion. From the standpoint of Islām, the *jāhilīyah* was a blind, savage passion which characterized those who 'did not know how to distinguish between good and bad, who never asked pardon for the evil they had done, who were deaf to the good, dumb to the truth, and blind to Heavenly guidance.'[8] And it was this dark, blind passion that had inspired endless blood feuds, and caused countless miseries and disasters in the history of the pre-Islamic Arabs.

The three remaining examples of the use of the word *jāhilīyah*

[8] Ibn Isḥāq, II, 603.

seem not so significant from the semantical point of view. They are all used to describe some aspects of either the moral attitude or the outward behavior of those who would not accept the monotheistic religion, or of those who, though Muslims on the surface, do not really believe in God at all and begin to waver on the first occasion.

I give next some examples showing the use of two other derivative forms of the same root: one is the participial-adjectival form *jāhil* (appearing mostly in the pl. form *jāhilīn*), and the other is the verbal form *jahila* in its various forms of conjugation.

In Sūrah XII, 33, Joseph in Egypt, who begins to feel himself defenceless before the onslaught of the temptation of women, addresses God and says:

> O my Lord! I would sooner be cast into prison than do that which these women urge me to do, yet if Thou turnest not from me their temptation, I shall surrender myself to the surge of lust for them and so become one of the *jāhilīn*.

This passage owes its particular interest to the fact that it is found in a non-religious context, thus showing a purely secular use, so to speak, of *jāhil*. In this context the word seems to mean the reckless behavior of one who easily falls a victim to the surge of lust and makes himself knowingly blind and deaf to the distinction between right and wrong, behavior which is evidently the exact opposite of *ḥilm* as explained above.

> And [remember] Lot, when he said to his people, 'How dare you commit such abomination while you can see? Do you indeed approach men with lustful desires instead of women? Nay, you are a people whose conduct shows every sign of *jahl* (*tajhalūna*).' (XXVII, 55–56/54–55)

In this passage we see the people of Lot, that is, the people of Sodom described as behaving in a characteristically *jāhil* way, 'approaching' as they do 'men lustfully rather than women', which is an 'abominable sin' *fāḥishah*. The semantic analysis of the latter word will be given in a later chapter. Here it may suffice to note that in this example too what is primarily understood under the word *jāhil* is a man who goes to any extremes at the mercy of his own passions, and that not ignorantly, 'while you can see', i.e. being fully aware that by acting in this way he is committing an abominable sin. This example is of particular significance in our present context because it shows clearly that *jāhil* has essentially nothing to do with 'ignorance' though it implies the act of ignoring wilfully the moral rule of *ḥilm*.

> We are well aware of the fact that thou [Muḥammad] art grieved to hear what they are saying. Yet it is not thee that they cry lies to; the signs of God it is that they deny, these wrong-doers (*ẓālimīn*)! Apostles before thee were also cried lies to. But, they proved patient of being cried lies to and of being hurt, until Our help came to them. . . . Now if it is hard for thee that they turn away from thee, well, if thou canst seek out a hole down into the earth, or a ladder up into the sky, to show them [something like] a divine sign, [attempt to do it thyself! But since as a matter of fact thou canst never do such a thing, it would be better for thee to remain patient]. Had God so willed He would have Himself brought them all to the guidance. So be thou not one of the *jāhilīn*. (VI, 33–35)

The commentary of al-Bayḍāwī explains this last sentence by paraphrasing it in this way: Be thou not one of the *jāhilīn* by desiring what is naturally impossible to obtain and by getting impatient in those situations to which patience is most befitting; for that is a characteristic act of those who are *jāhil*. It may be remarked that this is a passage in which Allāh at the same time consoles and admonishes the Prophet, who, utterly distressed and disappointed at the stubborn 'turning away' of his folk, is beginning to take a gloomy view of the future. God reminds him that there were many prophets before him who suffered from the same sort of adverse fortune and that they endured it patiently, putting absolute confidence in Providence. And He ends by commanding Muḥammad to follow their example and not to get impatient in vain. It will be evident, then, that *jāhil* in this passage also means a man whose mind tends to be easily thrown into agitation by anger, grief, desperation, or any other emotion.

> Even though We should send down the angels unto them, or the dead should speak to them, or We should gather against them everything in array, they would never believe—unless God so willed. After all most of them always prove themselves to be characteristically *jāhil* (*yajhalūna*). (VI, 111)

In this and the following examples *jāhil* has something to do in an essential way with belief-unbelief. The word, as is clear, describes here those people who are too haughty and arrogant to 'surrender' to the new religion whose spiritual ideal is in many important respects utterly incompatible with that of the old pagan Arabs. This of course implies that, viewed from the standpoint of Arabian paganism itself, they are the true representatives of its spirit, and, whatever should happen, would maintain unswerving loyalty to the traditional tribal virtues. They are the people who never respond to the call of Muḥammad except with sheer derision and contempt. In the next example the policy of remaining indifferent and 'turning away' is recognized as the ideal attitude for all pious believers to adopt towards people of this kind. It goes without saying that in point of fact this could not be the permanent policy of Islām towards the infidels, but the example is of particular interest in connection with our present problem, for it helps to bring out in a striking manner the fundamental opposition of *jahl* and *ḥilm*.

> When they [i.e. the pious believers] hear vain talk [i.e. what the misbelievers say about God, prophets, and revelation] they turn away from it saying, 'We have our deeds, and you have yours. Peace be upon you! We have nothing to do with the *jāhilīn*.' (XXVIII, 55)

> Say: 'What! Is it something other than God that you would have me serve, O you *jāhilūn*?' It has been revealed to thee as well as to those before thee, 'If thou dost associate aught with God, thy deed shall be lost, and thou shalt surely be in the number of those who lose.' Nay, but God do thou serve, and be of those filled with thankfulness. (XXXIX, 64–65)

In this example the word *jāhil* is used to denote those addicted to the idolatrous practices of paganism, who, not content with 'associating' other gods with Allāh, even bid others to do the same. Here, be it remarked in passing, the *jāhil* is opposed to *shākir*, one who is filled with gratitude. In discussing the problem of the semantic category of *kāfir* we have already remarked that in Islamic religion belief was fundamentally and originally conceived of in terms of gratitude for benefits received. Exactly the same use of *jāhil* is found also in the following passage in which the idolatrous inclination of the Israelites of Moses' time is described.

> And We made the children of Israel pass across the sea, and they came upon a people addicted to the worship of idols that were in their possession. 'Moses,' they said, 'prepare for us a god like the gods they have.' He replied, 'Verily you are a people who act in a *jāhil* way (*innakum qawm tajhalūna*).' VII, 134–136/138–140)

> And We sent Noah to his people, 'I am obviously for you a warner admonishing you to worship none save God. Verily I fear for you the chastisement of a painful day.' . . . Then said the chiefs of the people, who were *kāfir*, 'As we see, thou art nothing more than a mortal like ourselves. As we see, you [Noah and his followers] have no claim to superiority over us. Nay more, we think you are liars!' [To this Noah replies in v. 31] 'As I see, you are a people who act in a *jāhil* way.' (XI, 27–29/25–27 and 31/29)

The next example also places a particular emphasis on the very strong and tenacious nature of the resistance to the revealed religion on the part of the *jāhilīn*.

> And recall also the brother of ᶜĀd [i.e. the Prophet Hūd] when he warned his people in the district of winding sandhills, saying, 'Worship none save God. I fear for you the chastisement of a painful day.' They said, 'Hast thou come in order to turn us away from our gods? Well, then, bring us what thou dost warn us against, if thou speakest the truth.' He said, 'No one knows the truth save God. My task is only to convey to you what I am sent with. But I see now you are a people who act in a *jāhil* way.' (XLVI, 20–22/21–23)

I have mentioned earlier the 'arrogance' of heathendom (*ḥamīyat al-jāhilīyah*), the haughty spirit of resistance to all that threatens the foundation of tribal life, that vehement arrogance, as Professor A. J. Arberry has put it,[9] which, after having caused in earlier times countless bloody feuds in the desert, now drove the pagan Arabs, alike of town and desert, to the relentless persecution of Muḥammad and his followers. The last two quotations illustrate this phase of the meaning inherent in the word *jahl*, for 'to act in a typically *jāhil* way' (*jahila*) means this type of conduct on the part of the Kāfirs.

All things considered, it will be clear by now that in the semantic category of *jahl* there is comprised the central notion of a fierce, passionate nature which tends to get stirred up on the slightest provocation and which may drive a man to all sorts of recklessness; that this passion tends to manifest itself in a very peculiar way in the arrogant sense of honor characterizing the pagan Arabs, especially the Bedouin of the desert; and lastly that in the specifically Qurᵓanic situation the word refers to the peculiar attitude of hostility and aggressiveness against the monotheistic belief of Islām, which was, to the mind of most of Muḥammad's contemporaries, too exacting ethically and which, moreover, called upon them to abandon their time-honored customs and their idols.

I have conducted a somewhat detailed semantic analysis of the words derived from the root *JHL* for two main purposes: first, in order to describe an important feature of the moral climate of Arabia at the time immediately before the rise of Islām and thus to give some preliminary notion of the fundamental principles underlying its moral attitude; and secondly, in order to show by a concrete example the general characteristics of my method of analysis. I have, I believe, made sufficiently clear that this method is a sort of contextual interpretation. It is to be noticed that the materials gathered are not

[9] A. J. Arberry, *The Seven Odes* (London, 1957), p. 263.

all of equal value: they differ from one another in the degree of contextual relevance, and consequently they must be assessed and utilized each according to its worth.

What are the practical rules for such contextual interpretation? In a very valuable booklet which is designed to give some 'practical advice' for those wishing to become good translators of Classical Latin, Professor J. Marouzeau says that the best way to clarify the meaning of an obscure word is first and foremost 'rapprocher, comparer, mettre en rapports les termes qui se ressemblent, qui s'opposent, qui se correspondent'. To this he does not forget to add: 'A propos de chaque mot non compris, appelons à notre secours tout l'ensemble du passage où il figure.'[10] This piece of 'conseil pratique', which may seem at first a needless commonplace, is in reality a very clever resumé of all the essential points in the procedure of contextual interpretation. Its tremendous importance will leap to the eye when we amplify it by illustrations. 'To bring together, compare, and put in relation all the terms that resemble, oppose, and correspond with each other'—there can indeed be no better maxim for us to adopt in our attempt to analyze the Qurʾanic data.

As the maxim just quoted suggests, the mere fact of a given ethical term appearing repeatedly in one and the same passage is not in itself of any strategic importance for semantics. For any passage to acquire a peculiar semantic significance, it must work as a specific context revealing in a full light some aspect or aspects of the semantic category of a given word. In Sūrah XXXV, 37/39, for example, the root *KFR* appears six times in succession. As the fundamental semantic structure of the root is quite clear now, I see no harm in translating it provisionally and for convenience of style by the English word 'disbelief'. The passage runs as follows:

> Who so disbelieves (*kafara*), his disbelief (*kufr*) shall be on his own head. Their disbelief (*kufr*) will only serve to increase for the disbelievers (*kāfir*) abhorrence in the sight of their Lord. Their disbelief (*kufr*) will serve to increase for the disbelievers (*kāfir*) naught but loss.

We can see that in this passage none of the words derived from the root *KFR* gives us any information worthy of notice concerning the basic sense of *KFR* itself. True, this verse may further our knowledge of the causal relationship in which the human act of *kufr* stands to divine anger and chastisement. But this is the utmost we can make out of it, and we must not forget that for any reader of the Qurʾān, this point is abundantly clear even without the aid of this example, a fact which reduces its strategic value for semantic analysis almost

[10] J. Marouzeau, *La Traduction du latin* (Paris, n.d.), p. 38.

to nullity. When, in the following chapters, I try to analyze the key ethico-religious terms of the Qurʾān, I shall intentionally leave out all examples of the kind just described.

There are, roughly speaking, seven cases in which any passage clearly assumes a strategic importance for the method of semantic analysis.

1. The simplest case in which a passage is semantically relevant occurs when the precise meaning of a word is elucidated concretely in its context by means of verbal description. This is what may best be termed 'contextual definition'. A very good case in point is furnished by the following example. It is found in Sūrah II, 172/177, and the word in question is *birr*, which is translated in English sometimes by 'piety', sometimes by 'righteousness'.

> The *birr* does not consist in your turning your faces towards the East or the West, but [true] *birr* is this, that one believes in God, and the Last Day, and the angels, and the Scripture, and the prophets; that one gives one's own wealth, howsoever cherished it may be, to kinsfolk, orphans, the needy, the wayfarer, and beggars, and also for the sake of [the liberation of] slaves: that one performs the ritual prayer, pays the alms [i.e. the poor-rate]. And those who keep their covenant when they have once covenanted and are patient in distress and hardship: these are they who are sincere (*alladhīna ṣadaqū*); these are they who are godfearing (*muttaqūn*).

The passage declares most emphatically that *birr*—'piety' we might roughly say—in the true sense does not consist in observing outwardly the rules of religious formalism, but is that kind of social righteousness that naturally arises from a deep monotheistic faith in God. It is to be remarked also that in the last sentence of this verse, the concept of *birr* is explicitly put in a close relationship with the concept of *ṣidq* 'sincerity' in belief and that of *taqwá* 'pious fear of God'. The problem of *birr* itself will come up for further consideration at a later stage. Here it is sufficient to draw attention to the significance of this kind of example from the point of view of our method of analysis.

2. We may note the particular value of synonyms for the purpose of analysis. When a word *X* is substituted for a word *Y* in the same passage or in exactly the same kind of verbal context, whether its range of application be wider or narrower than that of *Y*, the substitution is helpful to us in investigating the semantic category of either word. See, for example, Sūrah VII, 92–93/94–95:

> We [God] have not sent any prophet unto any town but We seized the people thereof with distress (*baʾsāʾ*) and adversity (*ḍarrāʾ*),

> that haply they might grow humble (v. 92). Then did We change evil (*sayyiʾah*) for good (*ḥasanah*) so that they increased in number, and said, 'adversity (*ḍarrāʾ*) and happiness (*sarrāʾ*) did touch our fathers'. (v. 93)

From a comparison of verse 92 and verse 93 it will be readily seen that the whole phrase '*baʾsāʾ* and *ḍarrāʾ*' in the former is replaced in the latter by *sayyiʾah* without any essential change of meaning. And to see this is to know for certain that the word *sayyiʾah*, which is recognizedly a near equivalent of 'evil' or 'bad', may be used in certain contexts to convey the meaning of something like 'hardship', 'misery', or 'distress'. We observe further that this *sayyiʾah* is contrasted in 93 with *ḥasanah*, usually meaning 'good' or 'goodness', which is in turn replaced in the same passage by *sarrāʾ*, meaning approximately 'joy' or 'happiness'.

Here is another example. In Sūrah XII, the Chapter of Joseph 28–29, the Egyptian Governor says to his wife, who, having failed to (tempt and seduce) young Joseph, has tried to bring him under a false charge of an abominable act:

> 'This is an example of your women's deceit; verily how prone you are to deceit! Joseph, turn away from this. And thou, woman, ask forgiveness of thy sin; verily thou art of the sinners.'

The meaning conveyed by the word which I have provisionally translated 'transgression', *dhanb*, reappears in the next sentence in another form: 'thou art a sinner', more literally, 'thou art one of the *khāṭiʾīn*', i.e. one of those who commit or have committed a *khaṭīʾah*, a word which is usually translated as 'fault' in English. From this we may feel justified in establishing, as far at least as this and similar contexts, the formula of equivalence: *dhanb* = *khaṭīʾah*. Are the two perfect synonyms in the present context? This is a point which we cannot decide at this stage. Suffice it to note that the famous commentator al-Bayḍāwī says[11] that *dhanb* is a concept standing on a higher level than *khaṭīʾah* and gives as the differentia of *khaṭīʾah* the element of intentionality. In other words, according to him, *khaṭīʾah* is a *dhanb* committed wilfully and deliberately.

3. We might mention the case in which the semantic structure of a given term is elucidated by contrast. The word *khayr*, for instance, is perhaps the nearest equivalent of the English word 'good' in the moral sense. But there are in Arabic many other words that appear to participate concurrently in the general connotation of goodness, of which we have actually seen one in the preceding section—*ḥasanah*. The difference between *khayr* and *ḥasanah* will be made clear to a

[11] al-Bayḍāwī, *Anwār al-Tanzīl wa-Asrār al-Taʾwīl* (Cairo, 1939), *ad loc.*

considerable extent by the knowledge that *khayr* is generally used in opposition to *sharr* whereas *ḥasanah* is opposed to *sayyiʾah*. If we can ascertain the precise meaning of any one of the four terms, we shall become surer also about the meaning of the remaining three.

Sometimes we find two different words standing in opposition to a third term. Thus *kāfir*, whose basic meaning I have explained earlier in this chapter, is most commonly contrasted with *muʾmin*, 'believer'. But there is another word, *fāsiq*, which is also contrasted in many places with *muʾmin*. Since it is opposed to *muʾmin*, and stands on the same footing as *kāfir*, the word *fāsiq* must refer to some detestable property of a man with regard to religious matters, and presumably a man characterized by a peculiar attitude of enmity towards God. If that is right or wrong we shall see in a later chapter. Here I shall content myself with remarking that in al-Bayḍāwī's opinion *fāsiq* is substantially the same as *kāfir*; only, *fāsiq* is a particularly obstinate type of *kāfir* (*mutamarrid fī al-kufr*). We may also note that in post-Qurʾanic times this word becomes a technical term designating an independent class that stands between *muʾmin* and *kāfir*, 'a *muʾmin* who has committed a grave sin less than that of *shirk* "associating", i.e. polytheism'.

4. As a special sub-class of the last group I should like to mention the case in which the semantic structure of an obscure word *X* is cleared up in terms of its negative form, *not-X*. The attempt, it may be argued, is mostly doomed to failure, since *not-X* may logically be anything whatsoever outside *X*. Fortunately, however, this does not apply to those cases where the field of reference is narrowly limited, that is, where the number of the possible referents is not very great. When the topic for discussion is a kind of flower which can be either red or blue, the very fact of being told that a particular specimen is not-red is enough to give the hearer much positive information about it. And this is almost always true of moral vocabulary in any language. In point of fact, in the limited field of reference of moral evaluation, knowledge about *not-X* tends to prove a very effective means in determining the semantic category of *X* itself. To know what types of conduct are generally referred to by the expression 'This is not good', is as important for the semanticist as to know what types of conduct are generally called 'good'.

The verb *istakbara* is one of the most important terms of negative evaluation in the Qurʾān. Roughly it means 'to be big with pride', 'to act haughtily and scornfully', and is used to refer to a characteristic feature of the *kāfir*. In the following example this verb appears in its negative form and describes from behind, so to speak, the conduct of one who behaves 'haughtily'.

> Only those believe in Our signs [i.e. revelations], who, when they are reminded of them, fall down prostrate and celebrate loudly the praise of their Lord, never getting puffed up with pride. (XXXII, 15)

What line of conduct do 'those who are *not* haughty' adopt? How do they actually behave when they find themselves face to face with divine signs? To know something positive and concrete about this is to know many things about the nature of that special kind of haughtiness which is designated by the word *istakbara*.

5. We call a 'semantic field' any set of patterned semantic relations between certain words of a language. A very simple example of this is provided in English by the peculiar relationship holding between 'wind' and 'to blow'. In every language we encounter such semantic 'clusters' of words. A word rarely stands aloof from others and maintains its existence all alone; on the contrary, words manifest everywhere a very marked tendency to combine with certain others in the contexts of occurrence. Every word has, as it were, its own choice of companions, so much so that the entire vocabulary of a language forms an extremely tangled web of semantic groupings. To disentangle it constitutes one of the important tasks of a semanticist. So, from his standpoint, any passage is semantically significant that contributes in some way or other towards determining the bounds of a field of meaning. Thus in the Qurʾān the verb *iftará* ('to invent', 'to forge') most frequently takes as its grammatical 'object' the noun *kadhib* (a 'lie'), thus forming a well-nigh inseparable group. To join this group comes the word *ẓālim*, whose basic meaning I have discussed earlier. In fact the expression 'Who does more wrong, or who is more unjust, (*aẓlam*), than he who forges (*iftará*) against God a lie (*kadhib*)?' is one of the set phrases of our Scripture. This makes it clear that the three words *iftará–kadhib–ẓālim* form in the Qurʾān a peculiar group or combination, a semantic field in the sense just explained.

6. Very often the rhetorical device of parallelism reveals the existence of a semantic relationship between two or more words. It is widely known that in Biblical Hebrew and even more in Classical Chinese, parallelism in poetic style furnishes not infrequently the key to the meanings of many words which would otherwise remain obscure. This is not the case to the same degree in the Qurʾān. And yet there are a number of passages where parallelism helps to bring out a particular aspect of some semantic field. In Sūrah XXIX, for instance, we see the following two sentences appearing side by side:

> And none denies Our signs save the *kāfir*. (v. 46/47)
> And none denies Our signs save the *ẓālim*. (v. 48/49)

The parallelism of construction is in itself a clear proof of the fact that *kāfir* ('disbeliever') and *ẓālim* ('wrong-doer') are semantic equals in so far at least as the act of refusing to believe in divine signs is concerned. To this group of *kāfir* and *ẓālim* we may add one more member, *fāsiq*, if we note another instance of parallelism which is found in Sūrah V.

> Whoso judges not by what God has sent down: such are *kāfirūn*. (v. 48/44)
> Whoso judges not by what God has sent down: such are *ẓālimūn*. (v. 49/45)
> Whoso judges not by what God has sent down: such are *fāsiqūn*. (v. 51/47)

Here the three words *kāfir*, *ẓālim*, and *fāsiq* are put semantically on a par with one another in respect to not giving judgment according to what God has revealed. Thus it will be evident that these words define a specific phase of a wider semantic field, that of 'unbelief', whose fundamental features will occupy us in a later chapter.

7. As one might expect, the key ethical terms in the Qurʾān are generally used in contexts of deep religious import. Sometimes, however, we find them used, even within the bounds of the Qurʾān, in non-religious contexts which reveal the purely secular aspects of their meanings. These cases naturally furnish the semanticist with extremely valuable material for advancing his studies of the structure of the words concerned. In point of fact we have already seen an example of this in the word *jāhil*.[12] Generally speaking Sūrah XII, the 'Chapter of Joseph', is semantically of particular interest in that it provides us with many good examples of this kind of secular use of words. I shall give here another example from another Sūrah. The word in question is *kāfir*.

> And he said, 'Did we not bring thee up amongst us as a child? And didst thou not dwell amongst us for many years of thy life? And yet thou didst do the deed which thou didst. Thou art of the ungrateful (*kāfirīn*).' (XXVI, 17–18/18–19)

This is said by Pharaoh to Moses in a patently non-religious context of meaning, when the latter has slain an Egyptian subject of the former. Nothing indeed throws such a clear light on the basic element of 'ingratitude', which, as we saw earlier, constitutes the original semantic core of the root *KFR*.

12 See the first example taken from Surah XII, p. 32.

# FROM TRIBAL CODE TO ISLAMIC ETHICS

# III. The Pessimistic Conception of the Earthly Life

PERHAPS THE MOST CONSPICIOUS FEATURE OF THE DEVELOPMENT OF moral ideas in ancient Arabia is that Islām proclaimed a new morality entirely based on the absolute Will of God, whilst the guiding principle of the pre-Islamic moral life had been tribal tradition, or 'the custom of our forefathers'.

There should be no misunderstanding here. We would be doing gross injustice to the pre-Islamic Arabs if we maintained that there was among them no distinction between right and wrong, between what is good and what is bad. On the contrary, a careful perusal of a document such as the famous 'Book of Songs', *Kitāb al-Aghānī*, will at once convince us that the pagan Arabs were in reality richly endowed with an acute sense of morality. Even the so-called 'free children of the desert' had their own meticulous rules of conduct, by the standard of which any action, whether personal or tribal, could be judged to be right or wrong, good or bad. Only their 'good' and 'bad', 'right' and 'wrong' lacked a consistent, theoretical basis. They could hardly be justified except by what is reducible to a useless tautology of the type '*X* is good because it is good'. Besides, these ethical properties were as a matter of actual fact often quite powerless to regulate the conduct of men in time of crisis when tribal interest was at stake, as the well-known maxim of the desert shows: 'Help your brother [i.e. fellow-tribesman] whether he is being wronged or wronging others.'

The only form of argument the pagan Arabs could use, and in fact were willing to use in ethical matters was: *X* is good (or right) because we found our fathers and forefathers doing it.

> When it is said to them [i.e. the pagans], 'Follow that which God has sent', they reply, 'Nay, we will follow what we found our ancestors doing.' What, even if their ancestors were all ignorant folk erring away from the true path? (II, 165/170)

> They [i.e. pagans] argue, 'Lo! we found our ancestors holding fast to a certain form of religion, and we are guided by their footprints.' Just in the same way We never sent before thee [Muḥammad] any warner to any city, but that the people thereof who lived in luxury said, 'We found our ancestors holding fast to a certain form of religion, and we are following their footprints.' Ask them, 'What, even if I bring you what will give you better guidance than that you found your ancestors clinging to?' But they will only say, 'Nay, we in what you were sent with do disbelieve!' (XLIII, 21–23/22–24)

This type of argument naturally implies on its negative side that everything is bad (or wrong) in their eyes, which would involve any break with the existing social order, or which would shake and damage in however slight a manner the prestige of customs inherited from their tribal ancestors. And such was precisely the nature of the moral reform which Islām inaugurated. The principle of morality which its Prophet so energetically championed had its origin in his glowing belief in the one and only God, in Whose eye all the customs and traditions of the tribes could never be anything more than insignificant worldly affairs having nothing 'sacred' about them. It was only natural that this led Islām to a radical break with the fundamental assumptions underlying all the moral ideas of the pagan Arabs.

From among the various features that characterize the spirit of the age of Jāhilīyah, I would like to draw attention to the two following as being of particular relevance: its worldliness and its tribalism. The first of these will form the subject of the present chapter. The principle of tribalism will be dealt with in the following chapter.

The sober realism characterizing in a very peculiar way the Bedouin world-view is now well-known among those who are interested in the nature of Arab culture. It seems to be connected most intimately with the climate of the land. Indeed, it has something which evokes in our minds the arid sands of the desert. At all events it is a fact that lack of imagination has stamped its mark on almost everything that may be recognized as purely Arabic. To the realistic Arab mind this present world with its myriad colors and forms is the only world that exists. Nothing is more remote from such a mind than a belief in eternal life, the life to come. There can be no existence beyond the limits of this world.

> They assert, 'There is our life in this present world; we die, we live, and naught destroys us but Time (*Dahr*).' (XLV, 23/24)

> They assert, 'There is only our life in this present world; we shall never be raised.' (VI, 29)

Here the monotheism of Islām came inevitably into serious conflict with the old pagan conception of existence. The divine message the Prophet brought to his countrymen about the resurrection and the world to come provoked everywhere scorn and derision.

> They say, 'What, when we are dead and have become dust and bones, shall we then possibly be raised? A promise like this we and our ancestors have been given before. These are all merely fantastic old tales.' (XXIII, 84–85/82–83)

> The Kāfirs say, 'This is indeed a wondrous thing! What? when we are dead and have become dust? That would indeed be a long way to return!' (L, 2–3)

> The Kāfirs say, 'Hey! Shall we show you a strange fellow who will assure you that, after you have been utterly torn to pieces, you shall then be created anew?' (XXXIV, 7)

To be sure, even the pagan Bedouin knew and made much use of the word *khulūd*, meaning 'a long life,[1] so long indeed that it will never come to an end' (i.e. eternal existence), but their all too realistic minds could hardly go beyond the horizon of the immediately present; in other words, *khulūd* should be something of this world. The

[1] To be more exact, the 'length' of this 'long life' must be taken in a relative sense, varying from case to case. In the following verse of the Jāhilī poet ʿAbīd b. al-Abraṣ (*Dīwān*, ed. & trans. Ch. Lyall (Leiden, 1931), poem XLVII, v. 9), for instance, the same verb *khalada* is used twice in succession: in the first case it means 'to live longer than others' 'to remain alive after others are gone', and in the second 'to live for ever'.

*Fa-khaladtu baʿdahum wa-lastu bi-khālid,*
*Fa-al-dahr dhū ghiyar wa-dhū alwān.*

Thus I remain after them [i.e. after they have died], but I myself am not to live forever, for Time is ever full of vicissitudes and changes.

'eternity' of which there is much talk in pre-Islamic poetry, and which undoubtedly constituted one of the most serious human problems among the pagan Arabs just before the rise of Islām, meant primarily an eternal life on this very earth. A glance at the literary works they left makes it abundantly clear that they were aware that all the treasures amassed and all deeds done would be ultimately meaningless and vain if there could not be found something which would confer immortality to the whole life of this world. Some such principle of immortality, *mukhlid* (lit. an 'eternalizer'), they sought for everywhere. But it was, of course, so much labor lost. With biting sarcasm the Qur'ān speaks of 'everyone . . . who gathers wealth and counts it over as if his wealth could "eternalize" him'. (CIV, 1–3) and the poet al-Aʿshá says 'Never, never think that riches can make their possessor immortal.'

It is interesting to notice that in Jāhilī literature the idea that wealth is the most important thing in the world, that it *is* the 'eternalizer' is presented by women, usually wives, while men hold such a 'base and silly' idea in scorn and simply ignore it, for it goes against the ethical principle of *karam* 'generosity'. The wife of the famous poet al-Mukhabbal reproaches her husband for his spendthrift habits and says:

*Inna al-tharā' huwa al-khulūd wa-i **
*-nna al-mar' yuqribu yawmahu al-ʿadam*

Verily wealth means *khulūd*, and lack of wealth brings near to him his day, i.e. death.

To this the poet replies:

*Innī wa-jaddiki mā tukhalliduni **
*mi'at yaṭīru ʿifā'uha udm*

By my troth, never shall I be made to live eternally by a hundred fat camels whose hair is carried away by the wind.[2]

It is important to remark also that this bitter consciousness of the absolute impossibility of finding 'eternity' in this world was at once the dead end into which heathenism drove itself and the very starting point from which Islām took its ascending course. Indeed, Jāhilīyah and Islām unite in the recognition of the evanescence of human life. The pessimism arising from the consciousness of the essential vanity of life is common to both pre-Islamic poetry and the Sacred Book. Every reader of the Qur'ān knows that this is a theme of incessant recurrence.

[2] Mufaḍḍal, *Mufaḍḍalīyāt* Cairo, 1942), poem XXI, 36–37.

> The life of this present world is naught but a play and a pastime. (XLVII, 38/36)

> Know that the life of this present world is naught but a play and pastime, an outward show, and vainglory among you, and a rivalry in wealth and children. All this is like vegetation after rain, whose growth rejoices the *kāfir*; then it withers away and thou seest it become sere and yellow; then it becomes straw. . . . Thus the life of this world is but an illusion of joy. (LVII, 19–20/20)

This pessimistic conception of the earthly life, it would seem, has nothing in itself to differentiate it from that expressed by the poets. Throughout pre-Islamic poetry there runs a dark note of pessimism. It is, we might say, the natural basic mood of the literature of Jāhilīyah. The works of the great pre-Islamic poets invariably resound with bitter cries of despair at the emptiness of human life. Thus, to give one example, ʿAbīd b. al-Abraṣ says:

> I pondered on thoughts of my people, the kind ones who dwelt at Malhub, and my heart was sore for them, overwhelmed with sorrow;
>
> . . . . . . . . . . . . . . . . . . . . . . . .
>
> And as remembrance filled me, the tears streamed ceaselessly like a water-runnel watering the seed-plots of one who has come to decay.
>
> Yea, many the tent from whose chambers the scent of musk floated forth have I entered, mayhap in secret, mayhap as an open wooer;
>
> And many the songstress whose voice the wine had rendered hoarse, who sings to the strings stretched over a hollow curved lyre,
>
> Have I listened to with companions, all men of noble race, who count themselves bound without stint to all seeking help.
>
> . . . . . . . . . . . . . . . . . . . . . . . .
>
> And now all these things are gone, and I am left to mourn—nay, what man on earth is there whose hopes are never belied?
>
> . . . . . . . . . . . . . . . . . . . . . . . .
>
> Thou seest a man ever yearn and pine for length of life: but what is long life's sum but a burden of grief and pain?[3]

In the first poem of the Dīwān the same old poet, after giving a detailed picture of the desolation that has spread over the place of his youthful memories, goes on to moralize on the vanity of all earthly things[4] and concludes: 'All that is pleasant must be snatched

[3] ʿAbīd b. al-Abraṣ, IX, 31.
[4] *Ibid.*, p. 19.

away, and every one that gathers spoil is spoiled in turn' (v. 14); 'Man as long as he lives is a self-deceiver: length of life is but increase of trouble.' (v. 24)

Thus in the recognition of the vanity, emptiness, and ephemerality of life Islām and Jāhilīyah evidently stand on a common ground. And yet the conclusions they draw from this are poles apart. For Jāhilīyah did not and would not know anything beyond the world of present existence, whereas Islām was a religion that was precisely founded on a glowing belief in the life to come. The pivotal point of Muḥammad's message lies decidedly in the hereafter. And once we recognize, and believe in, the existence of the world to come, failure in the attempt at seeking out *khulūd*, 'eternity', in this world need no longer drive us into the depths of despair. So the *khulūd* which presented such an awful, insoluble problem to the men of Jāhilīyah, is now transposed without any difficulty to a sphere that lies beyond the horizon of existence.

> Nay, but you prefer the life of the present world, when in reality the world to come is far superior and everlasting. (LXXXVII, 16–17)

> You desire the perishable goods of the present world, while God desires [for you] the Hereafter. (VIII, 68/67)

> Wealth and children are but an adornment of the present world. The good deeds that remain for ever are better in the sight of thy Lord for reward and better in respect of hope. (XVIII, 44/46)

This world is transitory and vain, Islām teaches, and so you must never count upon it; if you really desire to obtain immortality and enjoy eternal bliss you should make the principle of other-worldliness the very basis of your life. All is vain in this world, Jāhilīyah preaches, and nothing is to be found beyond it, so you must enjoy your ephemeral life to the utmost limit of its capacity. Hedonism is the only possible conclusion for the worldly-minded people of Jāhilīyah.

The following two verses from the famous Ode of Ṭarafah reveal better than anything else the relation between their consciousness of the impossibility of binding *khulūd* in this world and the principle of hedonism.

> Well now, thou who censurest me because I attend the turmoils of war and because I cease not to pursue pleasures, canst thou then 'eternalize' (*mukhlid*) my existence? But since thou art unable to defend me from death, pray allow me to forestall it with what wealth I possess.[5]

[5] Ṭarafah, *Muʿallaqah*, vv. 56–57, in *Septem Moallakat*, ed. Aug. Arnold (Leipzig, 1850).

Pre-Islamic poetry is studded with hymns of voluptuous pleasures and enjoyments. In another passage (46–51) of the Ode Ṭarafah says:

> Seek me in the assembly of my people, and you will find me there. Hunt me in the taverns, and you will surely capture me there.
>
> Come to me in early morning, I shall fill you a cup of wine to the brim. If you decline, then decline as you like and be of good cheer.
>
> . . . . . . . . . . . . . . . . . . . . . . .
>
> My boon companions are youths white as stars. And at eventide a singing-girl comes to us in robes striped and saffron-colored.
>
> Wide is the opening at her bosoms, delicately soft her nakedness when the fingers of my companions touch it and caress.
>
> When we say, 'Pray let us hear a song', she begins gently to sing, with a voluptuous languidness, in a voice subdued.

The passage just quoted refers to the habit of winebibbing, which was for the men of Jāhilīyah a source of highest pleasure. Nothing shows better to what extent the principle of *carpe diem* was exercising an active influence on the moral phase of the Jāhilī life. Wine was in their eyes one of the supreme gifts of fortune. The men of Jāhilīyah were mostly winebibbers; they indulged in it habitually; they made it even their real boast and a point of honor to be able to indulge themselves freely with wine, for that was considered an unmistakable evidence of a 'generous nature', which constituted one of the personal virtues most highly prized by the Arabs in the days of paganism.

> I am a *karīm* ('man of a noble nature'), one who remains soaked in drink all his life. If we die tomorrow you will know which of us is the thirsty fellow.[6]

Great was the number of those who ruined themselves by dissipation on account of wine, for, as ᶜAbīd says in one of his poems (VIII, 3). 'High was the price of wine, and great was the gain of the merchants.' In another poem he also says:

> We bid up the price of all old wine,
> strong and fragrant, while we are sober;
> And we hold of no account, in pursuit of its delights,
> the mass of our inherited wealth, when we are drunken.[7]

And Labīd b. Rabīᶜah, another famous poet of Jāhilīyah who lived long enough to die as a Muslim, had chanted in his springtide days

[6] Ṭarafah, v. 63.
[7] ᶜAbīd b. al-Abraṣ, VII, 17–18.

the praises of the delight of wine-drinking. Here is a passage from his great Ode, in which he addresses his sweetheart Nawār:

> Ah, thou hast no idea how many serene nights of joyous merry-making and mirthful cheer
> I have passed in convivial gatherings; how I have frequented the hoisted flag of the wine-merchant when the price of wine was dear;
> How I purchase wine at a high price in skin bags old and black, or, sometimes, in jugs smeared with pitch, whose seals I break;
> How I take pleasure in quaffing pure wine in the morn, holding close a girl while her nimble fingers touch the strings of her lute;
> How often I rise before the cock to take my own morning draught and to take a second draught when the sleepers do awake.[8]

Ṭarafah, to whom reference has been repeatedly made, was a representative man of this type. In vv. 53–54 of his Ode, he describes the hapless fate which has put an end to all his enjoyments:

> Thus I went on drinking wine, and pursuing the pleasures of life, selling, dissipating both my own earnings and my patrimony,
> Until at last the whole tribe deserted me, and here I am left all alone like a dirty mangy camel.

According to an old tradition, the famous poet al-Aᶜshā set out for Muḥammad with a firm intention of becoming a Muslim. On his way a pagan friend met him and asked him what was the matter. The poet told him that he was going to the Prophet to accept Islām. On being told that Islām prohibited fornication, he declared that it did not matter to him at all. When, however, his friend said, 'Ah, but do you know that Muḥammad prohibits wine?' he said, 'That is a thing I cannot give up so easily. Well, in that case I will go back and drink heavily for a whole year and after that return and accept Islām.' So he went, and died in the very year, so that he never came back to the Prophet.[9]

It was precisely in the midst of such a thoughtless generation that Muḥammad arose to proclaim the new belief in the future life and the final judgment. He saw around him nothing but levity, worldliness, and pleasure-seeking.

> They only pursue pleasures of the life of this present world, when, in reality, the whole life of this world is naught but transient enjoyment compared with the future life. (XIII, 26)

[8] Labīd, *Muᶜallaqah*, vv. 57–61, in *Septem Moallakat*.
[9] Ibn Isḥāq, I, 256.

> The life of this world is naught but a play and a pastime; surely the next abode is better far for those who are godfearing. What, have you then no sense? (VI, 32)

For the godless and frivolous generation whom this world's life has completely deceived, it is, on the contrary, religion that is but a play and pastime (VI, 69/70, VII, 49/51). The determining mood of the spiritual situation of Jāhilīyah is, from the point of view of the Qur'ān, that of jollity and complete indifference to the serious matters of religion. At these careless people who are now laughing, jesting, and playing, the Apostle of God throws the 'good tidings' of the approaching torments of Hell. The calamitous Day of Judgment is threateningly near. And on that day the godless will have to pay dear for their thoughtlessness in this world.

> On the day when those who disbelieve (*KFR*) shall be exposed to the Fire [of Hell]: 'You squandered your good things in your earthly life and found enjoyment in them. Wherefore this day you are recompensed with a humiliating chastisement, for that you grew arrogant in the earth without any right, and for that you transgressed.' (XLVI, 19/20)

> Lo! This is a man who once lived among his family joyfully. Verily it never occurred to him that he should return to God. (LXXXIV, 13–14)

In view of this state of affairs, the basic attitude of man in this present world should be, from the Qur'anic point of view, not the desperate sort of hedonism which we have just encountered among the pre-Islamic Arabs, but absolute earnestness that stems out of the keen consciousness of the approach of the Last Day. The fear of God, a reverent awe before the Lord of the Day of Judgment, must act as the determining motive of all conduct of the religious man, nay rather it must determine the whole of human existence. The key word here is *taqwá*. The proof of a man's being genuinely noble (*karīm*) of character and personality should not be sought in the direction of audacity in mundane affairs. The real *karīm* is not a man who dares to squander impulsively and thoughtlessly all the riches in his hand. The real *karīm* is he who lives with great moral earnestness, being ever conscious of the approaching Day of horrible catastrophe. It is extremely significant that the Qur'ān in one of its most important verses defines the word *karīm* in terms of the concept of *taqwá* 'pious fear of God'.

> Surely the noblest [*akram*, the superlative form of *karīm*] of you all in the sight of God is the one who is most godfearing [*atqá*, the

superlative of *taqī* meaning 'god-fearing'] among you. Verily God knows everything. He is aware of everything. (XLIX, 13)

We can hardly overemphasize the revolutionary nature of this attempt to re-evaluate semantically an old moral word. Already in the day of Jāhilīyah *karīm* was one of the highest value-words, meaning roughly both nobility of birth and generosity. But no one before Islām could have thought of defining 'nobility' in terms of 'fear of God'.

Of course it should be kept in mind that this emotion of 'fear' meant in this case far more than being afraid of punishment. As Tor Andrae pointed out years ago[10], the deep ethico-religious value of the fear of God, the Lord of the Day of Judgment, is largely due to the fact that it cannot but arouse in the mind of the believer a clear consciousness of the tremendous seriousness of life and thus incite him to moral earnestness and responsibility. Act always as if you were standing at this very moment before the Divine Judge, before the judgment seat of Allāh on the Day of the great reckoning—this was the first of the cardinal rules of conduct which Islām laid down in the earliest period of its development.[11] But all this would be utterly impossible and absurd where there was no faith in the world to come. Fear of God could only become a principle of ethics on the basis of a monotheistic belief in which God is represented as the Lord of the Judgment Day.

10 Tor Andrae, *Mohammed, sein Leben und sein Glaube* (Göttingen, 1932), Chapter III.

11 *Taqwā* in this sense becomes in the post-Qurʾanic period the central theme of the early ascetics. Ḥasan al-Baṣrī is one of the outstanding examples of this attitude. For details see H. Ritter, 'Studien zur Geschichte der islamischen Frömmigkeit, I', *Der Islam*, XXI (1933), 1–83.

# IV. The Spirit of Tribal Solidarity

We shall turn next to the problem of tribalism. It is a commonplace to say that the social structure of pre-Islamic Arabia was essentially tribal. It has often been pointed out by various writers on Arabia that the lifeblood of pagan ethics was the feeling of solidarity existing between all the members of the tribe. The tribe, or its subclass, the clan, was for the pre-Islamic Arabs not only the sole unit and basis of social life but represented first and foremost the highest principle of conduct, evolving a comprehensive pattern for the whole of life, both individual and public. Tribal spirit was no doubt the fountainhead of all cardinal moral ideas on which Arab society was built. To respect the bond of kinship by blood more than anything else in the world, and to act for the glory of the tribe, this was by common consent a sacred duty imposed on every man, that is, every individual member of the group.

Nothing expresses better and more tersely the deep, irrational nature of this sentiment of tribal connection than a verse of Durayd b. al-Ṣimmah which Nicholson cites: 'I am of Ghaziyya: if she be in error, then I will err; And if Ghaziyya be guided right, I go right with her!'[1] This illustrates remarkably well how tribal solidarity

[1] Nicholson, p. 83.

dictated the actions of the heathen Arab, and how he had to obey through foul and fair the categorical imperative of tribalism. As R. Dozy remarked, 'this limitless and unshakable attachment, which is called *ʿaṣabīyah*, that a pagan Arab feels for his fellow-tribesmen, this absolute devotion to the interests, prosperity, glory, and honor of the community into which he was born and in which he will die—this is not in any way a sentiment like our patriotism, which would appear to a fiery Bedouin too lukewarm. It is a violent and terrible passion. It is at the same time the first and most sacred duty of all duties; it is the real religion of the desert.'[2] Even if there is some exaggeration in this last statement, yet it remains true that *ʿaṣabīyah* was incomparably stronger and more influential than the pagan religion of the desert, which never rose above the level of primitive polydaemonism and which, by the time of Muḥammad, was showing signs of degenerating more and more into sheer magic.

Of course, as a matter of actual fact, this rule of tribal solidarity, as every other rule of conduct, was sometimes transgressed. Sporadically there appeared, even in the desert, persons whose individuality was too strong and too marked to remain always loyal to the tribal cause. Such a person naturally tended to produce trouble by his reckless deeds inside and outside the tribe and might even involve his tribal 'brothers' in the bloodiest kind of warfare, for in pagan days a man's whole tribe or clan had to assume the responsibility for his disgraceful doings. In such a case the only way open to the tribe for evading all responsibility for him is to proclaim him as having been formally disowned, whereby he becomes an 'outlaw' (*khalī*). The whole procedure was known under the name of *tabarruʾ*.[3] A large number of such homeless outlaws, known as *ṣaʿālīk* (sg. *ṣuʿlūk*), appear to have been roaming the desert in the days of Jāhilīyah, some of them quite abject, base, and humiliated, but some others men of remarkable valor and dignity, a real embodiment of the spirit of independence.

Here is a song of such vagabondage, a poem by ʿUrwah b. Ward al-ʿAbsī, himself one of the most outstanding figures in the history of Arab outcasts (*ṣaʿālīk*). He describes in this famous poem the two types of *ṣaʿālīk* which I have just mentioned.

2 *Histoire des Musulmans d'Espagne*, 2nd ed., ed. E. Levi-Provencal (Leiden, 1932), I, 7.

3 From the verb *tabarraʾa* 'to declare oneself *barīʾ* from somebody or something'. *Barīʾ* means 'completely free from something undesirable, and having nothing to do with it'. It is extremely interesting to observe that this old word, so characteristic of the pagan tribal life, was later in the Islamic age turned into a technical term in theology meaning something like 'excommunication' from the Muslim community. The first theologians in Islām, the Khawārij, greatly abused this notion and 'declared themselves free' from the majority of Muslims, i.e. declared the latter to be Kāfirs.

God's curse on the poor vagabond who under cover of night
roams about slaughter-places in search of heads of bones.
At eventide he lies down exhausted, to awake the morrow still drowsy,
shaking off wearily the gravel from his side covered with dust.
But the real *ṣuᶜlūk* is this: the breadth of his face glows
like the flame of a shooting star blazing in the darkness,
Towering over the neighborhood, striking his enemies with horror.
All people curse him between the tents, as losers curse their unlucky lot.
Even when they live far from his haunts, they never relax their guard
against his coming nigh, as a family looking out for one whom they love.[4]

If we can judge from the poets, it even happened not infrequently that actual experience taught the Arabs a better wisdom. Often, says a poet, the roaming stranger (*nāziḥ*) proves a near friend, and the nearest kinsman is cut off to become a stranger.[5]

But taken all in all, these cases were all anomalies and were certainly in a small minority. And the life of these homeless outlaws was, as might be expected in desert conditions, always on the brink of death either from natural causes or by the hand of the human enemy. For it is almost a commonplace that, without a high degree of solidarity, there can be hardly any hope of facing with success the fierce struggle for survival under the climatic and social conditions of the desert. Even those strangers who were formally adopted among a tribe, and who consequently were in a position far better than that of outlaws, were often hard put to it only because they were 'outsiders'. Such an adopted member of the tribe was called *zanīm*. It is extremely significant in this connection that this word developed a very marked secondary meaning of 'base', 'ignoble', and a 'a man of evil character'. So much so that Ibn Isḥāq feels himself obliged to make a particular remark, concerning a passage from the Qurʾān (LXVIII, 10–13) where this word occurs, to the effect that *zanīm* here is not used in the sense of a man of ignoble birth (*li-ᶜayb fī nasabihi*), because it is not for God to insult the pedigree of anyone, but it is used in its original sense of a stranger adopted by a tribe. As a pagan poet, al-Khaṭīm al-Tamīmī, said a *zanīm* was a useless, superfluous addition to the body of the tribe, and anyone who dared to exhibit

The physical world shapes the needs of the people living in it

[4] In Abū Tammām's *Ḥamāsah*, with comm. of al-Khaṭīb al-Tibrīzī (Bulaq, A.H. 1296), I, 219–220.
[5] ᶜAbīd b. al-Abraṣ, I, 22.

preference for such an 'addition' over his kinsmen by blood was sure to arouse a storm of reproach. It was for exactly the same reason that those of the Arab tribes in Medina, who fervently took the side of Muḥammad incurred stinging reproaches from the opposite camp. This feeling of indignation has found a genuine expression in the following verses of ᶜAsmā b. Marwān:

> O how I despise you, sons of Mālik and an-Nabīt,
> and you, tribes of ᶜAwf and sons of Khazraj!
> You have obeyed an outsider coming from afar,
> belonging not to Murād nor to Madhḥij![6]

Thus the social structure of Jāhilīyah was essentially tribal in the sense that the ideal of the tribe was the Alpha and Omega of human existence. The bond of kinship by blood, the burning sense of honor based on the all-importance of blood relations, which required that a man should take the side of his tribal brothers regardless of whether they were right or wrong, love of one's own tribe, bitter scorn of the outsiders; these furnished the final yardsticks by which the people of Jāhilīyah measured personal values. There appears to have been practically no supratribal standard of good in pagan days.

It is of supreme importance for the right estimation of Muḥammad's religious movement to realize that it was just in such a circumstance that he declared the definite superiority of religious relationship over the ties of blood. His was indeed a daring attempt to establish an entirely new community on the basis of a common faith in the one and only God, whose members, as Professor Gustave Von Grunebaum has put it, were kin by faith rather than by blood. According to Von Grunebaum,[7] the most effective factor in attracting men to Islām was, apart from the religious truths contained in the message of Muḥammad, its ability to serve as a point of crystallization for a novel socio-political unity. But it had to overcome tremendous difficulties before it could begin to function as such a center of crystallization.

Abū Jahl, a sworn enemy of the Prophet, is reported to have described him once as 'one who more than anyone else has cut the bond of kinship by blood and wrought that which is scandalous'. And the tribal bard of Quraysh in Mecca, al-Ḥārith b. Hishām said after the battle of Badr in praise of those slain on the battlefield fighting against Muḥammad and the Muslims:

[6] Ibn Isḥāq, II, 995.

[7] G. E. Von Grunebaum, *Islam, Essays in the Nature and Growth of a Cultural Tradition,* 1st American ed. (New York, 1961), p. 31.

They were slain as noble warriors, they did not sell their tribe to
side with aliens who are no kith and kin of theirs.
But you sold your own tribe when Ghassān became your true
friends
in place of us [Quraysh]; what a scandalous act it was!
An act of treason, a glaring crime, a cutting of the ties of
kinship!
Your injustice all men endowed with reason will perceive.[8]

It is interesting to notice that *politically* Muḥammad himself profited to no slight extent from the existence of the rule of tribal solidarity even in the city community of Mecca, particularly during the first years of his prophetic activity. For, as Professor Montgomery Watt has pointed out,[9] it was largely due to the fervor of *ʿaṣabīyah* shown by the powerful subdivision of Quraysh, Banū Hāshim, who were there ready to protect him at any moment, that he could continue preaching in Mecca despite the indignation against him of the leading circles of Quraysh. The Prophet, according to orthodox tradition, belonged by birth to this illustrious family of Mecca, being one of the grandsons of Hāshim.

And yet, Muḥammad made a daring attempt to abolish the principle of tribal solidarity and to replace it by that of monotheistic faith which would make possible a new organization of society with a wholly ritualized way of life as a manifestation of the eternal order here on the earth. It is clear that this revolution—for 'revolution' it certainly was—was prompted at first by a purely religious motive, though as time went on the principle of kinship by faith began to assume more and more a rich political coloring.

kinship by faith rather than blood

Be that as it may, it is a fact that Islām ordained a new type of brotherhood based on faith between all the members of the community and declared that henceforward this brotherhood was to be regarded as closer and stronger than the bond of kinship by blood. For the purpose of this study it is particularly important to remark that the motive of this abrogation of the age-old rule of *ʿaṣabīyah* may be traced ultimately to the terrifying eschatological vision of the Last Day. For on that day, all blood relationships that are now so much prized, will turn utterly meaningless and useless.

the worldly - even blood/family - will be gone on the Last Day

> But when the trumpet sound [ushering in the Judgment] shall come, on the day when a man shall flee from his brother, his mother, his father, his spouse, and his sons, every man among them on that day shall have no time to care for others. (LXXX, 33–37)

[8] Ibn Isḥāq, I, 519.
[9] W. Montgomery Watt, *Muhammad at Mecca* (Oxford, 1953), p. 18.

> Thou shalt never find a people who believe in God and the Last Day loving anyone who opposes God and His Apostle, even though it be their own fathers, their sons, their brothers, or their fellow-tribesmen. (LVIII, 22)

> It is not for the Prophet and those who believe to ask pardon for the polytheists, even though they be the nearest in blood, now that it has been made clear to them that these are destined for Hell. Abraham did ask pardon for his father, but that was only because he had to fulfil a promise he had made. So once it became clear to him that his father was an enemy of God, he formally declared that he had nothing to do[10] with the latter's acts. (IX, 114–115/113–114)

Ethically, this is nothing but a proclamation of the principle of individualism. On the Last Day, men are summoned to come to their Lord as individuals. Everybody has to bear his own burden. And this begins at the very moment of his death, as ᶜAmr b. ᶜUbayd said, 'Fear (*ittaqi*) God, for you will die alone, you will be asked to settle accounts alone, you will be raised from the grave alone, and no one of those who surround you now will be of any avail to you in the presence of your Lord.'[11]

However, the new principle could not displace at one stroke the standard of tribal ethics based on the natural tie of the kindred, and age-old tribal feuds were carried over far into the Islamic ages. We have seen how the rival tribes of Aws and Khazraj in Medina lived in a precarious sort of unity after they had become friends and brothers by faith under the Prophet. And we find, Abū Qays, a well-known ascetic who adopted Islām after Muḥammad migrated to Medina, still saying in the spirit of tribalism:

> Sever not, my sons, the ties of kinship.
> Be magnanimous to your kindred though they be narrow of mind.[12]

The feeling of tribal solidarity tended to control a man's actions towards his kinsmen even when they joined the banner of his enemy, a phenomenon that occured very frequently in Arabia after the rise of Islām. Speaking of the Prophet's companions who had fled from Mecca for refuge with the king of Abyssinia, and trying to calm down an angry friend who was going to resort to violent

[10] *Tabarraʾa minhu*. The concept of *tabarruʾ*, has been explained earlier in this chapter (see note 3).

[11] ᶜAmr b. ᶜUbayd, a famous Muᶜtazilah, who, together with Wāṣil b. ᶜAṭāʾ, laid the foundation of Muᶜtazilism. He is reported to have said this when he admonished the Khalīfah al-Manṣūr. See Sharīf al-Murtaḍá, *Amālī* (Cairo, 1954), I, 175.

[12] Ibn Isḥāq, I, 347.

measures in order to 'uproot all these fellows', a 'godfearing' person says, 'Don't do such a thing. They are related to us by blood even though they are now on the opposite side.'[13] On the day of Uḥud, ᶜAlī, who was in charge of the standard of the Muslims, and Abū Saᶜd, who carried the banner of the pagans, fought in single combat, and the former smote the latter down on the ground. But he refrained from giving him the finishing stroke. When asked later why he did not do so, he replied, 'The bond of blood kinship it was that made me faint-hearted at the last moment.'[14]

So Muḥammad, when he migrated to Medina, tried at first to establish, in accordance with his newly proclaimed principle, a supertribal unity of all believers, and declared that the Muhājirīn (i.e. those who had shared from the very beginning in his hardship and migrated with him from Mecca) and the Anṣār (i.e. those who newly became Muslims in Medina) should regard themselves as 'brothers' in religion, and that this brotherhood should abrogate all the ancient customs and rules of blood kinship. Believers should be friends of believers, and disbelievers of disbelievers, regardless of all relationships by blood and ancestry; if not, 'there would arise in the land an irreparable moral corruption'. For all this, tribal feuds were carried on before his very eyes as in pagan days, if not of course to the same extent, and it became clear in the course of time that some concessions had to be made. Sūrah XXXIII, 6, of the Qurʾān may be taken as a record of a concession of this kind.

> The Prophet is closer to the believers than their selves, and his wives are their mothers. But those who have kinship by blood are closer to one another in the Book of God than the believers who are not kindred and the Muhājirīn. Nevertheless you have to behave with kindness towards your companions.

The key to this passage seems to lie in the meaning of the phrase 'the Book of God'. The commentators are in agreement that it refers to the right of inheritance. If this interpretation is admitted, then the meaning of the passage as a whole would amount to this: those who are related by the bond of blood are closer to one another so far as inheritance is concerned. And this statement would naturally place a limit upon the absoluteness of the principle of brotherhood among all Muslims, whether they be related or unrelated by blood. In any case, we see very often in the history of Islām old tribal interests cutting across religious relationships.

On the other hand, Arabia in that age of transition exhibits certain remarkable features which were opposed to the spirit of conservative

13 *Ibid.*, I, 220.
14 *Ibid.*, II, 547, according to Ibn Hishām.

tribalism. There were, about the time of Muḥammad, clear signs of a weakening of the tribal or clan kinship and a growing tendency to a certain individualism. Professor Watt[15] has remarked that the growing awareness of the problem of personal immortality, *khulūd*, which I have approached from a somewhat different angle in the last chapter, marks the breakdown of what he calls 'tribal humanism' as a vital religious force; for, he says, the problem of the cessation of a man is in the last analysis the problem of the ultimate destiny of the individual as distinguished from, and opposed to, the subsistence of the tribe. He argues that this growth of individualism at the cost of tribal spirit was probably fostered by the circumstances of commercial life in Mecca. In this center of mercantile life it was natural that financial and material interest fostered individualism and began to exercise a strong influence on the social life of the day as a possible new basis of community.[16] If these arguments are valid, we might perhaps safely say that there was in the air a presage of a new age with new ideals of life, which helped to create a religio-political society by means of a passage from tribal humanism to individual humanism.

I have given what may seem a rather lengthy description of the tribal spirit in Jāhilīyah. My purpose has been to furnish an appropriate background which will bring out by contrast the characteristic features of Islamic moral ideas. It will be clear that in a social pattern where the tribal ethos was the only possible principle of unity by which to preserve a balance and good order among the people, all the noble qualities were considered to reside not so much in the individual members of the tribe as in the tribe itself. We are now accustomed to think of moral virtues as personal qualities inherent in the individual. This was not the case with the pagan Arabs. For them, moral virtues were rather precious communal possessions inherited from fathers and forefathers. A man's honor or glory (*majd*) always came to him as an inheritance within the tribe. He felt himself charged with the sacred duty of transmitting it unharmed, or even greatly increased, to his posterity.

> We inherited our glory from our fathers.
> Lo! it has grown in our hands to a lofty height.[17]

In such a social system personal values could not be thought of apart from the nobility of the tribe to which one belonged, except in the exceptional case of those who built up their fame by their own personal effort and valor, without getting any support from an

[15] Watt, pp. 19, 25.
[16] *Ibid.*, p. 72.
[17] The poet is Muḥāfir b. Abī ʿAmr, cited by Ibn Isḥāq, I, 96.

illustrious family. Such a man was known as a *khārijī*.[18] But, after all, such original types were extremely rare and sporadic phenomena. In normal cases, noble ancestry was the sole unmistakable warrant of the excellence of a man. This explains why pagan poetry is so full of boastings of the ancestral virtues of one's own tribe. Thus, Abū Ṭālib[19] says in praise of Quraysh:

> If we are to value all men, you are a jewel,
> You preserve people noble and excellent,
> With an honorable lineage, with no stain of mixture.

The glorious deeds of the tribe are respectfully handed down by word of mouth from father to son, and as they are thus transmitted from generation to generation they go on increasing like a snowball. The tribal glory thus formed is designated by the word *ḥasab*, which may be approximately rendered by 'ancestral honor'.[20] Every noble family has its own *ḥasab* to boast of. *Ḥasab* is the final yardstick by which the value of a tribe, and consequently the personal excellence of every member of the tribe, is measured. Viewed from a somewhat different standpoint the *ḥasab* may be said to represent the only possible guide to moral conduct in the tribal pattern of society. For every individual member of the tribe sees in the glorious *ḥasab* left by his fathers a body of the highest ideals, a perfect model of behavior to be imitated in all circumstances of life. It tends to govern all his actions, and conversely, all his actions are judged right or wrong by the unique standard it offers. Thus it constitutes for him an unwritten code of law:

> He belongs to a tribe whose fathers have laid down
> for them a way of life.
> Every folk has its own traditional way of life,
> every folk has its objects of imitation.[21]

A way of life or code of law of this kind, as the reverse side, so to speak, of the ancestral honor, was called *sunnah*. We now see why *sunnah* was held in such high esteem in ancient Arabia, why there was even something 'sacred' about it.

That this peculiar passion for *ḥasab* continued to exist with almost unabated vigor even in the later years of Islām is shown by many occurrences. The most interesting of them all is perhaps the rise of Shuʿūbīyah in the early ʿAbbasī period. Here we see the old inter-tribal antagonism transformed into a grand-scale opposition of the

[18] See, for example, *Mufaḍḍalīyāt*, XXII, 11.
[19] Ibn Isḥāq, I, 180.
[20] A good example revealing the structure of the concept of *ḥasab* is found in *Mufaḍḍalīyāt*, XXV, 3.
[21] Labīd, *Muʿallaqah*, v. 81.

Arabs and the non-Arabs within the Islamic community. The Shuʿūbīyah was a movement inaugurated by those who claimed a complete equality of all Muslims, irrespective of race, nationality, and lineage. Their contention, according to *ʿIqd al-Farīd* by Ibn ʿAbd Rabbih, amounts to this: the Prophet forbade the Muslims to boast about their ancestors; and yet, the Arabs still pride themselves on their noble lineage and keep on looking down upon non-Arabs with the characteristic haughtiness of Jāhilīyah; but when it comes to that, we can establish logically and factually that we have in reality better grounds for boasting.

The Shuʿūbīyah could quote in support of this argument the famous words of the Prophet, which he is said to have uttered in his Farewell Pilgrimage: 'O men, verily God has eradicated from your minds the sense of honor and the inflated pride in ancestry, which are both peculiar to the people of Jāhilīyah. You have all sprung from the common stock of Adam, and Adam sprang from dust.'

This point is of basic importance for the right understanding of the position of Islām in ethical matters. If it dared to deny all value to ancestral honor despite such a deep-rooted attachment of the Arabian aristocracy for it, it was solely because of its belief that all this was groundless vainglory, an empty illusion created by the outward show of earthly life, and that it would never stand the divine test on the Day of Judgment. On that terrible day, when every person will be called out from the grave and will have to stand naked before the Judgment Seat, nothing will count among his merits except his personal faith and the good works which he has done in the world from purely religious motives.

We have seen that the principle of tribal solidarity among the pagan Arabs owed the greater part of its vital force and authority to the sentiment of pride arising from the consciousness of belonging to a noble stock. Noble blood in one's veins was the prerequisite to the development of noble personal qualities. 'Honor' was certainly one of the key concepts of pre-Islamic society. It is important to remember that 'honor' in those days was mainly based on and kept unsullied by heroism and valor, which, again, were maintained by the spirit of *ibāʾ* meaning literally 'refusal', that is, more concretely, 'refusal to bow before any authority, be it human or divine'. It was, in short, the spirit of independence, abhorrence of being dominated, haughtiness and pride standing on the consciousness of one's power and courage. And such a consciousness was to be expected only from a 'noble' man. If tribal solidarity could work in the days of Jāhilīyah as the effective religion of the Arabs, it was after all a religion of the aristocracy. The weak and poor, the baseborn, people of no descent, the



but didn't they still bow to the authority of the tribe?

slaves—in a word, the proletariat—were allowed no share in this religion.

Nothing was so intolerable for such a 'noble' and 'free' man as to be in the position of a servant (*ᶜabd*) whose job was to serve his master obediently. It was intolerable to him whether the master were a human being or a god. This, however, was exactly what Islām demanded of him. For in the Qurʾanic conception, God is the Lord and man is and should be nothing but His humble servant.

In the preceding chapter we have seen how the Qurʾān makes the fear of God, a reverent awe before the infallible and unrelenting Judge, the basic mood of human existence. And we have quoted a remarkable verse in which 'nobility' is defined in terms of 'fear of God': 'Surely the noblest (*akram*) of you all in the sight of God is the one who is most godfearing (*atqá*) among you.' (XLIX, 13). We may make another observation concerning the same passage. The Islamic position as represented by these words collides head on with the old ideal of Jāhilīyah in two points; first, that it places the locus of personal qualities in the individual as distinguished from the tribe and secondly, that it introduces what may seem to the haughty and proud warriors of Jāhilīyah an element of weakness or humility into the notion of virtue. The first point has already been discussed. So I shall turn to the problem of humbleness as an essential element of the Islamic idea of moral virtue. The problem has two different but closely related aspects, one social, the other spiritual.

In the social system of Jāhilīyah the weak and oppressed, the base-born and slaves had no share at all in the glorious 'honor' handed down from generation to generation.

Islām, on the contrary, stressed from the very outset the universal grace and goodness of Allāh. The awful Lord of the Last Day is at the same time the most merciful and the most compassionate God, who makes no distinction at all between rich and poor, the powerful and the uninfluential. In the presence of this God, all men are equal, irrespective of distinctions of rank and lineage. Nay, He even prefers the weak and insignificant to the arrogant aristocrats. 'O most Merciful', so Muḥammad prays, 'Thou art indeed the Lord of the oppressed. Thou art my Lord!'[22] It is easy to see that this involves, on the part of the believers, the moral duty of treating the poor and weak with utmost tenderness. The Qurʾān is replete with commands and injunctions that are immediate manifestations of this spirit.

> All things God has given as spoils of war to His Apostle from the people of the cities belong to God, and His Apostle, and the

[22] Ibn Isḥāq, I, 280.

near kinsfolk, the orphans, the poor and wayfarers, so that wealth should not become an exclusive possession of the rich of you. Whatever the Apostle gives you, take, and whatever he forbids you, abstain. And fear God. (LIX, 7)

Those who do not honor orphans and refuse even a small kindness to the poor and needy are not simple niggards. From the viewpoint of Islām, the cause lies much deeper than that. The characteristic mercilessness of their attitude originates in their *kufr*, their lack of gratitude to God for His grace and goodness. They behave in a niggardly fashion because they are at heart incorrigible Kāfirs.

Hast thou observed him who cried lies to the Judgment? He it is that repels the orphan, and urges not the feeding of the poor. So woe to those who pray [i.e. as a matter of outward form as if they were Muslims] but are in truth heedless of their own prayers; woe to those who make a show [of belief] yet refuse to show kindness. (CVII, 1–7)

In the following passage such conduct of the Kāfirs is made more directly the object of a severe reprimand.

Nay, but you show not any tenderness to the orphan, you urge not the feeding of the poor. You devour the inheritance [of the defenceless] with unbounded greed; you love wealth with a blazing love. (LXXXIX, 18–21/17–20)

The Qurʾān tells us that the Prophet himself was once severely rebuked by God for his merciless conduct towards a poor blind man. The Sūrah in which this event is related carries the significant title of 'Frowning'. One day, a certain blind man, Ibn Umm Maktūm by name, came to Muḥammad while he was talking with some of the leading people of Quraysh, and began to put importunate questions about the creeds of Islām. Muḥammad, annoyed at the interruption, turns away from him with a frown. Immediately a divine revelation is sent down to reprimand him for his tendency towards doing despite in such a way to the insignificant men while being ready at all times to attend respectfully to the wealthy and powerful.

He [i.e. Muḥammad] made a grimace and flatly turned his back, for that the blind man came to him. But who knows? Perchance he [i.e. the blind man] too may make a pure Muslim [lit. will purify himself], or may come to remember. But as for him who is rich and powerful, to him dost thou [Muḥammad] attend with care and respect, though at bottom thou art not concerned, whether he will purify himself or not. But as for him who comes to thee in earnest and in fear, to him thou payest no attention. (LXXX, 1–10)

*has to convince Muḥammad to fight against his cultural inclination to ignore poor/lowly*

In a number of other passages God admonishes Muḥammad in a gentler, and sometimes even coaxing tone not to despise and reject the poor ones; after all it is they, if anybody, who may turn out to be most receptive to the teaching of self-surrender.

> Keep thyself patient in company with those who call upon their Lord morning and evening, desiring His countenance. Let not thine eyes be turned away from them, desiring the pomp of the life of this world. (XVIII, 27/28)

In Sūrah XCIII, 6–11, God addresses His Apostle and tells him not to oppress orphans and drive away beggars mercilessly. The tone here, be it noted, is extremely intimate:

> Did He not find thee an orphan and give thee shelter?
> Did He not find thee erring, and guide thee?
> Did He not find thee poor, and give thee wealth?
> Therefore the orphan, oppress him not.
> Therefore the beggar, rate him not.

It is noteworthy that in these verses a very personal fact about Muḥammad's unhappy childhood is particularly evoked to remind him that he has always been the object of God's special care and protection, and that this is made the reason why Muḥammad should act towards the poor and needy with kindness. Translated into more general terms, this would mean that man should show tenderness and mercifulness because Allāh Himself is the merciful, gracious, and infinitely loving God. Human goodness is the counterpart—though of course it cannot be anything more than an incomparably poor and imperfect counterpart—of divine goodness. In another place it is expressly stated:

> Be thou kind and good [*aḥsin* from *ḤSN*] even as God has been good to thee. (XXVIII, 77)

It is very important to keep this point in mind, because in the matter of sheltering the weak and providing for the needs of orphan children, Jāhilīyah too could boast of having produced many examples of extravagant generosity. Outwardly, the Jāhilī mind shows signs of being even more liberal and charitable than the Muslim mind. Only the underlying motives are completely different, the motive in the former being essentially self-complacency and vainglory, and in the latter *Imitatio Dei*.

*2 diff. reasons*

Thus it comes about that the element of meekness, or humbleness, as the human counterpart of the benevolence of God, is made the very pivotal point of Islamic ethics. Most, though not all, of the

*gratefulness*

recognized moral duties of Islām derive in fact from this pious benevolence. Kindness is enjoined upon the believers on every possible occasion. Kindness should be the governing principle of all human relations in society as well as in family. Thus one should be humble and tender towards one's parents, and always treat them well.

> Thy Lord has decreed that you should serve none save Him, and that you should be kind to parents. If one or both of them attain old age with thee, say not 'Fie!' unto them nor chide them, but speak unto them respectful words, and lower unto them the wing of humbleness out of mercy, and say, 'My Lord, have mercy upon them, just as they raised me up when I was a small child.' (XVII, 24–25/23–24)

> We have enjoined upon man kindness towards his parents. His mother bore him with pain, and with pain did she give birth to him; it took thirty months for his bearing and his weaning. (XLVI, 14/15)

The mitigating policy adopted by Islām with regard to the age-old custom of the blood vengeance was another obvious manifestation of the same principle. It is well-known that blood vengeance was a supreme law of the desert, connected most closely with the Arab idea of 'honor'. Persistence in seeking revenge was an essential constituent of the conception of *murūwah*, or the highest moral ideal of the Bedouin, of which I have given a summary explanation in an earlier chapter; it was regarded in Jāhilīyah as an important 'virtue' of man. Nicholson has tried to give a vivid representation of the true Arab feeling of vengeance by saying that 'it was a tormenting thirst which nothing would quench except blood, a disease of honor which might be described as madness.'[23] It was so deep-rooted in the soul of the pagan Arabs that it could not be extirpated all at once. Islām attempted to calm down this raging madness by imposing upon it some severe restrictions. Hence the ordinance that only the person of the culprit himself is liable to the justice of the vendetta; that only one life can be taken, a freeman for a freeman a slave for a slave, a woman for a woman; and that, moreover, it would be better for the kinsmen of the murdered man to accept a bloodwit and settle the matter in a peaceful way.[24]

There is something much more noteworthy here. In Islām, we see the right of taking vengeance transposed from human to divine hands. In the days of Jāhilīyah, bloody vengeance was always sought by a man upon a man; vengeance was carried out within the bounds

[23] Nicholson, p. 93.
[24] See Sūrah II, 173–174/178.



murūwah → manliness:
bravery in battle
patience
persistence seeking revenge
protecting weak
defying the strong
great generosity
loyalty to tribe

of humanity, on the strictly human level. In Islām, the direction of vengeance became vertical; or rather, a new vertical direction made its appearance and began to run across the horizontal line. God was declared to be the supreme Avenger of all evils and wrongs done on the earth. It stands patent from a number of Qurʾanic passages[25] that the chastisement of Hell was represented as the divine act of retaliation on an infinitely grand scale. And in Sūrah XIV, 48/47 and XXXIX, 38/37, Allāh is called the mighty 'Lord of Vengeance' (*dhū intiqām*). Since, then, there is God who 'never wrongs anybody, who is 'aware of all that men do', and who promises to take vengeance on those who have done any wrong, what better policy for man to follow than to submit all these matters to Allāh's Will? Though in practice the problem of vengeance was still studded with all sorts of difficulties, theoretically at least the conclusion was clear and simple: here too, benevolence and love should be made the guiding principle of human conduct.

All this is another way of saying that the principle of *ḥilm* was adopted by Islām as the central point of its moral system. We have seen that *ḥilm* is an Arabic equivalent of the Greek *ataraxia*, a freedom from being moved and stirred up on the smallest provocation.[26]

> The [true] servants of the Merciful God are they who walk on the earth quietly and gently; and who, when the *jāhilūn* address them, reply 'Peace!' (XXV, 64/63)

The demand to adopt the principle of *ḥilm* and to endeavor to live up to its highest ideal must have seemed particularly harsh to the pagan Arabs born with an extremely passionate and irascible nature. So in fact this way of life is compared in the Qurʾān to the most difficult place of ascent of a mountain-road, *ʿaqabah*. But we are told at the same time that those who have overcome all its difficulties are to become the 'companions of the Right' on the Last Day; that is, they will go to Paradise and enjoy its everlasting bliss, while the 'companions of the Left' are destined for the eternal torment of Fire.

> What is the meaning of the Steep Ascent (*ʿaqabah*)? It is to set free slaves, or to give food on the day of famine to an orphan who is akin, or a poor man reduced to beggary. And then it is to become of those who believe and encourage each other to patience, and encourage each other to acts of kindness. (XC, 13–17)

[25] See, for example, XV, 79; XXX, 46/47; XLIV, 15/16.

[26] The reason why the word *ḥilm* itself does not play an important role in the Qurʾān, in spite of the tremendous importance of the concept in the Qurʾanic thought, has been elucidated in detail in my *God and Man in the Koran*, pp. 216–219.

So much for the social side of the problem of pious benevolence. Turning now to the second of its aspects as distinguished above, the spiritual, we may begin by remarking that here again the principle of 'humble-mindedness' collides head on with the unyielding spirit of the desert Arabs, the sense of honor, the fierce arrogance, that *ḥamīyat al-jāhilīyah* which, as we have seen in some detail earlier, is so characteristic of the Bedouin mind.

*Islām*, as its name itself suggests, insists first and foremost on the absolute necessity of humble submission to God. *Muslim* means literally a 'submitter', he who has submitted himself and surrendered his heart and mind to Allāh's Will. A total, voluntary self-surrender is the basic characteristic and the first condition of Islamic piety. It need not surprise if this aroused in a peculiar manner the 'pique of Jāhilīyah'. Humbleness, patience, trembling fear, avoidance of ostentation—all these cardinal virtues of a Muslim must have appeared to the mind of a truculent pagan Arab as nothing but manifestations of natural weakness and humility.

> When it is said to such a man 'Fear God', then the sense of honor[27] takes him to sin. So Hell is enough for him. How evil a couch it will be! (II, 202/206)

We have already seen how the Qur'ān makes 'fear of God', *taqwá*, the very basic mood of religion. The most fitting definition of the true believer is 'one who trembles in fear before God'. 'O men! fear your Lord!' (XXII, 1) 'O you who believe! fear God. Let every soul look to what it has sent on for the morrow. And fear God. Verily, God is well aware of all you are doing.' (LIX, 18) And it is also said: 'The flesh and blood of the sacrificial offerings reach not God: it is pious fear (*taqwá*) only that reaches Him from you.' (XXII, 38/37) As is easy to see, in these contexts 'fear' is almost synonymous with 'faith' or 'devotion'. The 'submission', the humble obedience to whatever God commands, to which reference has just been made, is but an aspect of this basic mood.

> They assert, 'None shall enter Paradise unless he be a Jew or a Christian.' This is nothing but their heart's desire. Say thou, 'Then bring your proof, if what you say is true.' Nay, but whosoever submits his face [i.e. his whole self] to God and show kindness [to his neighbors], he shall have his reward from his Lord. (II, 105–106/111–112)

The same is true of the absolute reliance which any believer who is at all worthy of the name is expected to place upon the goodness of God. The attitude of maintaining unshakable reliance (*tawakkul*)

[27] *ʿIzzah*, i.e. *ḥamīyat al-jāhilīyah*, as al-Bayḍāwī remarks, *Tafsīr*, *ad loc.*

whatever may happen is one of the fundamental properties of a true Muslim.

> Verily, the final decision is only with God. Upon Him do I rely, and upon Him let all rely who would rely. (XII, 67)

> Upon God let the believers rely. And why should we not place reliance upon God when He has shown us the ways to follow? We will surely endure with patience whatever hurt you do us. Upon God let all rely who would rely. (XIV, 14–15/11–12)

> Upon God do you rely if you are believers. (V, 26/23)

The last-quoted passage is of particular importance in that it brings out most clearly and tersely the semantic relationship between 'reliance', *tawakkul*, and 'belief', *īmān*, in the Qurʾanic conception. In just the same way the following example reveals the close interconnection between 'fear of God' and 'humble-mindedness':

> Give good tiding into the humble-minded whose hearts, whenever God is mentioned, tremble with fear. (XXII, 35–36/34–35)

Here the word actually used for 'fear' is not *taqwá*, but the verb *wajila* which means 'to palpitate with fear', 'to entertain an acute fear'. As for the 'humble-mindedness', the word used in this passage is *mukhbit*, the adjectival-participial form of *ikhbāt*. There are a number of other terms expressing nearly the same thing. The root *KH-SH-ᶜ* is one of the commonest. Here I give two examples of its usage, whose general contextual situations bring out admirably well what kind of human character and what type of conduct are considered most deserving of the adjective 'humble'.

> Seek help patiently and in prayer. Verily, this will appear extremely difficult save to the humble-minded (*khāshiᶜ*) who are well aware that they shall meet their Lord [on the Day of Judgment], and that unto Him they are all going back. (II, 42–43/45–46)

> You may believe in it [i.e. the Qurʾān], or believe not. Those who were given the knowledge before this, whenever it is recited to them, fall down prostrate upon their beards, and say, 'Glory be to our Lord! Verily, the promise of our Lord will come to pass.' And so they fall down prostrate upon their beards weeping the while, and it makes them humble-hearted ever more. (XVII, 108–109/107–109)

Another important word for humbleness is *taḍarruᶜ*. The example which follows is of particular significance for our purpose because, by putting this word in sharp contrast with its antithesis, it throws a revealing light on the structure of its semantic category.

> We have sent [Apostles] unto peoples before thee, and seized them with distress and hardship, in order that they might be humble (*yataḍarraʿūna*). Ah, if only they had been humble when Our might came upon them! But their hearts became [the more] hardened, and Satan embellished to their minds what they were doing. (VI, 42–43)

'His heart becomes [or is] hard' is a standing expression in the Qurʾān used to denote the peculiar mental attitude of the *kāfir*. This we know from other evidences, as we shall see in full detail in a later chapter dealing with the concept of *kufr*. So we have here a very significant formula of semantic antithesis: 'humbleness' (*taḍarruʿ*) is opposed to 'ungratefulness' (*kufr*). And since, as we already know, ungratefulness is, in the Qurʾanic conception, the very basis of 'unbelief', we may safely conclude that 'humbleness' is an essential part of 'belief'.

It is highly important to remark in this connection that the Qurʾān employs constantly the verb *istakbara* describing the usual attitude of the pagan Arabs towards the evangelistic preaching of Muḥammad. *Istakbara* is a verb derived from the root *KBR* 'big' and means something like 'to consider one's self big', 'to be haughty, insolent, or arrogant'. I have already referred to the negative side of its semantic structure, and much more will be said in a later context. Here it must suffice to note that Islām and Jāhilīyah stood at antipodes with each other as regards the principle of submission and humbleness as a fundamental way of life. As a matter of fact all the Islamic virtues deriving from this principle are the exact opposites of the cardinal virtues which the Arabs of the desert were so proud of. Indeed, submission is the last thing which might be expected of a pagan Arab. As a poet said:

> We refuse to all men submission to their leading
> till we lead them ourselves, yea, without reins![28]

And he will stubbornly refuse to change this attitude even in the presence of God. For, to his mind accustomed to the lukewarm and halfhearted worship of idols, a god, after all, is not and cannot be an absolute being, absolutely superior to human beings.

As for the virtue of 'humble-mindedness', it goes without saying that for a Jāhilī Arab it was nothing but an evidence of base-mindedness. In his view, only those who were baseborn and, consequently, had no natural right to be haughty and proud could, and indeed should, make themselves humble.

'Reliance' was held highly valuable in desert conditions; only it

28 ʿAbīd b. al-Abraṣ, IV, 20.

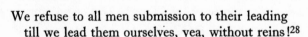

was not such submissive reliance on a superior being as Islām demanded, but a more human kind of reliance subsisting among the members of the tribe, and, in particular, reliance on one's self. Self-reliance was a mark of a noble nature. It was a basic attitude which was expected to manifest itself in all phases of human conduct. It was designated by the word *istighnā'*. This word derives from a root meaning 'free from want' and is used to denote the attitude of a man who considers himself absolutely free in all his doings, who stands completely independent, or dependent only upon himself. Such an excess of self-confidence, viewed from the standpoint of Islām, represents a glaring case of insolence and presumptuousness because it implies ultimately denying the fact of man's creatureliness. The Qur'ān emphasizes repeatedly that the only One who has the full right to take pride in being self-reliant or independent in the true sense is God. But to this point we shall have occasion to return later.

# V. The Islamization of Old Arab Virtues

HITHERTO IT HAS BEEN MY CONSTANT ENDEAVOR TO BRING TO LIGHT the basic antagonism that exists between Islām and Jāhilīyah regarding the fundamental principles of life. We would do a grave injustice, however, to the spirit of Jāhilīyah and even to the position of Islām itself if we supposed that the latter denied and rejected without discrimination all the moral ideals of pre-Islamic Arabia as essentially incompatible with its monotheistic faith. There is clearly recognizable a certain continuity between the Qurʾanic outlook and the old Arab world view, as much as there is a wide cleavage between them. This is particularly noticeable in the sphere of ethical qualities. In this chapter we shall deal with this aspect of the problem.

It is true that in many important respects Islām broke completely with the old paganism; but it is, we should not forget, no less true that, in spite of the bitter attacks on the pagans and their idolatrous customs, the Qurʾān adopted and revived, in a new form suited to the needs of monotheism, many of the outstanding virtues of paganism. There is a certain respect in which we might perhaps speak of the moral aspect of Islām even as a restoration of some of the old Arab ideals and nomadic virtues which had degenerated in the hands of the wealthy merchants of Mecca before the rise of this religion.

It is quite significant in this connection that, in the pictures of Muḥammad which the pious Muslim writers of later ages have left, we often see a typical hero of the Arabian desert. Interestingly enough, the personal characteristics attributed to Muḥammad in the books of Tradition are quite in line with the old nomadic ideals of man that we find so highly praised in the works of pre-Islamic poets. Take for example the following description of the personality of the Prophet by ᶜAlī b. Abī Ṭālib, given by Ibn Hishām[1] in the *Sīrah*: 'He was of all men the most open-handed, most stout-hearted, most truthful of tongue, most loyal in the keeping of his trusts, most serene of mind, and the noblest in friendly intercourse. Those who saw him for the first time feared him, but those who got acquainted with him loved him. Indeed, a man like him I have never seen.' This is nothing but a picture of an ideal man, containing no element at all that might have been repugnant to the moral sense of a Jāhilī Arab.

Be that as it may, we encounter in the Qurʾān many of the moral ideals of the desert in the new garment of Islām. We have already seen that the highest ethical ideal of the Jāhilīyah was *murūwah*, and that it included such various virtues as generosity, bravery and courage, patience, trustworthiness, and truthfulness. In fact, to all these virtues the Muslims are exhorted very earnestly in the Qurʾān. What is much more important to note, however, is that Islām did not revive or restore these nomadic virtues as it found them among the Bedouin. In adopting and assimilating them into its system of moral teachings, Islām purified and freshened them, making their energy flow into certain channels which it had prepared. Linguistically we may say that with the advent of Islām some of the key ethical terms of Jāhilīyah underwent a specific semantic transformation.

Of the semantic categories of these words some became thereby considerably expanded, some were narrowed down and some were developed in entirely new directions. In any case, in the Qurʾanic teaching the old *murūwah* was made to abandon all its harmful excesses and to assume a more civilized form. It began to work as a new moral energy in the midst of the growing community of the Muslims. And undoubtedly this has given a very specific coloring to Islamic ethical culture.

## Generosity

We shall begin with the virtue of liberal-mindedness or generosity, to which reference has often been made in the foregoing pages. It is quite natural that under desert conditions the spirit of charity

[1] Ibn Isḥāq, I, 266.

and generosity should be given an exceedingly high place in the list of noble qualities. In the desert, where even the basic material necessities are very scarce, acts of hospitality and helpfulness are beyond any doubt a necessary aspect of the struggle for existence. But there is something more than that. We may observe first of all that generosity in the minds of the pagan Arabs was closely connected with the Jāhilī conception of 'honor'. As a great poet of Jāhilīyah, Zuhayr b. Abī Sulmā, said:

> Whoever makes of generosity a shield for his personal honor makes it grow. But whoever neglects to guard himself from blame, will be blamed.[2]

Acts of generosity were held as a proof of genuine nobility. And the more extravagant and impulsive an act of generosity was, the more it tended to arouse admiration. For a pagan Arab, charity was not simply a natural manifestation of his feeling of tribal solidarity, for very often it extended beyond the members of his own tribe to the strangers who happened to be there. Nor was it always dictated by the motive of benevolence and kindness. It was first and foremost an act of chivalry. A man who could make a royal display of his generosity was a true dandy of the desert. Generosity in this sense was a master passion of the Arabs. It was not so much a 'virtue' as a blind, irresistible impulse that was deeply rooted in the Arab heart. We may profitably recall at this point the fact already referred to, that the pre-Islamic poets used to boast of their habit of excessive wine-drinking as a mark of a genuinely generous nature, that is, as a mark of nobility. A man of noble nature, so they sang, should not care for the morrow. The true meaning of this is that he should perform acts of liberality for the joy of playing the dandy. And, to inspire the greatest degree of admiration in the minds of the onlookers, not to speak of the guests themselves, the liberality should naturally go to the extreme of thoughtless prodigality. Ḥātim Ṭā'ī, of whom many half-legendary stories have been handed down to us by tradition, was acknowledgedly a perfect embodiment of the Bedouin ideals of generosity. We should remember in this connection that the adjective *karīm* is just the word in Old Arabic for such a combination of the ideas of lavish generosity and nobility. *Karīm*, in other words, is a man who is acknowledged by everybody to be 'noble' just because he proves his own noble birth concretely in his acts of limitless generosity. We have already seen how the Qur'ān dealt a blow to the semantic category of this adjective by redefining it forcibly in terms of the fear of God and piety.

Basically the position adopted by the Prophet of Islām agrees

[2] Zuhayr b. Abī Sulmā, *Muʿallaqah*, v. 51, in *Septem Moallakat.*

with the outlook of the pagan Arabs in that it, too, places a high value upon charity. For him, no less than for a Jāhilī, generosity represented an important virtue. The sole fact that he made it the economic basis of his new religio-political community goes to show clearly how high it stood in his estimation. Besides, in itself the nomadic ideal of generosity contained nothing offensive to, and incompatible with, the central tenets of the Islamic faith.

> I am not a man who lurks about fearfully among the hills.
> I am here ready to help, whenever people call for my charity.

So the Jāhilī poet Ṭarafah once declared boastingly.[3] 'Fearfully', that is, through fear of guests who might come to his tent expecting hospitalities. Nothing prevents such an attitude from being honorable and praiseworthy in the eyes of the Muslims. In fact, we see the famous panegyrist of Muḥammad, the poet Ḥassān b. Thābit, describing him in an encomium as a man who 'is lavishly generous with his possessions, whether inherited or newly gained, even in times of hardship when an admittedly liberal man would hesitate to give of his wealth.'

Only there is a fundamental difference between the two positions. The difference lies in this, that Islām denied all value to acts of generosity originating in the desire to make a show. Dandyism or chivalry for its own sake was in this view nothing but a satanic passion. What is important is not the act of generosity, but the motive underlying it. All acts of generosity are absolutely valueless that come from the source of vainglory and pride.

> O believers, you must not make your charity vain by grudging and making disagreeable remarks, as one who expends of his wealth simply for the pleasure of an ostentatious display, and not from his belief in God and the Last Day. Such a man may be compared to a smooth stone covered with soil; a rainstorm smites it and leaves it smooth and bare. Though they have amassed great wealth, they can make naught out of that, for God guides not the Kāfirs. (II, 266/264)

It follows that, although generosity *is* a virtue, it ceases to be a virtue and even becomes positively a vice if it goes to the length of wastefulness. It is significant that in this verse he who does this is explicitly called a Kāfir. In another verse a prodigal is formally declared the Devil's brother:

> Give the kinsman his due, and the poor, and the wayfarer. But never waste in sheer waste, for those who squander are brothers

[3] Ṭarafah, v. 45.

of Satan, and Satan is ever ungrateful (*kāfir*) to his Lord. (XVII, 28–29/26–27)

Niggardliness is of course dishonorable, it is admittedly a moral defect or a vice. But the excess of lavishness is no less a dishonorable moral defect. Keep always to the happy medium; this is the rule of conduct that must control believers in matters concerning private property.

Keep not thy hand fettered to thy neck, nor yet spread it out too widespread, lest thou shouldst become an object of reproach or stripped naked. Lo, thy Lord spread out His provision to whomsoever He will or again straitens it as He will. (XVII, 31–32/29–30)

The true servants of the Merciful God are . . . those who, when they spend, are neither prodigal nor miserly, but who ever take the constant mean between the two. (XXV, 67)

In order that generosity may become a genuine Islamic virtue, it must first of all be deprived of the thoughtlessness which characterized it in the days of Jāhilīyah. One who goes to the length of slaughtering on the spur of the moment, or worse still merely for display, all his camels without stopping a moment to think that his act may reduce him and his family to misery and perdition on the morrow—such a one may very well have been a model of *murūwah* or *karam* in Jāhilīyah, but is no longer to be considered a man of true generosity. A man of true generosity is he who 'expends his wealth in God's way', that is, from a pious motive.[4] And being founded on piety, it must be something well-controlled and restrained. Generosity in Islām is something essentially different from the boastful and excessive charity of which the pagan Arabs were so fond. Thus the duty of almsgiving was offered to the Muslims as the most suitable mold into which they might pour their natural generosity without being led into the satanic vices of haughtiness and extravagance. Almsgiving provided in this way a new outlet for the old instinct of generosity that was deeply rooted in the Arab soul, but it was so calculated, at the same time, as to work as a powerful regulator of its excessive energy.

As is well known, in the Muslim empire after the Prophet's death, almsgiving developed rapidly into a legalized tax known under the name of *zakāt*. There is evidence that this development was already in process during his lifetime. And yet, in the Qur'ān itself we find

[4] 'The expending of one's wealth deserves [the divine] reward only when it is accompanied by the wish to seek after God's countenance, to worship Him and to obey Him. When it is not accompanied by all this, the doer does not deserve any reward by his action.' Sharīf al-Murtaḍá, I, 204.

no precise indication as to how and how much alms should be paid. The believers are strongly exhorted to almsgiving as an act of pious benevolence; it still belongs to the sphere of personal ethics rather than that of social duties; it is a religious duty. It should be noted in this connection that those verses in which almsgiving is enjoined upon the believers—and which, by the way, are extremely numerous—contain almost always some reference to 'faith' as its ultimate source and 'eschatological reward' as its final result.

> Believe in God and His Apostle, and expend [i.e. give alms] of that which He has given you in inheritance. Those of you who believe and give alms, for them there shall be a great reward. (LVII, 7)

> Those who expend their wealth in God's way may be compared to a grain that sprouts seven ears, in every ear a hundred grains. God will increase for whom He pleases. For God embraces all and knows everything. Those who expend their wealth in God's way, and then follow not up what they expended with grudging and the making of disagreeable remarks, those shall have their wage with their Lord, and no fear shall come upon them, neither shall they grieve. (II, 263–264/261–262)

From some passages of the Qurʾān we gather that there were people, particularly among the Arabs of the desert, who, though outwardly good Muslims, regarded the alms they gave as a sort of fine (*maghram*) or compulsory donation, whereas the Muslims worthy of the name should regard all that they expended in alms as a means of approaching God.

> Of the Bedouin there are some who regard what they expend [in the way of God] as a forced donation, and wait [in secret] a turn of fortune against you [i.e. the Muslims]. Against them shall be the turn of evil fortune, for God hears all and knows all.
> Again of the Bedouin there are some who believe in God and the Last Day, and take what they spend for a means of approach to God and to the prayers of the Apostle. And so it really is a means of approach. (IX, 99–100/98–99)

But even here, even in the way of God, thoughtless extravagance is to be avoided. Almsgiving is a religious duty imposed on every Muslim, but to give out all one has too liberally and thoughtlessly until one is cast by one's own hands into perdition is neither more nor less than to fall back into the godless folly of Jāhilīyah. The following passage from Sūrah II is best understood, I think, as referring to this point, though according to the old commentaries it is capable of being explained in several other ways.

> Expend your wealth in God's way, but cast not yourselves by your own hands into perdition.[5] Try to do good,[6] for God loves the good-doers (*muḥsinīn*). (II, 191/195)

If it is disgraceful to be cast by one's own hands to ruin, it is much more disgraceful to be called a 'niggard'. Niggardliness (*bukhl*), as the opposite of the virtue of generosity, was looked upon as a glaring case of shamelessness and ignominy. In view of the highest estimation in which generosity stood, it is indeed quite natural that in both Jāhilīyah and Islām niggardliness was regarded as a most despicable quality; and to show even the slightest sign of it was held as something of which a 'manly' man should be ashamed. The poet Zuhayr in a famous passage of his Ode, known as an epitome of the desert ethics says:

> He who, being in possession of great wealth, shows himself niggardly of it towards his folk shall end by being shunned and reviled.[7]

It is told that Muḥammad once asked the people of Banū Salamah, 'Who is your chief?'; when they replied, 'al-Jadd b. Qays, though he is a niggard', the Apostle said 'There is no disease more malignant than niggardliness.'[8]

It is highly probable, as Professor Watt suggests,[9] that about the time of Muḥammad the conduct of the rich Meccans particularly tended to show signs of such a dishonorable nature, and that it is chiefly these rich Meccan merchants that are so severely rebuked in the Qur'ān as 'niggards' who are incorrigibly rotten to the core. We should remember, however, that even in the desert in the days of Jāhilīyah there appear to have been a large number of persons who were conspicuous by their niggardliness and covetousness. The very fact that so many poets in so many passages of their works declare emphatically that they are perfectly free from the vice is good evidence of the existence of it in the society.

A contemporary Arab scholar,[10] writing about the life of the pre-Islamic Arabs has drawn our attention to a very curious fact that, as far as one can gather from the poetry of Jāhilīyah and old traditions

[5] i.e. 'by squandering it thoughtlessly so as to endanger your own livelihood'; al-Bayḍāwī's *Tafsīr, ad. loc.*

[6] i.e., your aim in expending in alms should be solely to do an act of kindness, and not to make a show of extravagant liberality.

[7] Zuhayr b. Abī Sulmā, v. 52.

[8] Ibn Isḥāq, I, 309.

[9] Watt, Chapter III, Section 3, pp. 72–79.

[10] Aḥmad Muḥammad al-Ḥūfī: *Ḥayāt al-ᶜArabīyah min al-Shiᶜr al-Jāhilī* [The life of the Arabs as mirrored in pre-Islamic poetry] (Cairo, 1952), pp. 252 ff.

contained in the 'Book of Songs' and others, this was particularly the case with women. From abundant evidence he draws a conclusion to the effect that in the time of Jāhilīyah women generally tended to be niggards, or at least they had to show themselves more niggardly than men because of their particular position in society and in the home. In their eyes, the principle of unrestrained generosity was not a praiseworthy virtue at all; it was, on the contrary, an incurable vice of the other sex, which was all the more to be repressed because it was by nature harmful and destructive to the happiness of family life. From the feminine standpoint, generous hospitality—particularly when it was too generous—was nothing more than stupidity and foolishness (*safah*). In fact, in old poetry we see wives described as incessantly casting reproach on their husbands for their carelessness in squandering away their precious things, and men, on their part, as busy making attempt to justify their extravagant generosity, the only excuse they can afford being that such generosity is the sole way to an eternal fame, while wealth is the way to blame and shame.

It would be extremely interesting to observe that the point of view of the rich Meccan merchants at the time of the rise of Islām was exactly the same as that of the Jāhilī housewives just referred to. Here, in the essentially mercantile community of Mecca, the ideal of *murūwah* had lost its all-powerful influence. The tribal sense of honor was no longer capable of functioning as the real basis of human life. Wealth, not honor, was now the ideal of life. Wealth, of which the desert Arabs used to speak in such disparaging terms as a way to blame and shame, was regarded here as the only way to glory. Far from being a vice, niggardliness was now a sign of a good financial ability, the real source of power and eminence in society. It is natural that the rich Meccans, even after they adopted Islām, still continued to 'clench their hands', to use the Qur'anic expression (IX, 68/67), and grudged giving the prescribed alms or even flatly refused to give anything. It is also natural that the Qur'ān should accuse them of niggardliness.

> Some of them have given a solemn pledge to God that 'if He give us of His bounty, we will surely give alms and become of the good believers.' And yet, when He actually gave them of His bounty, they showed themselves niggardly (*bakhilū*, a verbal form of *bukhl*) thereof, and turned away and swerved aside. (IX, 76–77/75–76)

The Qur'ān does not hesitate to threaten them with the most dreadful eschatological punishment.

> Let not those who show themselves niggardly (*yabkhalūna*, a verbal form of *bukhl*) of what God has given them of His bounty

count that it is better for them. Nay, it is worse for them, for on the day of Resurrection they shall have hung around their necks all that they have been so niggardly of. (III, 175–176/180)

> Those who store up gold and silver, and expend it not in God's way—give them the good tidings of a painful torment! On the day when they shall be heated in the fire of Hell, and their foreheads shall be burnt therewith, and their sides and their backs likewise. 'This is [the reward] of what you have stored up for yourselves; so taste you now what you stored up!' (IX, 34–35)

I should like to draw attention to the small phrase 'in God's way' in this passage. It shows that there again what is made the target of condemnation is not niggardliness in general, but niggardliness in the specific sphere of religious activity. It is, in other words, those who are niggardly in the way of God, those who reveal their niggardly nature particularly in the fulfilment of the duty of almsgiving, that are sentenced to the eternal punishment of Hell. For the same Kāfirs themselves were quite ready and willing to spend their wealth generously when they knew that they were thereby aiding the cause of resistance to Muḥammad's new religious movement. Many verses of the Qur'ān bear witness to this:

> 'Lo! Kāfirs spend their wealth freely for the purpose of debarring men from God's way.' (VIII, 36)

The vigorous denunciation by Islām of niggardliness as a vice worthy of severe punishment had nothing novel and unfamiliar about it in the social circumstances of the day, particularly among the desert Arabs. It was in a certain respect nothing but a revival of an important aspect of the old nomadic ideal. And if we take into account the tendency towards niggardliness among Jāhilī women, we might perhaps speak of it as a restoration of the specifically 'manly' aspect of the ideal of *murūwah*. But it was not simple revivification of the old Bedouin sentiment of hatred towards all that debars men from lavish generosity. It is highly characteristic of Islām that it tried to revive this sentiment not as it was there, but in a form best suited to its own requirements. To the old inveterate hatred of niggardliness in the Arab mind it gave a fresh stimulus, giving it a new direction and furnishing it with a new invigorating ideal.

This, however, should not make us forget that this condemnation of niggardliness 'in the way of God' was backed by a deep insight into the essential feature of human nature. Man is by nature niggardly, covetous, and greedy. Niggardliness in God's way is, viewed from this point, but a manifestation of the more fundamental tendency of the human soul.

> Say, 'Even if you were in possession of the treasuries of my Lord's mercy, yet you would surely remain tight-fisted, ever afraid of expending. Verily man is niggardly.' (XVII, 102/100)

The word here translated 'niggardly' is *qatūr*, which means the same as *bakhīl*, that is, one who is characterized by *bukhl*, a niggardly, avaricious, or stingy person. The root *QTR* appears in a verbal form in Sūrah XXV, 67. There it is used very significantly in antithesis to *isrāf*, the act of squandering away one's wealth carelessly. 'The true servants of God are . . . those who . . . neither squander (*yusrifū*) nor yet behave too niggardly (*yaqturū*), but who ever take the constant mean between the two extremes.' From this it is clear that *qatr* represents the other extreme of the scale starting from prodigality in the direction of non-prodigality, that is, niggardliness in the utmost degree.

The Qurʾān offers in this sphere another important word, *shuḥḥ* (or *shaḥḥ* or *shiḥḥ*), meaning the utmost degree of niggardliness or covetousness. The word tends to carry an element of strong deprecation and disapproval; it presents niggardliness as a reprehensible state of mind. Concerning the difference between *shuḥḥ* and *bukhl*, it is said[11] that *bukhl* denotes the very act of niggardliness whereas *shuḥḥ* refers to the particular state of the soul that necessitates acts of niggardliness. This interpretation appears to be confirmed by the Qurʾanic usage of the word in question. It is at any rate highly significant that the Qurʾān uses *shuḥḥ* in reference to the essential nature of the human soul.

> *Shuḥḥ* is in the very nature of the souls. But if you do acts of charity through fear of God, verily God will never fail to take notice of what you do. (IV, 127/128)

> Fear God as much as you can, and give ear, and obey, and expend willingly for the sake of your souls. And whosoever is saved from the *shuḥḥ* of his soul, such are the prosperous. (LXIV, 16; see also LIX, 9)

## (2) Courage → fear of God + Last Day spurs bravery in defense of/for Islam + God

I have tried to show how the Qurʾān revived the old ideal of generosity in the religious atmosphere of the newly formed Muslim community and succeeded in developing the peculiarly Arab impulse to generosity into a genuine Islamic virtue. Practically the same thing is true of the virtue of bravery.

Now it was natural that in desert conditions courage or bravery

11 *al-Bukhl: nafs al-manᶜ; al-shuḥḥ: al-ḥālah al-nafsānīyah allatī taqtaḍī dhālika al-manᶜ*. al-Bustānī's *Muḥīṭ al-Muḥīṭ*, I, 69.

was given the highest place among the virtues. It was admittedly an essential ingredient of the *murūwah.* In the Arabian steppes where the forces of nature were so severe against human beings and where brigandage, far from constituting a crime, was often almost the only alternative to death, nothing could excel in importance physical strength and military prowess. The tribal honor among the pagan Arabs, of which I have given above a somewhat detailed description, was to a large extent a matter of prowess. For the Arabs of the desert, the bloodiest fight, whether tribal or personal, was the very source and mainspring of life as well as of honor. The time was indeed hard for weaklings and cowards.

> My lineage goes not back to weaklings and the unarmoured
> Nor to some abject, miserable cowards on the battlefield,
> But a son of those warriors am I, who used to smite
> The streaks of the helms whenever they met them,
> Who with long sword-belts, imperturbably went to death.

So says Ḍirār b. al-Khaṭṭāb with evident pride. In the desert where, as the poet Zuhayr says, 'he who defends not his watering-place with his own weapons will have it devastated, and he who wrongs not others will himself be wronged', bravery was not simply a defensive weapon; it was something much more positive and aggressive. Zuhayr does not mind declaring openly in his moral teaching that it is not enough for 'a warrior, fierce as a lion, to strike back and chastise his enemy when the latter has struck him a blow; he should rather take the initiative and become an aggressor when no one wrongs him.'[12] Thus the virtue of courage and bravery among the pagan Arabs was often no better than cruelty and inhuman ferocity in tribal feuds. We have already seen that this is precisely what characterizes *jāhilīyah* as opposed to *ḥilm.*

Islām does not differ from Jāhilīyah in its praise of courage and scorn of cowardice. Here too, as in pagan times, it was the highest honor for men to be described as 'unfaltering in danger, no weakling they; bold and intrepid against their enemy in every arena of battle' (Kaʿb b. Mālik), and it was no less a disgrace for the Muslims than for the pagan Arabs to have it reported: 'They shrank from death; that is why their private pasture land was taken as a spoil. They did the act of base and mean cowards.' Just as in the case of generosity, however, Islām cut off all excessive elements from this Jāhilī virtue and made out of it a typically Islamic virtue. In the days of paganism courage was displayed, as it were, for courage's sake. A broad survey of pre-Islamic poetry creates an impression that the Jāhilī warriors showed dauntless, reckless courage on the battlefield only to gratify

12 Zuhayr b. Abī Sulmā, *Muʿallaqah*, vv. 38–39.



NOT for it's own sake, must have piety + humbleness + fear of God as the base

an irresistible desire; courage was then largely a matter of unrestrained and unrestrainable impulse. In Islām this underwent a peculiar transformation, without, however, losing an atom of its original energy. It was no longer a blind, unruly impulse. It was now a noble, well-disciplined courage with a lofty aim serving the cause of the right religion: courage 'in the way of God.'

> O you who believe, smite the Kāfirs in your neighborhood until you bring them to cry mercy. But always remember that God is with the god-fearing (IX, 124/123)
>
> Will you not smite a people who broke their pledges and intended to expel the Apostle? They attacked you first. What! Are you afraid of them? God deserves more that you should be afraid of Him, if you are really believers.
>
> Smite them! God will chastise them at your hands, and disgrace them, and help you against them towards victory. He will heal the breasts of a people who believe, and will remove the burning rage from their hearts. God turns into whom He pleases. (IX, 13–15)

Rumor spread incredibly fast in the desert. For a Jāhilī warrior it was an unbearable shame to have it said that he had turned his back upon the enemy on the battlefield and fled before them, for it was sure to bring the deepest disgrace not only upon his own head but also upon the tribal honor itself. For a Muslim, too, to fly before the enemy when fighting in the way of God was to commit the most infamous offence against religion and God. To be called a runaway (*farrār*) was a moral stain that could not be wiped off easily. Thus in the battle of Muʾtah in A.H. 8, the Muslim army was severely smitten by the overwhelmingly numerous enemy. The famous 'Sword of Allāh', Khālid b. al-Walīd, being a great commander, decided to beat a hasty retreat in order to avoid spilling Muslim blood to no purpose. When, however, the army came back to Medina, the enraged crowd threw dirt at them, shouting, 'O you runaways! How durst you flee in the way of God?' And even Muḥammad could not allay the excitement. It is related about a certain Salamah b. Hishām that he could not go out of his house even a step. His wife, when asked, 'How is it that I do not see your husband at prayers with the Apostle together with other believers?' is said to have replied, 'By God, it is actually impossible for him to go out. For every time he does the people shout, "Coward! You fled in God's way!" so much so that he remains nowadays in his house and never goes out.'[13] We find the same state of mind expressed in the Qurʾān, though with a mitigating reservation which is intended to justify the cases in which the Muslims have to beat a retreat for some strategic purpose.

[13] Ibn Isḥāq, II, 798.

> O you who believe, when you encounter the Kāfirs marching against you, turn not your back to them. He who on such a day turns his back to them—unless he be escaping by stratagem to attack them afresh or withdrawing to join another troop—has incurred the wrath of God; his final habitation will be Hell; an evil journey, indeed! (VIII, 15–16)

Those who show reluctance in going forth in the way of God disclose by that very attitude that they are not true Muslims.

> No matter how they may swear by God that they belong to your community [i.e. that they are Muslims], they are in reality not of you, for they are a people of a cowardly nature (*yafraqūna: faraq* meaning 'to be timorous, pusillanimous') (IX, 56)

In the following passage it is categorically affirmed that the true believer (*muʾmin*), that is, 'he who is god-fearing' (*muttaqī*) does not fear his human enemy, and is ready to fight strenuously with his wealth and his person, while he who does not fear God does fear to fight in His way.

> Those who believe in God and the Last Day will never beg off from going to fight; they will strive with their wealth and their lives. God is aware of those who fear Him. They alone beg off from thee who believe not in God and the Last Day, and whose hearts are in doubt, so that they waver in their doubt. (IX, 44–45)

To put it in a nutshell, what is now demanded of a true believer is no longer that brute courage of which the poets of Jāhilīyah spoke so boastingly, but an entirely new kind of military prowess born of, and based on, a firm belief in God and the Last Day. In Jāhilīyah courage was something groundless and without direction. The Qurʾān provided it with a definite direction, and succeeded, as the subsequent history of the Islamic empire affords abundant proof, in creating out of it the most formidable weapon in the hands of the believers for fighting the enemies of Allāh.

## Loyalty

That faithfulness or trustworthiness was one of the highest and most characteristic virtues in the desert is known to every reader of pre-Islamic poetry and traditions. As might be expected, the Jāhilī virtue of loyalty was largely a matter of kinship by blood. It was mostly practiced within the bounds of the tribe; and within this narrow sphere, loyalty ruled absolute and supreme. It manifested itself as the most disinterested self-sacrifice on behalf of one's kinsmen, the most faithful devotion to one's friends, and also as the greatest fidelity shown in the keeping of a covenant plighted and trust committed. Very often a solemn compact could extend the sphere of effectiveness of this virtue even beyond the limits of the tribe. This is illustrated by the typical example of Samawʾal b. ʿĀdiyā, which is too well-known now to be repeated in detail here.[14] Demanded by a besieging tyrant to surrender the coats of mail which the poet Imruʾ al-Qays had committed to him, Samawʾal, though no relative of the poet by blood, refused to do so and finally saw his son slaughtered before his own eyes. Even today the name of Samawʾal survives on the lips of the Arabs as the highest embodiment of the Bedouin ideal of loyalty. And the poet Zuhayr, in the oft-quoted verse says concerning *wafāʾ*:

> He who proves faithful to his covenant escapes blame, and he whose heart aims at the calmness of integrity will never have to falter.[15]

This fervent veneration of faithfulness and loyalty Islām inherited from Jāhilīyah, in its original nomadic vigorousness. It is clear from both the Qurʾān itself and Apostolic Tradition that the virtue of loyalty peculiar to the desert Arabs was adopted by Islām as an important item of its moral code and was even given there a very high place of honour. Just as in the case of other nomadic ideals, however, Islām did not remain content with simple adoption, but developed this old virtue in a peculiar way, and succeeded in leading it into the groove of monotheistic faith. This islamization of the nomadic virtue of *wafāʾ* was effected in two distinct but closely related directions: in the sphere of ordinary social relationships among the believers themselves, and in the properly religious sphere concerning the vertical relationship between God and man.

On the first of these two points little need be said here. For any detailed discussion of this aspect of the question would be nothing more than tedious repetition of what was already said in the preceding chapter concerning the abolition of tribal solidarity in Islām. The virtue of *wafāʾ*, having been born of a particular consciousness of blood fellowship produced by a solemn ceremony of sacrifice, was primarily a tribal or intertribal affair. It was first of all the most chivalrous devotion to each other between the members of one and the same tribe. It was, secondly, the sacred covenant connection between different tribes and clans. Any two tribes that happened to agree on anything, friendship, for example, or marriage, trading, etc., offered a common sacrifice to some deity, and entered thereby into a solemn agreement. Islām, by breaking down all limitations due to the tribal

14 See for instance Nicholson, pp. 84–85.
15 Zuhayr b. Abī Sulmā, v. 43.

pattern of society, put the virtue of fidelity on a wider basis, transformed it into something supertribal, truly human. *Wafā*ʾ thus became a moral force capable of operating in an individualistic society.

What is much more important is the second of the two points distinguished above: the Islamic transformation of *wafā*ʾ in the religious sphere. Here we see the Prophet transcending all the crude ideas of primitive nomadic religion and betaking himself to the characteristically Semitic conception of Covenant, as a formal expression of the religious bond between God and men. It goes without saying that this conception of religion is most typically exemplified by the Old Testament. The most fundamental and most general frame within which the religious consciousness of Israel moved and developed was the idea of the covenant between Yahweh and the people of Israel as a whole. 'I will be your God, and you shall be My people.' The covenant was first imposed on Israel by Yahweh Himself by His act of pure grace in redeeming them out of Egypt. This point is repeatedly emphasized in the Qurʾān, too. 'We delivered you from Pharaoh's family who were inflicting atrocious tortures. . . . We tore in two the Red Sea and delivered you, and drowned Pharaoh's family before your own eyes.' (II, 46–47/49–50) But every covenant, inasmuch as it is a covenant, puts both parties under obligations. By the very act of imposing His covenant on His people, Yahweh also laid Himself under obligation to fulfill the covenant conditions; He gave His word that He would be God of Israel, love them, deliver them, guide them to salvation, with all that is implied by 'being the God of a people'. And, it should be remembered, 'God never breaks His promise, though most men do not know it.' (XXX, 5/6). Thus Yahweh and Israel contracted themselves into a mutual relationship of claims and rights. It is quite significant that this basic relation between Yahweh and Israel is referred to very frequently in the Qurʾān.

> O children of Israel, remember My blessing with which I blessed you, and fulfill My covenant and I shall fulfill yours. Me you should fear. (II, 38/40)

It is beyond doubt also that the Qurʾān transferred this particular relationship between Yahweh and Israel into the very center of Islām and made it the basic form of the relationship between Allāh and the Muslims.

> Verily, those who swear fealty to thee [Muḥammad] swear fealty by that very act unto God. The hand of God is over their hands [representing the ritual ceremony of covenant-making]. So whosoever breaks his oath [after that] breaks it only to his own hurt,

and whosoever fulfills his covenant with God, on him will God bestow a great reward. (XLVIII, 10)

The conception of religion as based on a covenant between two parties is indeed no less characteristic of the Qurʾān than of the Old Testament. And practically all the moral values that developed in Islām may be said to have something to do with the covenant-idea, directly or at least indirectly. The virtue of *ṢDQ* is perhaps the first of those that are most intimately related to this basic conception.

This root, *ṢDQ*, appears in the Qurʾān in a number of forms: *ṣadaqa*, verbal, *ṣidq*, nominal, *ṣādiq*, participial-adjectival, *ṣiddīq*, emphatic-adjectival, and so on. We may make a beginning by noting that among the old Arab lexicographers *ṣidq* is recognized by common consent to be the exact opposite of ***kadhib*** ('falsehood', 'lie'). According to Ibn Fāris b. Zakarīyāʾ, the famous author of one of the earliest alphabetical dictionaries, the basic meaning of the root is 'strength', or 'hardness', whether of language or other things. This original meaning, he says, is still to be seen in the adjective *ṣadq* meaning 'hard, vigorous'. *Ṣidq* is the 'truth' of language, so named because of its 'strength' as opposed to the weakness of falsehood.[16]

In effect, the most usual sense of *ṣidq* is to 'speak truth', to give information which is true, i.e. which conforms to the reality. This meaning of the word is clearly seen in the most ordinary sentences of the type: 'They investigated the report closely and found that the reporter had spoken truth (*ṣadaqa*).' In sentences of this kind *ṣidq* means beyond any doubt conformity of language to reality. This, however, does not exhaust the whole of its meaning.

Now the truth of language, that is, the process by which any speech becomes true, may be looked at from two opposite sides, subjective and objective. The objective pole is the reality to which language conforms. In Arabic this pole is designated by the word *ḥaqq*, a word which is also generally translated 'truth'. *Ḥaqq* then, represents the specifically objective side of the truth. *Ṣidq* is the opposite pole; it refers more particularly to a property in the speaker, which tends to make his words correspond with the reality, i.e. his truthfulness. The following example taken from Ibn Isḥāq brings out this point admirably well. 'The Apostle of God informed the people of what they knew was truth (*ḥaqq*) and so they recognized at once his truthfulness (*ṣidq*).'

subjective

Equally interesting in this respect is the following verse by Ṭarafah:

[16] Ibn Fāris, *Muʿjam Maqāyīs al-Lughah*, ed. ʿAbd al-Salām Hārūn (Cairo, A.H. 1366–1371), III, 339.

*Wa-al-ṣidq yaʾlafuhu al-labīb al-murtajá* *
*wa-al-kadhib yaʾlafuhu al-danī al-akhyab*[17]

Truthfulness is a constant quality of a man who is persevering, always to be trusted, while falsehood is a constant quality of a man vile and deceptive.

It is interesting to notice in this connection a very curious observation made by some Arab lexicographers about the semantic structure of *ṣidq*. For a given statement to be *ṣidq*, we are told, it is not enough that the words used conform to reality; they should also conform to the idea of reality in the mind of the speaker. It is the existence of the intention or determination to be true that constitutes the most decisive element in the semantic structure of *ṣidq*. But the formula 'the intention to be true to reality' may, as a matter of actual fact, be understood in various ways and may cover wider or narrower areas of meaning, because the 'reality' admits of considerable variety. It may be simply an objective fact, popular custom, a rule of conduct, a treaty, or again the words one has uttered oneself. In all these cases *ṣidq* acquires very obvious implications of sincerity, steadfastness, honesty, and trustworthiness. Thus we encounter many examples of actual usage of *ṣidq* in the Qurʾān as elsewhere, which mere 'speaking the truth' could in no way account for.

The most remarkable of all—and that not only from the specific standpoint of the present chapter, but more generally—is perhaps the case in which *ṣādiq* is used in the Qurʾān in contrast to *kāfir* or *munāfiq*, 'perfidious'.

And when We [Allāh] imposed a covenant upon the Prophets, and upon thee [Muḥammad], and upon Noah, Abraham, Moses, and Jesus son of Mary, We imposed upon them a solemn covenant, that He [Allāh] might question [on the Last Day] the *ṣādiq* concerning their *ṣidq*. He has prepared for the *kāfir* a painful chastisement. (XXXIII, 7–8)

We are told here that on the Day of Judgment all men will be divided into two categories: the class of *ṣādiq* and the class of *kāfir*. The *ṣādiq* are those who have remained throughout their life unswervingly true to the covenant obligations, while the *kāfir* are, as we already know very well, those who have always shown themselves ungrateful to the grace of God, and have been, by implication, untrue and unfaithful to the same covenant. It is highly significant that in this passage *ṣidq* is spoken of in particular reference to the covenant between God and His people. Here the contextual situation forces us to translate *ṣādiq* by 'faithful', and *ṣidq* by 'faithfulness' or 'loyalty'.

[17] Ṭarafah, *Dīwān*, ed. M. Seligsohn (Paris, 1901), XII, v. 7.

In the following passage, in which *ṣādiq* stands opposed to *munāfiq* 'perfidious', the verb *ṣadaqa* (in m. pl. form *ṣadaqū*) should be rendered as 'they remained true to', or, 'they fulfilled' (their covenant).

> There are amongst the believers men who have remained true (*ṣadaqū*) to their covenant with God, and there are some who have fulfilled their vow [by martyrdom], and some who still wait and have not changed lightly; that God might reward the *ṣādiq*, and punish the *munāfiq* if He please, or turn again unto them. (XXXIII, 23–24)

The word *ṣidq* must perhaps be understood in the same way when it appears alongside of *ʿadl* 'justice' in Sūrah VI, 115. This interpretation becomes the more probable if we, as I think we should, take the latter half of the passage, indicating the absolute unchangeableness of divine words, as a kind of periphrasis for what is implied by *ṣidq*.

> Perfect are the words of thy Lord in *ṣidq* and *ʿadl*. Naught can change His words.

Here we see *ṣidq* used in reference to the words of God. This means simply that God as an active participant in the 'covenant' remains true to His own words. And this is nothing other than a particular way of expressing the thought that God's words once uttered cannot be changed with fickleness, that, in other words, they are absolutely trustworthy.

However this may be, it is certain that *ṣidq* in the sense of 'being true to one's words' comes very near the word *wafāʾ* which, as we saw, also denotes the quality in man of being faithful and loyal. And in fact we encounter very often these two terms employed side by side synonymously, e.g. 'I am in covenant with Muḥammad and I do not wish to break my word because I have never seen in him except faithfulness (*wafāʾ* and *ṣidq*).'[18] And a poet contemporary with Muḥammad says in a passage of his poem composed after the battle of Uḥud: 'We parted with Abū Sufyān on the promise that we should meet again at Badr; but we did not find him to his promise true (*ṣidq*) nor was he a man of faithfulness (*wāfī*, participial-adjectival form of *wafāʾ*).'[19]

It would not be without interest to note in this connection what Abū Bakr is said to have remarked concerning *ṣidq*. It is related that, when he was elected Khalīfah after the Apostle's death, he declared in a passage of his speech, 'The essense of *ṣidq* is *amānah*, while the essence of *kadhib* is *khiyānah*.' *Amānah* is another word meaning the

[18] Ibn Isḥāq, II, 674.
[19] *Ibid.*, p. 620.

human quality of being trustworthy, trustworthiness, or honesty, while *khiyānah* denotes its opposite, namely, treacherousness, betrayal, or perfidy. It will be easy to see how closely *ṣidq*, truth, was related to the idea of trustworthiness in the linguistic consciousness of the old Arabs, and also how high a place it occupied among the nomadic as well as the Islamic virtues.

There remains to explain one more important form derived from the same root, *ṣiddīq*. It is extremely difficult to state in a definite manner the exact meaning of this controversial term. One thing is certain: that this is a *mubālaghah* (intensive, lit., exaggerating) form of *ṣādiq*. It denotes, in other words, the highest possible degree of *ṣidq*; but this is still very ambiguous because *ṣidq*, as we know, has two distinguishable aspects. According to the commonest view among the Arab philologists, it refers specifically to the element of speaking the truth. *Ṣiddīq* in this view means 'highly veracious', 'who speaks nothing but truth', 'who never lies'.

Now the term *ṣiddīq* is widely known as the honorary epithet of the Khalīfah Abū Bakr, and is generally understood in this sense. A closer examination, however, of the traditional account of the occasion on which Abū Bakr received this honorific would lead us to a somewhat different interpretation. Tradition relates that, when Muḥammad, immediately after the famous experience of the ascension to Heaven and the miraculous night journey to Jerusalem, gave a detailed account of this experience, grave doubts were aroused in the minds of all Muslims who were there with regard to its truthfulness. The only person who did not allow his faith to be shaken by Muḥammad's account was, we are told Abū Bakr. He alone kept on saying, while the Apostle described in detail what he had seen in Jerusalem, 'That is true. I testify that you are the Apostle of God.' At the end of his account Muḥammad said, 'And you, Abū Bakr, are indeed *ṣiddīq*.'

If we are to take this tradition as it is, it would follow that *ṣiddīq* does not mean 'one who speaks the truth', but rather 'one who testifies to the truth of something.' It does not matter very much whether this tradition be authentic or not. It is valuable for our present purpose in that it gives us an important key to the meaning attached to the word *ṣiddīq* in the minds of the Arabs of those days. But the Qur'ān itself must have something to say about it.

In the Qur'ān this epithet is applied to the Virgin Mary, Abraham, Joseph, and more generally to all true believers.

> The Messiah, son of Mary, was no more than an Apostle, just like other Apostles who had passed away before him. And his mother

was [simply] a *ṣiddīqah* (fem. form of *ṣiddīq*). They both ate [ordinary] food. (V, 79/75)

The purport of this passage is to deprive Jesus and his mother, the Virgin Mary, of the halo of sanctity which is essentially incompatible with the idea of the absolute Oneness of God, and to declare that they both were no more than simple mortals who ate food like other mortals. The only point in which they differed from common people was that Jesus was one of the Apostles of God, and Mary was an eminently virtuous woman. As to the exact meaning in which we should understand the word *ṣiddīqah*, the context affords practically no explanation. We are left embarrassingly at liberty to interpret it in terms of truth-speaking, trustworthiness, or honesty.

'Joseph, thou *ṣiddīq*! Give us your opinion on [the strange dream] ... so that I may return to the people and let them know the truth.' (XII, 46)

Usually it is taken for granted that the word *ṣiddīq* in this passage means 'veracious'. Is the word meant to refer to the previous experience of the speaker—to the fact that the interpretation of a dream concerning his future course of life, which Joseph had given him, really came true—so that it denotes a 'man who spoke the truth'? Or does it, more generally, mean the quality of veraciousness itself? Or, again does it mean 'trustworthy'? At all events there remains considerable uncertainty about the real meaning of the word.

The following example, which concerns Abraham, is of particular importance semantically, for the whole passage forms, as it were, a very detailed explanation of why he came to be called a *ṣiddīq*. True, it is not a real verbal definition, but at least it gives us a clue as to what kind of conduct entitled one to this honorific.

And mention in this Book [i.e. Qurʾān] the affair of Abraham; verily, he was a *ṣiddīq*, a Prophet.
He said to his father, 'O my father, why dost thou worship that which can neither hear nor see nor avail thee aught? O my father, I have received knowledge such as thou hast not received yet. So follow me, and I will guide thee to a straight path.... O my father, worship not Satan; verily, Satan has ever been rebellious against the Merciful God. O my father, verily, I fear that there may smite thee some chastisement from the Merciful God, so that thou shouldst become a client of Satan.' He [father] said, 'What! art thou averse from my Gods, Abraham? Stop, or surely I shall have to stone thee to death. Rather, depart from me for a while.'
He [Abraham] said, 'Fare thee well, then! I will ask forgiveness

for thee from my Lord; verily He has ever been benevolent to me. I will go away from you and all these things [i.e. idols] that you pray apart from God. My Lord I will pray. In praying [only] to my Lord I think I shall never be unfortunate.' (XIX, 42–49/41–48)

Here we see Abraham described as a determined champion for monotheism against the surrounding forces of idolatrous polytheism; a zealous and fearless believer in God, who remains loyal to the last to his religion even if he is forced thereby to part with his own father and be condemned to exile. Such is a man who is fully entitled to the name of *ṣiddīq*. It will be clear that this passage helps us a step forward in understanding the semantic core of the word. In the next example the same word, presumably with the same meaning, is applied to true believers in general. It should be noticed as a fact of particular relevance that the *ṣiddīq* are here opposed to the *kāfir*.

Those who believe in God and His Apostles, they are the *ṣiddīqūn* (pl. of *ṣiddīq*) and the [true] witnesses in the view of their Lord; for them is an appropriate reward and they have their light. Those, on the contrary, who have shown themselves Kāfirs and cried lies to Our signs, they are the inhabitants of Hell. (LVII, 18/19)

The last two passages would seem to suggest that the word *ṣiddīq*, at least in the Qurʾanic context, means a zealous persevering believer who remains unswervingly faithful to his monotheistic belief in God whatever happens, rather than a man who always speaks truth.

In the saying of Abū Bakr quoted above (p. 791) we saw *ṣidq* opposed to *kadhib* and, through this latter, to *khiyānah* ('treacherousness'). Now if *ṣidq*, in the sense of remaining unswervingly true to one's promise, oath, treaty, covenant, and the like, constitutes such a high moral quality, it is only natural that its opposite, *khiyānah* should be considered one of the most sinful qualities man can ever possess. In Islām no less than in Jāhilīyah the act of treachery was an atrocious sin, and a man qualified by such a property was abhorred as a viper.

If thou fearest treachery (*khiyānah*) from any folk [with whom thou art in treaty], then throw it back to them [i.e. dissolve the treaty without compunction] in fairness. For verily, God loves not the treacherous (*khāʾinīn*, pl. of *khāʾin*, lit. 'those who are prone to *khiyānah*'). (VIII, 60/58)

In the following passage in which the integrity of Joseph is confessed through the very lips of the wife of the Egyptian Governor, we see *khāʾin* 'treacherous' standing significantly in opposition to *ṣādiq*, a fact which, by the way, goes to confirm the view that *ṣādiq* in this context means a man who remains loyal and true to the covenant between master and servant.

> Said the wife of the Governor, 'At last the truth (*ḥaqq*) is out! Yes, it is I who tempted him. He [Joseph] is surely a *ṣādiq*.' [Then said Joseph,] '[All this has happened] in order that he [my master, the Egyptian Governor] may know that I betrayed (*khāna*, verbal form corresponding to *khiyānah*) him not behind his back, and that God guides not the evil design of the *khā'in*.' (XII, 51–52)

If treachery (*khiyānah*) is a grave sin in the sphere of ordinary social life, that is, in social ethics regulating the conduct of individuals among themselves within the same Islamic community, this is naturally much more the case in the sphere of the ethico-religious attitude of man towards God. In other words, *khiyānah* against God constitutes a more serious sin than *khiyānah* against man. To realize this, it will be enough to remember that the most characteristic type of the *khiyānah* against God is *nifāq* which denotes perfidy under the cover of hypocritical faith. Unlike the above-discussed *kufr* which, at least in its typical form, is not so much 'treachery' or 'betrayal' as downright refusal to enter into a covenant with God, or the open declaration of disbelief in God, *nifāq* is to act treacherously in the midst of Islām, under the guise of piety.

As a matter of fact, we have already met with the concept of *nifāq*. Briefly, *munāfiq* is one who, though outwardly a pious Muslim, remains at heart an infidel and is secretly an inexorable enemy of God and the Prophet. We might do well to recall also that in the passage quoted above (XXXIII, 23–24), *munāfiq* stood in antithesis to *ṣādiq*. Since, however, the topic of *nifāq* is so important for the specific purpose of this book as a whole as to warrant a much more detailed analysis, I shall leave further discussion of this problem to a later, more suitable occasion and bring this section to a close by simply quoting two characteristic passages which will throw further light on the meaning of *khiyānah* in the sphere of religion and faith.

> Act not as a pleader for the treacherous (*khā'inīn*) . . . and plead not on behalf of those who betray (*yakhtānūna*, a verbal form of *khiyānah*) themselves. Verily, God loves not anyone who is a sinful traitor (*khawwān*). (IV, 106–107/105–107)

The phrase 'who betray themselves' implies that those who act treacherously towards God are only being treacherous to themselves, because in the final resort their *khiyānah* comes back upon their own heads. As to the word *khawwān*, rendered here provisionally as 'traitor' we might remark that it is a *mubālaghah* (exaggeration)-form of *khāʾin*, denoting one who is characterized by an exceeding degree of treacherousness, one who, as al-Bayḍāwī put it, persists in doing acts of treachery and perfidy. It is noteworthy, moreover, that the word is here placed in further emphasis by the addition of another word, *athīm*, 'sinful'.[20]

> Surely God will defend those who believe. Surely God loves not any ingrate traitor (*kull khawwān kafūr*). (XXII, 39/38)

Here again one who proves unfaithful to the covenant with God is designated by the same strong term, *khawwān*. But this time it is accompanied not by 'sinful', but by a much more forcible word, *kafūr*, which is an emphatic epithet derived from the root *KFR*, and means 'extremely, or habitually ungrateful'.

There appears in the Qurʾān another word for 'traitor', which is no less forcible than *khawwān*: that is *khattār*, an emphatic epithet from *khatr*, which means one who acts 'with the foulest perfidy, treachery, or unfaithfulness'.[21] It is interesting to observe that this word, too, is found in the Qurʾān accompanied by *kafūr*. The passage in question is Sūrah XXXI, 31/32, where we are reminded of certain thankless people who, when they are overtaken by a storm on the sea, call on God, being utterly sincere in their piety, but as soon as God brings them safely to the shore, forget all about it and begin to act inimically against God.

> Hast thou not seen how the ships run upon the sea by God's favor ...? When waves like darkness cover them, they pray to God making their belief in Him quite sincere, but as soon as He brings them safely to the shore, some amongst them become cool and indifferent. No one, however, could deny our signs, except every ingrate traitor (*kull khattār kafūr*).

The parallelism of outer structure seems to give evidence that *khattār* and *khawwān*, although belonging to two entirely unrelated roots, are the nearest possible synonyms in every respect, whether in meaning, structure, or emotive force.

I should like to add that al-Bayḍāwī, commenting on the word *khattār* in this example, makes a very interesting remark: that it means *ghaddār* i.e. the most villainous traitor, and that those who do acts of the kind here described are called 'traitors' because the denial of the divine signs is in the last resort an act of treachery and unfaithfulness to religion as a 'natural covenant'. This is indeed a valuable piece of confirmatory evidence for our argument that the

[20] This word, *athīm*, will be dealt with later, in Chapter XI.
[21] E. W. Lane, *An Arabic-English Lexicon* (London, 1863–1893), II, 701.

conceptual opposition *ṣidq—khiyānah* should be understood primarily in terms of the Covenant between God and His people. Even where there is no explicit mention of a formal covenant, the idea itself is there, and this tends to give a very peculiar ethical coloring to the meanings of these words.

## Veracity

As I noted above we discern in the semantic category of *ṣidq* two different, though closely related, aspects: veracity or truth-speaking, and faithfulness (to one's promise, treaty, or covenant). In the latter half of the foregoing section we have concentrated our attention on the second aspect. Now it is time that we turned to the first to see if Islām has something peculiar to say about this old virtue of the desert.

That truth-speaking was considered an eminent virtue among the desert Arabs in Jāhilīyah will be clear without any lengthy discussion. It is so in all peoples, so far as I am aware. It is the commonest, most ordinary sort of human virtue, and as such it does not seem to offer any problem of particular interest. In the Qur'ān, however, it assumes a very remarkable peculiarity, and this point will leap to the eye when we approach the problem from its negative side, i.e. the sin of lying.

We may do well to call to mind again an important point which was casually referred to in an earlier passage: namely, that 'truth' is fundamentally a relationship between two poles, *ṣidq* and *ḥaqq*. As we saw there, *ḥaqq* represents the objective side of the truth, and language can be 'true' only when it conforms to it. 'Truth' as a subjective affair, then, consists in using language in such a way as to make it correspond with *ḥaqq*, the reality. This point begins to assume a tremendous significance when we turn to the problem of truth-speaking in matters that concern the religious relationship between God and man. For according to the Qur'ān, the Revelation is nothing other than *ḥaqq*, and God Himself is the absolute *Ḥaqq*. It is significant that in either case *ḥaqq* is opposed to *bāṭil* which means something essentially groundless, 'vanity' or 'falsehood'.

*God as the Truth or Reality*

> God is the Truth, whereas what they [i.e. the idolaters] call upon apart from Him is nothing but unreality (*bāṭil*). (XXII, 61/62; see also XXXI, 29/30)

*Bāṭil* in this passage clearly refers to the idols which the pagan Arabs worshipped alongside of Allāh. And since idols are, in the Qur'anic view, nothing but an absurd invention of the 'human caprice', a groundless fable, mere names, it will be evident that by the 'Truth' (*ḥaqq*) is meant something pre-eminently real, a living force which is operating in the very process of life and death in the world of existence. This point is brought out particularly well by the following example in which, through a very detailed description of the process whereby each one of the human beings is created from dust and grows up from a drop of congealed blood into a well-shaped infant, it is suggested that the same God who has the power of creating man from nothingness has also the power of causing the final resurrection.

> All this [wonderful process of creation] is possible because God *is* the Truth, and is [able to] bring the lifeless to life, and is able to do everything. (XXII, 6)

In the next example, too, the omnipotence of God in administering human affairs is greatly emphasized, and is made the evidence of His being really the Real. The quality of reality in God, in other words, is grasped chiefly in terms of His grand creative activity.

> Say, 'Who furnishes you with your provision from heaven and earth? Who can really hear and really see? Who brings forth the living from the lifeless and the lifeless from the living? Who administers all these affairs?' They will reply, 'It is God.'
> Then say at once, 'Are you not afraid [of Him]? Lo! such is God, your Lord, the Truth. And what is there beyond truth, but error?' (X, 32–33/31–32)

*Revelation as the Truth or Reality*

> They [i.e. the disbelievers] say: 'He [Muḥammad] is only possessed by a devil.' Nay, but he has brought them the Truth (*ḥaqq*), but most of them dislike the Truth. And had the Truth followed their caprices, the heavens and the earth and all those who are therein would have surely been corrupted. (XXIII, 72–73/70–71)

Verse 72 refers to the fact that the Prophet, particularly at the outset of his career, was often regarded by his compatriots as a sort of madman, *majnūn*—literally, a man attacked and possessed by a *jinn* or invisible spirit, of whose existence Muḥammad himself did not doubt. The passage denies this emphatically and declares that Muḥammad, far from being a *majnūn*, is a Prophet of God, who has brought the divine message, which is the 'Truth'. In a similar way, this 'Truth' was often reviled and laughed at as sheer 'magic', *sihr*.

> The Kāfirs, when the Truth reaches them, say of it, 'This is naught but sheer magic.' (XXXIV, 42/43)

Before the tenacious, vigorous onslaught of the Kāfirs, even Muhammad, so it appears, had to waver sometimes; and tradition tells us that he, particularly at the beginning of his prophetic career was sometimes driven into anxiety and doubt as to the real source of the mysterious voice which dictated to him the messages to deliver. In the two following passages God Himself assures Muḥammad of the never-to-be-doubted Truth-quality of the divine message.

> [This is] the Truth from thy Lord, so be thou never of those who doubt and waver. (III, 53/60)

> Those unto whom We gave the Scripture [i.e. the Jewish people who know what Revelation is] recognize it [the Qurʾān] as they recognize their own sons. And yet, a party of them conceal the Truth knowingly. [This is] the Truth from thy Lord, so be thou not of those who doubt and waver. (II, 141–142/146–147)

*Islām as the Truth*

If the revelation that came through the mouthpiece of the Prophet is the Truth, then it follows naturally that Islām, the religion based on this revelation, is also the Truth. In this sense, too, the word *ḥaqq* is constantly used in opposition to *bāṭil.*

> Say, 'Is there amongst your associates [i.e. the idols whom you worship alongside of Allāh in the capacity of His associates] any that guides you to the Truth?'
> Say, 'It is God [alone] who guides to the Truth. Is He who guides to the Truth worthier to be followed, or he who guides not unless he himself is guided? What is the matter with you then? How do you judge?' (X, 36/35)

> Say, 'The Truth has come and Falsehood has vanished. Surely Falsehood is ever bound to vanish'. (XVII, 83/81)

The upshot of all this is that a particular sacrosanctity is attributed in the Qurʾān to the word 'Truth', *ḥaqq*, and, consequently, all use of language which contradicts it in any way is considered to be glaring blasphemy against God and His religion. It is not at all surprising, then, that we find *kadhib*, 'falsehood' or 'lying', talked of in the Qurʾān as a heinous sin. It constitutes one of the most salient features of a Kāfir.

Now *kadhib*, as such a blasphemous attitude towards God, manifests itself mainly in two different ways. In the first place, it manifests itself as an open act of lying on the part of man, concerning God and His revelation. Secondly, it may take the form of 'giving God the lie'. The Qurʾanic word for the first kind is *iftirāʾ* (*al-kadhib*) 'forging (a lie)', and the second is designated by *takdhīb* which means literally 'to declare something a lie'.

*Takdhīb*, as the name itself suggests, is a flat denial of the divine revelation, refusal to accept the Truth when it is sent down, with an additional element of mockery and scorn. In other words, *takdhīb* in the Qurʾanic context denotes the characteristic attitude of those stubborn unbelievers who persist in their refusal to accept the revelation as really coming from God, and never cease to laugh at it as mere old folks' tales.

> Whenever a sign of their Lord comes to them they turn away from it. They [always] cried lies (*kadhdhabū*) to the Truth (*ḥaqq*) when it came to them. But [before long] there shall come to them news of that which they were laughing at [i.e. the announcement of the terrible divine punishment]. (VI, 4–5)

The phrase 'that which they were laughing at (*yastahziʾūna*)' describes, as is evident, the same thing as the phrase 'they cried lies to', and thus throws a strong light on the mental attitude underlying the act of *takdhīb*. *Istihzāʾ* or 'mockery' is the fundamental state of mind of those who deny the revealed Truth.

As to *iftirāʾ* 'forging' we may observe that, if *takdhīb* is the act of downright blasphemy against God, 'forging' is a more subtle kind of ungodliness consisting as it does in inventing groundless fables and pretending that they came from a divine source. *Iftirāʾ* is the word for such an act of forgery. It is a verb and is usually accompanied by the word *kadhib* as its 'direct object'. Those who commit *iftirāʾ* do in fact no smaller wrong than those who flatly deny God's signs, for it is plain that they are attempting thereby to forge 'divine' signs themselves. So it is no surprise to us to find that the act of *iftirāʾ* is condemned and censured in the Qurʾān in exactly the same terms as *takdhīb*.

What, concretely, is meant in the Qurʾān by *iftirāʾ*? The answer varies according to the specific context. But there can be no doubt that the most representative kinds of *iftirāʾ* are idolatry and the 'sacred' customs connected with the idolatrous worship of Jāhilīyah.

> Verily, those who took [to themselves] the Calf, wrath shall come upon them from their Lord and abasement [even] in the life of this present world, for such is the reward We confer upon those who forge (*muftarīn*, pl. of *muftarī*, he who is addicted to *iftirāʾ*). (VII, 151/152)

This is said in reference to Moses' folk who, in his absence, made a golden calf and began to worship this idol instead of God. It is clear that the word *muftarīn* denotes the idol-worshippers. From the point of view of Islām, idolatry is an obvious form of the 'forging of a lie', because it means inventing out of sheer fantasy strange beings and attributing to them reality quite arbitrarily, when, in truth, 'reality' belongs to God alone. The same word *muftarī* appears in the following passage with exactly the same meaning.

> And unto the people of ʿĀd [We sent] their brother [i.e. one of their fellow-countrymen] Hūd. He said, 'O my people, worship God. You have no other god save Him. Verily, you are only *muftarūn*.' (XI, 52/50)

As is well known, life in Jāhilīyah was regulated by an elaborate and intricate system of taboos that were prescribed by traditional customs. 'This is *ḥarām* (forbidden), and this is *ḥalāl* (lawful).' And this system of *ḥarām—ḥalāl* was imposed upon all men as something sacrosanct. For Islām, this of course constituted an unmistakable case of forgery against God, for He alone is really entitled to the authority of enjoining upon men any rules of conduct in the name of religion. Thus it comes about that in the Qurʾān the 'sacred' customs of Jāhilīyah are frequently condemned in the strongest terms as being 'forged lies' against God.

> You should not say of the lie (*kadhib*) which your own tongues describe, 'This is lawful, and this is forbidden.' This is to forge a lie against God. Verily, those who forge against God a lie shall not prosper. (XVI, 117/116)

> They [i.e. the idolaters] pretend, 'These cattle and tilth are sacrosanct; none shall eat thereof, save such as we please'—so they pretend—'and cattle there are whose backs are forbidden, and cattle over which the name of God is not to be mentioned.' All this is forgery (*iftirāʾ*) against God. He will surely reward them for what they have forged. (VI, 139/138)

Sometimes sorcery is also called *iftirāʾ*. The example which follows refers to the act of the sorcerers of Egypt who, in the presence of Pharaoh, wished to compete with Moses in the art of sorcery.

> Moses said unto them, 'Woe unto you! Forge not a lie against God, lest He destroy you with punishment. All those who have forged have ever failed.' (XX, 63–64/61)

In any case, *iftirāʾ*—and so too, *takdhīb*, which appears in the text just before it—constitutes in the Qurʾanic conception one of the most conspicuous features of the Kāfirs, and as such it will be dealt with more fully later when we come to the problem of the concept of *kufr* itself.

## Patience

*Ṣabr*, 'patience', 'steadfastness', or 'endurance', was a prominent virtue in desert conditions in the days of Jāhilīyah. It was part of the *shajāᶜah*, 'courage', which I have described, or rather it was an essential ingredient of it. In the desert where the conditions of living were so harsh, every man was constantly required to show extraordinary patience and endurance, if only for his mere existence and for the subsistence of his tribe. Physical strength was of course necessary, but it was not enough; it had to be backed up by something coming from within, namely patience, the inflexible determination to stand by one's cause whatever might happen.

Semantically, the word is the exact opposite of *jazaᶜ* which means the property of those who cannot bear patiently what befalls them and are quick to manifest violent agitation; this implies that *ṣabr* itself means having sufficient strength of soul to remain patient under adversity and suffering and to persevere amidst all the difficulties in championing one's own cause.[22] It will be easily seen that *ṣabr* was a representative manly virtue of the warrior on the battlefield. There could be no courage without the virtue of *ṣabr*.

This old nomadic virtue, too, Islām transformed into a one of its cardinal virtues by furnishing it with a definite religious direction: 'patience in the way of God'.

As in the days of Jāhilīyah, to begin with, *ṣabr* was enjoined upon the believers on the battlefield when fighting against the Kāfirs.

> Those [in the camp of David] who believed that they were to meet God said, 'How often a small host has overcome a mighty host by God's leave! God is always with the patient (*ṣābirīn*, participle, pl.).' And when they went forth against Goliath and his hosts they said, 'Our Lord, pour out upon us patience (*ṣabr*), and make our feet sure, and help us against the Kāfirs!' (II, 250–251/249–250)

> With how many a Prophet have myriads fought; they never gave way at what befell them in God's way, nor did they weaken, nor did they humble themselves. God loves the patient (*ṣābirīn*). (III, 140/146)

Such soldierly 'patience' develops quite naturally into the spirit of martyrdom, that is, the moral strength to undergo with amazing heroism death or any other torment for the sake of one's faith. In the following passage, the magicians of Pharaoh declare their fixed determination to remain faithful to Moses' God even if they have to suffer the most atrocious torture.

> Pharaoh said, 'You have believed in Him before I permitted you to. . . . You shall smart for it. I shall surely cut off your hands and

22 In Sūrah XIV, 25/21, we find these two properties set against each other. The words are supposed to be said by the Kāfirs who go to Hell on the Last Day: 'It is all the same to us [now] if we get impatient (*jaziᶜnā*) or if we are patient (*ṣabarnā*), we have no escape.'

feet on opposite sides. After that I shall crucify you all together.' They said, 'Verily, we turn unto our Lord. Thou dost take vengeance on us only because we have believed in the signs of our Lord when they came to us. Our Lord, pour out upon us patience (*ṣabr*), and receive us unto Thee in the state of Surrender.' (*muslimīn*, lit. as those who have surrendered) (VII, 120–123/123–126)

It should be noticed that here the virtue of 'patience' is made to stand in a manifest semantic relation to *islām* which we shall discuss presently. And a few lines down, we see the same 'patience' standing in an equally close relation to *taqwá* 'fear of God'.

Moses said unto his people, 'Solicit help from God, and be patient (*iṣbirū*). Verily, the whole earth is God's, and He gives it for an inheritance to whom He likes among His servants. The ultimate [felicity] will fall to the lot of the godfearing (*muttaqīn*).' (VII, 125/128)

The torment which the believers have to suffer is not in any way restricted to physical pains; it may also take the form of sneering, derision, and abuse on the part of the Kāfirs. In this sense, the *takdhīb* which we mentioned in the preceding section and all the marks of the overbearing haughtiness which as we saw in the preceding chapter, characterize the disbelievers, may be regarded as so many calamities falling on the believers and calling forth the spirit of martyrdom.

Apostles before thee were also cried lies to. But, they proved patient (*ṣabarū*) of being cried lies to and of being hurt, until Our help came unto them. (VI, 34)

Bear thou [Muḥammad] with patience (*iṣbir*) what they say against thee, and try to avoid [collision with] them graciously. Leave Me to deal with those who cry lies (*mukadhdhibīn*), lords of prosperity in this world, and do thou respite them for a while. (LXXIII, 10–11)

[God will say, on the Day of Judgment, to the Kāfirs in Gehenna], 'Verily, there was a party of My servants who used to say, "Our lord, we believe (*āmannā*), so forgive us, and have mercy upon us, for Thou art the best of the merciful ones." You, however, took them for mockery, and in laughing at them you forgot My remembrance. This day I have recompensed them for their patience (*bi-mā ṣabarū*, lit. for that they endured patiently). Now they are the happy people.' (XXIII, 111–113/109–111)

Thus 'patience' comes to represent an essential aspect of the genuine 'belief', *īmān*, in God. 'Patience' is that particular aspect of 'belief' which it shows when it finds itself in unfavorable conditions. And this, we must remember, was actually the case with Islām in the first period of its history. Living as they did in the midst of the Kāfirs and surrounded by all sorts of worldly temptations, the believers were forced to assume the attitude of determined resistance. It is to this inflexible determination to persist in the genuine faith in the face of unrelenting attacks of the enemy that the term *ṣabr* refers specifically. The point will come out most clearly in the following examples:

> Be thou patient (*iṣbir*) whatever they [the Kāfirs] say, and celebrate the praise of thy Lord before the rising of the sun and before the setting; in the night, too, do thou celebrate the praise of thy Lord. (L, 38/39)

> Keep thyself patient (*iṣbir nafsaka*, here the verb *ṣabara* is used transitively) in company with those who call upon their Lord morning and evening, desiring His countenance. Let not thine eyes be turned away from them, desiring the pomp of the life of this world. (XVIII, 27/28)

> O you who believe, seek [God's] help in patience (*ṣabr*) and prayer. Verily, God is with the patient (*ṣābirīn*, part. pl.). . . . We may try you with something of fear, hunger, and loss of wealth and lives and fruits, but give thou [Muḥammad] glad tidings to the patient (*ṣābirīn*), who say, whenever there befalls them a misfortune, 'Verily, we belong to God. Verily, unto Him do we return.' (II, 148–151/153–156)

The preceding account does not in any way pretend to exhaust the pre-Islamic moral ideas taken up by Islām and assimilated into the new conception of morality. But at least it gives the most remarkable examples, and shows us how the Islamization of non-Islamic elements was accomplished at this earliest period. In its long subsequent history Islām will have to pass through a similar process several times at a number of different levels of culture, when it will be faced with the problem of settling accounts with ideas of Greek, Persian, and Indian origins, and still later, with modern Western concepts.

# VI. The Basic Moral Dichotomy

Say, 'Listen, Kāfirs! I worship not what you worship.
You are not worshipping what I worship.
I am not worshipping what you worship.
Nor will you worship what I worship.
To you your religion, and to me my religion!'
(CIX, 1–6, the whole Sūrah)

THESE WORDS MARK IN A DRAMATIC WAY THE MOST RADICAL BREAK with the surrounding polytheism, to which Islām was led by its fundamental attitude in religious matters. This was, so to speak, the formal declaration of independence on the part of Islām from all that was essentially incompatible with the monotheistic belief which it proclaimed. In the domain of ethical practices, this declaration of independence involved a grave consequence. It suggested that henceforward all human values were to be measured by an absolutely reliable standard of evaluation.

The Qurʾanic outlook divides all human qualities into two radically opposed categories, which—in view of the fact that they are too concrete and semantically too pregnant to be called 'good' and 'bad', or 'right' and 'wrong'—we might simply call the class of positive moral properties and the class of negative moral properties, respectively. The final yardstick by which this division is carried out is the belief in the one and only God, the Creator of all beings. In fact, throughout the Qurʾān there runs the keynote of dualism regarding the moral values of man: the basic dualism of believer and unbeliever. In this sense, the ethical system of Islām is of a very simple structure. For by the ultimate yardstick of 'belief' one can easily decide to which of the two categories a given person or a given act belongs.

The significance of this fact, however, was very great for the moral development of the Arabs, because it meant the first appearance of moral principle which was consistent enough to deserve the name of 'principle'. A whole practical code of conduct, though as yet largely unsystematic, was imposed upon the believer, the moment he truly believed in the oneness of God and the truth of the prophetic message. As I remarked earlier, this was an unprecedented event in the spiritual history of the Arabs. In Jāhilīyah there were, as we have seen, a number of recognized moral values. But they were just there as *membra disjecta*, without any definite underlying principle to support them; they were based almost exclusively on an irrational sort of moral emotion, or rather, a blind and violent passion for the mode of life that had been handed down from generation to generation as a priceless tribal asset. Islām made it possible for the first time for the Arabs to judge and evaluate all human conduct with reference to a theoretically justifiable moral principle.

The basic dichotomy of moral properties to which I have just referred, appears in the Qur'anic verses in a number of different forms. It may, to begin with, assume the form of an essential opposition of *kāfir* and *mu'min* 'believer'.

> It is He who created you. But one of you is a *kāfir*, and one of you is a *mu'min*. God sees everything you do. (LXIV, 2)

> Those who disbelieve (*kafarū*, a verbal form corresponding to *kāfir*) and turn men away from the way of God, He will surely make all their works vain and futile.
> Those, on the contrary, who believe (*āmanū*, verbal form corresponding to *mu'min*) and do good works and believe in what is revealed unto Muḥammad inasmuch as it is the Truth from their Lord, He will surely remit from them their ill-deeds and improve their minds. All this is because those who disbelieve (*kafarū*) have adopted falsehood (*bāṭil*) whereas those who believe (*āmanū*) have adopted the Truth (*ḥaqq*) from their Lord. (XLVII, 1–3)

It may also take the form of an opposition of *kāfir* and *muttaqī* 'godfearing'. The religious meaning of 'fear' of God (*taqwá*) in Islām was elucidated earlier.

> Verily, this Qur'ān is a reminder to the *muttaqīn* (pl. of *muttaqī*), but We know that there are amongst you some who cry lies to it. Verily, it is a cause of sorrow to the *kāfirīn* (pl. of *kāfir*), although in reality it is the absolute Truth. (LXIX, 48–51)

Or it may take the form of an opposition of ***muslim***, 'he who has surrendered', and ***mujrim***, 'sinful' or 'guilty'.

> Shall We treat the ***muslimīn*** in the same way as the ***mujrimīn***? (LXVIII, 35)

Or, as an opposition of *ḍāll*, 'he who goes astray, errs', and *muhtadī*, 'he who is guided, who goes the right way'.

> Verily, thy Lord knows best who goes astray from His way, as He knows best those who are guided. (LIII, 31/30)

Or again, the 'positive' side may be called 'the Companions of Paradise' or 'the Fellows of the Right' and the 'negative' side 'the Companions of Hell' or 'the Fellows of the Left'.

> Not equal are the Fellows of the Fire and the Fellows of Paradise. The Fellows of Paradise, they alone are the blissful. (LIX, 20)

As we shall see later, this fundamental dichotomy of human properties appears in still other forms. But they are all rather marginal variations within the bounds of the essential opposition of belief and unbelief; the most basic fact remains always the same.

Sometimes, the Qurʾān seems to divide men into not two but three classes, recognizing an intermediate state fluctuating between both ends. This unstable middle ground where belief and unbelief overlap and fuse, is formed by those who remain very lukewarm in their faith although they have formally accepted Islām and become Muslims.

> We conferred the Book [of Revelation] as an inheritance upon those whom We chose of Our servants. But of them some there are who wrong themselves [by rejecting it and crying lies to it], and of them are some who are lukewarm [though they have accepted it outwardly], and, again there are some who vie in good works by the leave of God. (XXXV, 29/32)

We should remark that it was mostly the nomadic Arabs of the desert that formed this middle class, though of course there were among them city-dwellers, too, people who remained lukewarm and always wavering between belief and *kufr*. 'L'Arabe', says Dozy, 'n'est pas religieux de sa nature, et, sous ce rapport, il y a entre lui et les autres peuples qui ont adopté l'islamisme une énorme différence. . . . Voyez les Bédouins d'aujourd'hui! Quoique musulmans de nom, ils se soucient médiocrement des préceptes de l'islamisme. . . . En tout temps, il a été extrêmement difficile de vaincre chez les Bédouins leur tiédeur pour la religion.'[1] The Qurʾān itself attests to

[1] Dozy, I, 13, 24.

this. In a remarkable passage (XLIX, 14–15), where the basic difference between ***muʾmin*** 'believer' and ***muslim*** is brought out most clearly, it is declared that the Bedouins who have accepted Islām are not to be regarded, in virtue of that fact alone, as having become *muʾmin* in the true sense of the word.

It must be admitted, nevertheless, that, semantically at least the class of such doubtful Muslims is after all but a borderline case, whose value is to be determined in terms of either the one extreme or the other of the common scale running from true belief to downright unbelief. The existence of those lukewarm believers in a great number was no doubt a tough practical problem for Muḥammad himself to solve, but there can be no doubt that they did not constitute in any way an independent category. In the eyes of Muḥammad, they were in the last resort a variation of the positive class. They represented, in other words, an imperfect type of the believer; very imperfect, and yet believers in the sense that they obeyed—at least outwardly—God and His Apostle; and, as such, they were not to be denied the reward of their deeds.

Before we launch into a detailed analysis of the words standing for the most representative ethico-religious properties, both positive and negative, which are recognized as such in the Qurʾān, perhaps we may do well to make a more general survey of the characteristic features of the two fundamental types of man formed by various combinations of these properties. In plainer language we might formulate our problem by asking what, according to the teaching of the Qurʾān, a man should do in order to win the reward of Paradise, and what lines of conduct are characteristic of those who are bound to go to Hell. What is the ideal type of the believer, and what are the representative features of an infidel? By analyzing some of the relevant passages, we may hope to isolate the principal ethico-religious categories. We shall, at the same time, remark that the ethico-religious system of the Qurʾān is, very broadly speaking, based on the conception of eschatology. In other words, the ethics of the present world is not simply there as a self-sufficing system; on the contrary, its structure is most profoundly determined by the ultimate (eschatological) end to which the present world (*al-dunyā*) is destined. In the Islamic system the thought—or rather the vivid image—of the Hereafter should behave as the highest moral principle of conduct.

## The Companions of Paradise

In Sūrah LXX, 22–35, there is given a detailed description of those conditions, the fulfilment of which is deemed strictly necessary if one desires really to be in the number of 'those who will be allowed to live in Heavenly Gardens, high-honored'. There it is stated that the reward of Paradise is promised only to those worshippers (1) who remain constant at their prayers and observe them well (vv. 23, 34), (2) in whose wealth there is an acknowledged portion for the beggar and the destitute (v. 24–25), (3) who believe the Day of Judgment to be true (v. 26), (4) who are fearful of the chastisement of their Lord (v. 27), (5) who guard their pudenda (v. 29), (6) who keep faithfully their trusts and their covenant (v. 32), and (7) who give right testimonies (v. 33).

Thus this passage enumerates as the conditions necessary for winning the approval of God, constant and devout worship, almsgiving, eschatological belief in the final Judgment, fear of God, sexual continence, faithfulness, and truthfulness. The first two items chiefly concern ritual; they are destined to develop later into two statutory duties of Islām, and to constitute, together with fasting, pilgrimage, and the profession of faith in the oneness of God, the so-called five Pillars (*arkān*) of faith. The third and fourth items concern directly the central notion of 'fear' of which I have already given a detailed account. The sixth and seventh have also been fully discussed in Chapter V under the heading of *ṣidq*.

Sūrah XIII, 20–23 gives a list of Islamic virtues which is substantially the same as the preceding one. Here is the whole passage in translation.

> Those who fulfil the covenant with God, and break not the compact; who join what God has bidden to be joined; and dread their Lord and fear the evil reckoning; who remain patient, craving their Lord's countenance; and perform the prayer; and expend [in alms] of what We have provided them secretly and openly; and ward off evil with good—these shall have the recompense of the [eternal] abode, Gardens of Eden which they shall enter. (XIII, 20–23)

It is to be noticed that this second list adds 'patience' (*ṣabr*), which we have considered in the preceding chapter, to the items enumerated in the first passage. Patience is also given a place in the following list of the Islamic virtues which go to constitute the ideal type of Muslim: (1) Those who have surrendered, men and women alike (*muslim*), (2) those who believe, men and women alike (*muʾmin*), (3) those who are truthful, men and women alike (*ṣādiq*), (4) those who are patient, men and women alike (*ṣābir*), (5) those who are humble, men and women alike (*khāshiʿ*), (6) those who give alms willingly, men and women alike (*mutaṣaddiq*), (7) those who are punctilious in fasting, men and women alike (*ṣāʾim*), (8) those who guard their pudenda, men and women alike (*ḥāfiẓ al-furūj*), (9) those who remember God constantly, men and women alike (*dhākir Allāh*): for them God has prepared forgiveness and a great reward. (XXXIII, 35)

Thankfulness (*shukr*) and repentance (*tawbah*) must also be added to this list if we are to make it more complete. These two elements are made particularly prominent in the next quotation from the Qur'ān, which purports expressly to give an account of the characteristic features of the 'Companions of Paradise'. In this passage every true believer, when he reaches forty years, is charged to address his Lord with the following words:

> 'My Lord, arouse me that I may be thankful (*ashkura* from *shukr*) for Thy favor wherewith Thou has favored me and my parents, and that I may do good works that shall please Thee. Be Thou gracious unto me as regards my offspring. Lo, I have turned [repentant] unto Thee (*tubtu*, from the same root as *tawbah*). Lo! I am of those who have surrendered (*muslimīn*)!—Those are they from whom We accept the best part of what they have done, and overlook their evil deeds. They are amongst the Companions of Paradise.' (XLVI, 14–15/15–16)

The first of these two, 'thankfulness', *shukr*, has already been considered in Chapter IV. It will come up again for consideration in the following chapter. As to the second element, 'repentance' or 'penitence', *tawbah*, we might remark first of all that it is, as it were, a human counterpart of God's unfathomable mercy. God, although He is the terrible Lord of the Judgment Day, the most unyielding avenger of all evils done, is at the same time an infinitely merciful, and forgiving God. Throughout the Qur'ān it is constantly emphasized that 'God turns (*yatūbu*, from the same root as *tawbah*) towards whom He will. Verily, God is most forgiving (*ghafūr*), most merciful (*raḥīm*)!' (IX, 27). It is interesting to observe that the same word, *tawbah*, means 'repentance' on the part of man, and 'forgiveness' on the part of God. Man 'turns' towards God in repentance, and God 'turns' towards man with His grace. There is clearly a correlative relationship of 'turning' between God and man, and this is reflected in the semantic behavior of the word *tawbah*.

God's limitless goodness and grace extend even to those faithless who have fallen into the temptation to commit the most heinous sin against God, the sin of idolatry, provided that they repent of their evil ways and return to the faith. Thus, speaking of the people of Moses who worshipped the idol of the Golden Calf, it is said:

> Verily, those who took [to themselves] the Calf, wrath shall come upon them from their Lord [even] in the life of this present world, for such is the reward We confer upon those who forge (*muftarīn*).

> Those, however, who have done evil deeds, but repent (*tābū*) thereafter and have faith (*āmanī*), verily, thy Lord thereafter is Merciful. (VII, 151–152/152–153)

So all believers are strongly enjoined to turn to God in sincere repentance. It may be that God will forgive them their previous sins, committed consciously or unconsciously. A truly repentant heart merits even the reward of Paradise.

> O believers, turn (*tūbū*) unto God in sincere repentance (*tawbatan naṣūḥan*). It may be that your Lord will remit from you your evil deeds and let you enter gardens with rivers flowing underneath. (LXVI, 8)

The emphatic form from the same root, *tawwāb* is used very often. When applied to a man, it means 'one who repents very often'; when applied to God, it naturally means 'He Who is wont to turn to sinners in forgiveness, Who reverts very often from wrath to grace.' *Awwāb* is another word for one who repents frequently. This is the emphatic form from *AWB* which literally means 'to return'. He who repents his sin 'returns' from his sin unto God. Unlike *tawwāb*, this word is not applied to God in the sense of 'forgiving'. *Awwāb* appears in the following passage.

> [Upon the Day of Judgment] Paradise shall be brought nigh to the godfearing; [it will be there, before their very eyes,] not far off. 'This is what you were promised; [it is] for all heedful ones who have returned very often (*awwāb*).'
>
> He who fears the Merciful God and brings a repentant (*munīb*) heart: 'Enter it [i.e. Paradise] in peace! This is the day of immortality.' (L, 30–33/31–34)

In this quotation we find one more word with approximately the same meaning, *munīb*. This is the participial form of the verb *anāba* meaning 'to return unto God repentant' with an additional implication of 'from time to time', the original meaning of the root (according to the Arab lexicographers) being that of 'doing something by turns' or 'coming to someone time after time'.

## The Companions of Hell

Having seen the main qualities which go to form the Islamic virtue worthy of the reward of Paradise, it is no longer a difficult matter to guess the general features characteristic of those who will be thrown into Hell, 'the Fellows of the Left', as they are sometimes called.

> The Fellows of the Left—alas the Fellows of the Left!—in the midst of burning, poisonous winds and boiling waters, under the

> shadow of a choking smoke, which, though it is a shadow, is neither cool nor beneficent. (LVI, 40–43/41–44)

The Companions of Hell are those who are not qualified by any of the 'positive' properties, or are even marked by some of the characteristics that are the exact opposites of these good qualities. It goes without saying that the Kāfirs go at the head of this grand procession marching towards *Jahannam* (Gehenna).

> For those who reveal themselves ungrateful (*kafarū*) to their Lord, there is the torment of Gehenna—an evil end of the journey, indeed! (LXVII, 6)

The Kāfirs are thrown into the Fire as the just reward for their *fusūq*, that is, for their bad conduct in the present world against the commandments of God.

> On the day [of the Last Judgment] when the Kāfirs shall be exposed to the Fire: 'You squandered your good things in your earthly life and found enjoyment in them. Wherefore this day you are recompensed with a humiliating chastisement for that you grew arrogant in the earth without any right, and for that you transgressed (*tafsuqūna* from the same root as *fusūq*).' (XLVI, 19/20)

There participate in this procession to Hell all those who are related in some way or other with the Kāfirs, that is, those who embody and represent any of the many distinguishable aspects of *kufr*. Here I give a few quotations in which some of the 'negative' properties are explicitly brought into connection with the chastisement of the Fire.

There are those who are characterized by *takdhīb*, 'giving [God] the lie', which I have mentioned in the last chapter.

> 'Then lo! you who go astray and cry lies, (*mukadhdhibūn*, pl. participial form of *takdhīb*) you shall eat of a tree of Zaqqūm,[2] and you shall fill your bellies with it and drink thereon the boiling water, drinking like thirsty camels.' This shall be their entertainment on the Day of Judgment. (LVI, 51–56)

> Upon the day when the heavenly vault will swing from side to side, and the mountains will be moved from their places, woe that day unto the *mukadhdhibīn* who are now bathing joyously in the submerging floods [of vain discourse about God], the day when they shall be hurled into the fire of Gehenna. 'This is the fire that you used to cry lies to (*tukadhdhibūna*). Say, is this a piece of magic? Or have you not eyes to see? Roast well in it. Whether you endure

[2] The name of a monstrous tree which is found at the bottom of Hell, whose flowers are said to be the heads of demons.

patiently or endure not patiently, it is all the same to you. You are only going to receive your just recompense for what you were doing.' (LII, 9–16)

There is the *ẓālim*, 'wrong-doer', or 'evil-doer', to which passing reference was made earlier and of which much more will be said later. Here it is sufficient to note that the Zaqqūm tree which, as we have just seen, is said to await the arrival of those who cry lies to God, is mentioned in the following quotation as a special entertainment for the *ẓālim*.

Is that better as an entertainment, or the tree of Zaqqūm? Verily, We have prepared it as a special torment for the *ẓālim*. Verily, it is a tree that appears from the root of Hell, its spathes being as the heads of devils. They shall eat thereof and fill their bellies thereof. And afterward they are given a drink of boiling water. After that, they shall be brought back unto Hell. (XXXVII, 60–66/62–68)

The *mustakbir* (syn. *mutakabbir*) is one who is too big with pride to accept the teaching of the Qurʾān. The concept will be subjected to a detailed analysis in the following chapter.

Verily, those who are too proud (*yastakbirūna*, from *istikbār*) to worship Me shall enter into Gehenna, utterly mean and abject. (XL, 62/60)

So enter the gates of Gehenna, therein to dwell for ever. Evil indeed will be the abode of the *mutakabbir*. (XVI, 31/29)

Similarly the *ṭāghī* is one who is exceedingly insolent and presumptuous; the word will be analyzed semantically later.

Verily, Gehenna lies in ambush, the last resort for *ṭāghīn* (pl. of *ṭāghī*), therein to dwell for ages eternal. They shall not taste therein neither coolness nor drink, but only boiling water and pus. A fit recompense, indeed! (LXXVIII, 21–26)

The *fājir* (pl. *fujjār*) is one who, forsaking the commands of God or the rules of moral conduct, acts viciously, as opposed to the *bārr* (pl. *abrār*).

Verily, the *abrār* shall be in bliss, while the *fujjār* shall be in the Fire, to roast therein on the Day of Judgment, nor shall they ever be removed therefrom. (LXXXII, 13–16)

The *qāsiṭ* is one who deviates from the right course and acts wrongfully, as opposed to the *muslim*.

Verily, of us some are *muslimūn* (pl.), and some are *qāsiṭūn* (pl.). Whoso has surrendered (*aslama*, become Muslim), they have taken the right course. But as for the *qāsiṭūn*, they have become fuel for Gehenna. (LXXII, 14–15)

The *ʿāṣī* is one who rebels against God and His Apostle.

Whoso rebels against God and His Apostle, for him is prepared the fire of Gehenna to dwell for ever. (LXXII, 24/23)

The *munāfiq* is one who, though outwardly a pious believer, is in reality a most stubborn disbeliever, a 'hypocrite'. About the semantic structure of this important term more will be said later on.

O Prophet! Strive against the *kuffār* (pl.) and the *munāfiqīn* (pl.), and be harsh with them. Gehenna shall be their final abode, an evil journey's end. (LXVI, 9)

The *mustahziʾ*, the scoffer, is one who mocks at Revelation. The act of making a jest of God's words springs from *kufr*. It is, according to the Qurʾān, the most characteristic attitude of all Kāfirs towards prophetic messages.

That is the reward of such men [those who disbelieve in the signs of God], Gehenna, because they acted as Kāfirs and took My signs and My Apostles in mockery (*huzūʾ*) (XVIII, 106)

The *kharrāṣ* is condemned in the strongest terms. The word means one who says by conjecture, 'without knowledge' as the Qurʾān says all kinds of things concerning Revelation.

Accursed be the *kharrāṣūn* (pl.) who are heedless [of the warnings of God] in the abyss [of Kufr]! 'When is the Day of Judgment?' they ask. Upon the day when at the Fire they shall be tormented. 'Taste well your torment! This is what you wished [in the world] to hasten.' (LI, 10–14)

Finally there are those who, having no faith, never participate in social charity and relief work. Hailstones of abuse are hurled at these people, attesting to the extraordinary importance attached to being ready to offer a helping hand at any moment to the poor and needy.

Take hold of him, fetter him, then roast him in the Hell Fire, and put him in a chain of seventy cubits! Verily, he believed not in the Almighty God, nor did he ever urge the feeding of the destitute. So this day he has here no true friend nor any food except putrid pus which none but the sinners eat. (LXIX, 30–37)

In conclusion I shall give a few quotations in which several of the 'negative' properties are put together, whether unified in one single person or divided among a number of persons.

> Throw into Gehenna, you two [this is said by God to the two 'stokers' of Hell Fire], every stubborn *kaffār* (emphatic form of *kāfir*) who hinders by all means (*mannā*ᶜ) the good, transgresses (*mu*ᶜ*tadī*), entertains doubts [about God and His Revelation], who sets up another god besides God. So throw him, you two, into the dreadful chastisement! (L, 23–25/24–26)

Here we find four sins particularly pointed out as deserving the 'reward' of terrible torment in Gehenna: (1) *kufr*, (2) the act of hindering others positively from doing such works as are considered religiously good, (3) transgression against God's will, and (4) throwing doubt on the truth of God and turning to polytheism.

> Obey thou [Muḥammad] not those who cry lies (*mukadhdhib*); it is their wish that thou shouldst treat them gently, so that they, too, would be gentle to thee. And obey thou not any vile oath-monger (*ḥallāf*), a backbiter (*hammāz*) going about to spread abroad slanders, a hinderer of the good, a sinful transgressor, rough and rude (ᶜ*utul*) therewithal, ignoble (*zanīm*),[3] though he is possessed of wealth and sons. Whenever Our signs are recited to such a man, he always says, 'These are but old folks' tales.' We shall brand him on the snout. (LXVIII, 8–16)

In this passage, the features that are mentioned are seven: (1) *takdhīb*, (2) the act of swearing haphazardly, that is, lack of truthfulness, (3) backbiting, which is a special form of 'telling a lie (*kadhib*)', (4) the hindering of the good, (5) transgression, (6) the rudeness of manner, peculiar to Jāhilīyah, and (7) being of a base, ignoble nature such as is characteristic of an 'outsider' in the tribal system of society.

The following words are the imaginary confession of those who have been thrown into Gehenna on the Day of Judgment!

> 'We were not of those who observed the ritual of worship, nor did we feed the poor and needy. But we used to plunge together with other plungers [into the flood of vain discourse concerning God and Revelation], and we cried lies to the Day of Judgment, until at last the indisputable state of affairs has come to us.' (LXXIV, 44–48/43–47)

In this confession four things are made to stand out as most immediately responsible for the sinners' being punished with the torment of Hell; (1) their not having observed the ritual of worship, (2) the non-payment of *zakāt*, (3) vain discourse about religious matters, and (4) *takdhīb*.

[3] For this word see above, Chapter IV, p. 57.

Having obtained some general notions as to the distinguishing marks of those who go to Paradise and those who are bound for Hell, we are now in a position to proceed to a detailed analysis of the key value-words belonging to either of the two diametrically opposed categories. This will be the main task of the following chapters.

# THE ANALYSIS OF MAJOR CONCEPTS

# VII. The Inner Structure of the Concept of *Kufr*

In proceeding to give a detailed account of the principal ethico-religious values that are found in the Qur'ān, I begin with *kufr* rather than any of the positive virtues. I adopt this course because it has an obvious methodological advantage for my purpose: *kufr* not only forms the very pivot round which revolve all the other negative qualities, but it occupies such an important place in the whole system of Qur'anic ethics that a clear understanding of how it is semantically structured is almost a prerequisite to a proper estimation of most of the positive qualities. Even a cursory reading of the Scripture will convince one that the role played by the concept of *kufr* is so peculiarly influential that it makes its presence felt well-nigh everywhere in sentences about human conduct or character. In my opinion, even the concept of faith or belief, as the highest ethico-religious value in Islām, may best be analyzed not directly but rather in terms of *kufr*, that is, from its negative side.

Now concerning *kufr*, we already know many things, since frequent reference has been made to this or that aspect of its complex meaning. Let us summarize those points which have been established.

1. The basic meaning of the root *KFR*, as far as our philological knowledge goes, is most probably that of 'covering'. In contexts concerned especially with the bestowing and receiving of benefits, the word naturally comes to mean 'to cover, i.e. to ignore knowingly,

the benefits which one has received', and thence, 'to be unthankful'.
2. The Qurʾān emphasizes most strongly the Almighty God's being particularly a God of grace and goodness. Man, as His creature, owes everything, his very existence and subsistence, to the boundless mercy of God. This means that he owes Him the duty of being grateful for His goodness which is being shown him at every moment of his life. A Kāfir is a man who, having thus received God's benevolence, shows no sign of gratitude in his conduct, or even acts rebelliously against his Benefactor.
3. This fundamental attitude of ingratitude with regard to God's grace and goodness is manifested in the most radical and positive way by *takdhīb*, that is, 'giving the lie' to God, His Apostle, and the divine message he is sent with.
4. Thus it comes about that *kufr* is actually used very frequently as the exact antonym of *īmān* 'belief'. In the Qurʾān the most representative opposite of *muʾmin*, 'believer', or *muslim*, lit. 'one who has surrendered' is admittedly *kāfir*. It would appear that *kufr*, having been used so often in contrast to *īmān*, lost more and more of its original semantic core of 'ingratitude', and assumed more and more the meaning of 'dis-belief', until finally it has come to be used most commonly in this latter sense, even where there can be hardly any question of gratitude.
5. *Kufr*, as man's denial of the Creator, manifests itself most characteristically in various acts of insolence, haughtiness, and presumptuousness. *Istakbara*, 'to be big with pride', and *istaghná*, 'to consider oneself as absolutely free and independent', have been mentioned above; as we shall presently see, there are many other words standing for similar ideas. *Kufr* forms, in this respect, the exact opposite of the attitude of 'humbleness', *taḍarruʿ*, and clashes directly with the idea of *taqwá*, 'fear of God', which is indeed the central element of the Islamic conception of religion in general.

## The Element of Ingratitude in *Kufr*

I gave earlier an excellent example of the 'secular' use of the word *kāfir*, which brings out in a really striking way the element of 'ingratitude' as the semantic core of *kufr*.[1] Turning to the behavior of the term in specifically religious contexts, I shall begin by giving an example which is indeed a rarity of the kind. It concerns *kufr* not as an attitude of man towards God, but quite the other way round. It presents *kufr* as an attitude which it is absolutely impossible for God to adopt towards man. The passage reveals the remarkable fact that, just as it is a religious duty of man to be grateful to God

[1] See above, Chapter II, p. 41

for His acts of grace, so God, on His part, shows Himself thankful to man for all the good works he does as a pious believer in response to the divine call through His Apostle. God will never 'ignore' the good services rendered by a sincere believer, but He acknowledges them gratefully and records them for him.

> Whoso does good of his own accord, verily [to him] God is thankful (*shākir*, part. of *shukr*); He is aware of everything. (II, 153/158)

And the principle of non-*kufr* on the part of God will be manifested most visibly in the bestowal, on the Day of Judgment, of the reward of the Heavenly Gardens.

> Whoso does good works as a pious believer, there shall be no ingratitude (*kufr*) for his efforts. Verily, We Ourselves write them down for him. (XXI, 94)

This means in plain language that God will never bring any act of piety to naught, but will surely pay it back amply. Reduced to this form, the passage just quoted loses all its seeming strangeness and becomes completely of a piece with the general trend of thought in the Qur'ān. What makes this passage particularly interesting and important for our purpose is that it expresses this fundamental thought in terms of *kufr*, and bears thereby witness to the fact that the essence of *kufr* consists in 'ungratefulness' and that the word is applicable in the same sense even to the attitude of God towards the believers.

The examples that follow concern man's attitude towards the favors of God. God, with His inscrutable will, goes on bestowing upon man innumerable favors, but man remains stubbornly thankless to Him.

> Hast thou not seen those who paid back God's favors with ungratefulness (*kufr*), and induced their people to dwell in the abode of perdition? In Gehenna they shall roast—an evil resting-place indeed! (XIV, 33–34/28–29)

In the two following quotations *kufr* is put expressly in antithesis to *shukr* 'thankfulness'.

> Here is a similitude which God has just struck: [there was] a city, secure and in peace, its provision coming to it in abundance from all quarters. But it was ungrateful for God's favors, so God caused it to taste the garment of death and fear for what they were doing. . . . Eat, then, of what God has provided you with, lawful and good things, and be thankful for God's favors, if it is really Him that you worship. (XVI, 113, 115/112, 114)

[I have bestowed upon you favors.] So remember Me, and I will remember you. Be thankful to Me (*wa-ushkurū lī*), and be not ungrateful to Me (*wa-lā takfurūni*). (II, 147/152)

Man's *kufr*-nature becomes especially evident when one observes his conduct in time of distress. In the first two examples that follow the root appears in the form of *kafūr*, which, according to al-Bayḍāwī, suggests an exceeding degree of *kufr* and denotes the type of man who is forgetful of all benefits he has enjoyed, although he retains in memory the slightest hurt he has received.

Your Lord it is who drives the ships for you in the sea so that you may seek after His bounty. So merciful is He towards you. Moreover, when some affliction befalls you in the sea, those whom you call upon usually [i.e. the idols] forsake you, leaving Him alone. But when He brings you safe to shore, you turn away. Man is indeed an ingrate (*kafūr*). (XVII, 68–69/66–67)

So long as We let man taste of mercy from Us, he is very glad thereof. But the moment some evil befalls him because of that which his own hands have done, he shows himself to be an ingrate (*kafūr*). (XLII, 47/48)

When they ride in the ships they pray to God, holding out their religion sincerely to Him alone. But as soon as He has brought them safe to shore, behold, they return to polytheism. Let them act ungratefully (*yakfurū*, a verbal form of *kufr*) for what We [the subject here changes abruptly to the first person] have given them [i.e. Our favors]! Let them betake themselves to merry-making. Soon they will come to know. (XXIX, 65–66)

Sometimes God gives a very detailed list of the favors—called 'signs' *āyāt* (pl. of *āyah*)—which He has bestowed upon men (XVI, 3–18) and adds that in spite of such benevolence on His part most of them remain negligent of the duty to be grateful to Him. In the following quotation, be it remarked, man is accused of being 'unfair' or 'wrongful', *ẓalūm*,[2] because of his attitude of *kufr* toward God's gifts.

God it is who created the heavens and the earth, and sent down from heaven water, and produced therewith fruits as a provision for you. And He subjected to you the ships to run upon the sea as He commands. And He subjected to you the rivers. And He subjected to you the sun and the moon to run their fixed courses. And He subjected to you the night and the day. Yea, He gave you of all you asked Him. If you count God's favors, you will never

[2] For the more exact meaning of this word see below, Chapter VIII, pp. 164–172.

number them. Verily, man is too unfair, too ungrateful (*kaffār*, emphatic form of *kāfir*). (XIV, 37/32–34)

The following quotation brings out with clarity that God does expect man to be grateful to Him for all the favors He has given him. He enumerates in detail the items of His bounty; states that all these He has bestowed upon man 'that haply he may give thanks'; that man denies, however, the blessing of God, although he recognizes it clearly; and He reaches the conclusion that 'the great majority of men are Kāfirs.'

God brought you forth out of the wombs of your mothers when you knew naught about it, and He made for you hearing, and sight, and hearts, *that haply you will be thankful.* Have they not seen the birds subjected in mid-air? None holds them there but God. Verily, *this must be a* [*divine*] *sign for people who believe.* And God it is who has established for you as a dwelling-place your houses; and made for you houses out of the skins of cattle, very light to carry both on the day you journey and on the day you abide; and with their wool, fur and hair, He has prepared for you furniture and articles of enjoyment for a while.

And God it is, too, Who has made for you, of that which He created, shelter from the sun, and established the mountains as places of refuge, and made for you shirts to protect you from each other's violence. *Thus He fulfils His favors towards you, that haply you may surrender* [i.e. become good Muslims in return for this extraordinary benevolence of God]. But if, with all this, they still turn their backs, thy [i.e. Muḥammad's] mission is only to deliver the clear message. *They recognize the favors of God, and yet they deny them, for most men are ungrateful.*[3] (XVI, 80–85/78–83)

I shall conclude this section by remarking that there is in the Qur'ān another forcible word *kanūd* used with approximately the same meaning as *kafūr*. The root is *KND*, and means 'to be ungrateful, to refuse to acknowledge any benefit received'. The context seems to suggest that the word is here used with an implication that man tends to reveal his ingratitude by being avaricious and grudging others even a small portion of the good things which he has received from God. I have already pointed out that passing on some at least of the divine gifts to the poor and needy is considered in the Qur'ān to be part of the manifestation of gratitude one feels towards God for His grace.

[3] '*Yaʿrifūna niʿmat Allāh thumma yunkirūnahā, wa-aktharuhum al-kāfirūn.*'

Indeed, how ungrateful (*kanūd*) man is to his Lord! Verily, he himself is a witness of that! Indeed, how passionate he is in the love of good things! (C, 6–8)

## *Kufr* as Opposed to *Īmān*

The root *KFR* in the Qurʾān is semantically ambiguous in the sense that it can be used in either of the two basic meanings: 'ingratitude' and 'disbelief'. There is in the *Ṣaḥīḥ* of al-Bukhārī a very interesting Ḥadīth which shows that there was in the minds of the earliest Muslims a sort of fluctuation in the understanding of this root when the context did not make clear as to which of the two concepts was actually meant.[4]

> The Prophet (may God bless and give him peace!) said: 'I was shown the Fire [i.e. I saw in my dream, Hell], and lo! most of its inhabitants were women who had been [in this world] characterized by *kufr* (*yakfurna*).' It was asked: 'Does that mean that they used to disbelieve in God (*yakfurna bi-Allāh*)?'
> He [the Prophet] said: 'No, the word means that they used to be ungrateful towards the husband (*yakfurna al-ʿashīr*) and used to be ungrateful for acts of kindness (*yakfurna al-iḥsān*).' [4]

Concerning this Ḥadīth, the commentator al-Kirmānī remarks that the verb *kafara* has two different infinitives, one *kufr* and the other *kufrān*. The former, he says, is the opposite of *īmān*, 'belief', while the latter, being in the majority of cases opposite of *shukr*, 'gratitude', means usually 'ingratitude for a favor (*niʿmah*)'.[5]

In any case it is certain that the Qurʾān itself uses the root *KFR* in these two different senses, but sometimes we find it difficult to draw a sharp line of demarcation between them, for, as I said before, the two are connected with each other in Qurʾanic thought by a firm conceptual link. In order to understand this, we have to remember that the 'signs', *āyāt*, of God, which, in the last section, were chiefly understood as 'favors' conferred by Him upon men calling forth 'thankfulness', may also very well be interpreted as so many manifestations of the divine Majesty, the Almightiness of God. In this second aspect, the 'signs' are naturally expected to arouse wonder and awe in the minds of men, and to cause them to 'believe' in Providence. He who refuses to do so is a Kāfir.

> O people of the Scripture! why do you disbelieve (*takfurūna*) in the signs of God, when you yourselves bear witness to them? (III, 63/70)

[4] al-Bukhārī, *Ṣaḥīḥ*, Ḥadīth no. 28, in *Kitāb al-Īmān*.
[5] al-Kirmānī, *Sharḥ Ṣaḥīḥ al-Bukhārī* (Cairo, 1933–1939), I, 134.

> Indeed We have displayed for men in this Qur'ān all sorts of similitudes [to make them understand the truth of God's words], but most men refuse aught but disbelief (*kufūr*). (XVII, 91/89)

> Have not those who disbelieve (*kafarū*) seen that the heavens and the earth were [originally] stitched together, and We unstitched them asunder, and made out of water all kinds of living things? *Will they not believe for all this?* And We set on the earth mountains firm-rooted, lest it should totter with them, and We placed therein ravines for paths, *that haply they may be guided* [i.e. they may be rescued from error and perdition and find the way to salvation]. And We established the heaven as a solid roof. Yet *from Our signs they still turn away*. (XXI, 31–33/30–32)

> How can you disbelieve (*takfurūna*) in God, seeing that you were lifeless and He gave you life? He will give you death again, then He will give you life, then unto Him you shall all be brought back. (II, 26/28)

Sometimes the object of disbelief is the doctrine of Resurrection, which is one of the central tenets of Islām. Here *kufr* consists in the refusal to accept the doctrine on the grounds that it is completely absurd and fantastic. It has very little, if at all, to do with the emotional reaction of 'thankfulness', the issue hinges on the acceptability or non-acceptability of such a doctrine to human reason. The Kāfirs are those who definitely take the side of Reason in this issue and turn a deaf ear to Revelation.

> They assert, 'There is only our life in this present world; we shall never be raised.' If only thou couldst see them when they are set before their Lord [on the Day of Judgment!] He will ask, 'Is not this the truth?' And they will answer, 'Yea, by our Lord!' He will say, 'Then taste the chastisement for that you disbelieved [i.e. as the reward for your disbelief in Resurrection].' (VI, 29–30)

> 'What! when we are bones and rubbish, shall we really be raised up in a new creation?' Have they not seen that God, who created the heavens and earth, is able to create [again] the like of them? He has set for them a definite term, wherein there is no doubt. And yet the wrongful people refuse aught but disbelief (*kufūr*). (XVII, 100–101/98–99)

> If thou shouldst wonder, wondrous indeed is what they are saying: 'What! after we have become dust? Shall we then be created afresh?' These are they who disbelieve in their Lord. And these are they who shall be the Fellows of the Fire, therein to dwell for ever. (XIII, 5–6/5)

Their disbelief is not in any way confined to the doctrine of Resurrection. Being constantly pricked with the thorn of Reason, they keep doubting anything that contradicts what they believe to be reasonable. They are born sceptics; the attitude which characterizes them is just the opposite of the act of faith which consists in an unconditioned surrender to whatever God commands. Thus they cannot acknowledge as the Apostle of God a simple mortal, one from among themselves, who 'eats ordinary food and walks in the market-place'. To their sceptical minds it sounds strangely discordant with all reason that such an ordinary man who appears to possess no special claim to prestige should attribute to himself the prophetic authority.

> 'Are we to follow a single mortal from among ourselves? Then verily, we should be in error and folly. Is it possible that the Revelation should be cast upon him alone out of all of us? Nay, rather he is an impostor (*kadhdhāb*), a self-conceited fellow!' (LIV, 24–25)

A storm of indignation is raised when this 'impudent fellow' proclaims that there is only one god, that all the other deities are mere names, a doctrine which is indeed nothing but sheer absurdity for the idol-worshippers.

> They are astonished that a warner has come to them from among themselves. The disbelievers (*kāfirūn*) say, 'This is only a wizard, an impostor. What! has he made all the gods One God? That is indeed an astounding thing!' (XXXVIII, 3–4/4–5)

In these examples it is almost certain that *kufr* means the negation of 'belief' in God and Revelation. Here follow some examples, out of a great number, which serve to bring to light the basic semantic opposition of *kufr* and *īmān*, that is, *kufr* as opposed not to the concept of 'thankfulness', but to that of 'belief', because the antithesis is here emphasized quite explicitly.

> Many of the people of the Scripture would fain turn you back into disbelievers (*kuffār*, pl. of *kāfir*) after your profession of belief (*īmān*), through the envious nature of their souls, after the Truth has become manifest unto them. (II, 103/109)

> How shall God guide a people who disbelieved (*kafarū*) after having once believed and testified to the truth of the Apostle, to whom clear signs came? . . . Verily, those who disbelieve after their profession of belief, and go on increasing in disbelief, their repentance shall not be accepted. (III, 80, 84/86, 90)

Those who disbelieve say, 'We will never believe in this Qur'ān, nor in the Scriptures before it.' If only thou couldst see these wrong-doers set before their Lord, trying to attribute these words the one to the other! (XXXIV, 30/31)

When there comes to them [i.e. the people of Israel] what they know to be the Truth, *they disbelieve* in it. The curse of God be on *the disbelievers*. What a bad bargain they have sold their souls for, that *they should disbelieve* in that which God has sent down, mortally offended because God bestows of His bounty upon whomsoever of His servants He will. Thus they have brought on themselves [divine] wrath upon wrath. For the *disbelievers* there shall be a shameful chastisement. And when it is said to them, '*Believe* in that which God has sent down', they reply, '*We believe* only in that which was revealed unto us' [referring to the Bible], and *they disbelieve* in what comes after it, though it is the Truth that confirms what they possess [i.e. the Book of Revelation which they possess already]. (II, 83–85/89–91)

## The Heart of a Kāfir

The Qur'ān devotes a considerable number of verses to the description of the state of a *kāfir* mind. Let us begin by noting that the hearts of those who believe are described as finding a calm, sweet rest in remembrance of God: 'Those who believe, their hearts rest calmly in God's remembrance. Aye, in God's remembrance do their hearts rest calm and serene.' (XIII, 28) In contrast to this calm, peaceful state of the believing heart, the hearts of the Kāfirs are very often described as being 'hardened like stones'. *Qasat qulūbuhum*, 'their hearts are hard, or, have become hardened', is a standing metaphor for the state of the *kāfir* hearts which would stubbornly resist the call of the divine voice 'even though the mountains were moved, or the earth cleft' (XIII, 30/31) and 'even though We should send down the angels to them, or the dead should speak to them.' (VI, 111).

Even after that [i.e. after God has shown them many astounding miracles] your hearts were hard as rocks, or even harder still. For, in fact, rocks there are from which rivers gush forth, and others which split in two to let water flow out. Indeed there are even rocks that crash down for the fear of God. (II, 69/74)

Because they broke their covenant with Us, We cursed them and made their hearts hard (*qāsiyah*). (V, 16/13)

We may note in passing that in the last-quoted sentence, the hardening of the Kāfirs' hearts is attributed to God. The point is bound up with the well-known doctrine of foreordination, and it did lead to very serious debates in Islamic theology as to whether all evil including *kufr* might justifiably be attributed to God's will. As far as the Qurʾanic texts are concerned, however, this question is left undecided. And it would be far beyond the scope of the present inquiry to try to find some way of resolving this apparent theoretical paradox.

The second characteristic of the *kāfir* heart is that it is 'veiled' (*fī akinnah*), that there is a veil or partition curtain (*ḥijāb*) between it and Revelation.

> [This is] an Arabic Qurʾān for a people who have understanding, a bearer of good tidings and warning. Most of them, however, have turned away and will not give ear. They say, 'Our hearts are veiled from what thou callest us to, in our ears is deafness, and between us and thee there is a partition.' (XLI, 2–4/3–5)

> When thou recitest the Qurʾān, We place between thee and those who believe not in the Hereafter a partition curtain (*ḥijāb*), and We place veils (*akinnah*) upon their hearts lest they understand it, and in their ears deafness. (XVII, 47–48/45–46)

The same thought is expressed in various ways. It is for instance expressed by means of the metaphor of 'sealing'!

> As for the Kāfirs, whether thou warn them or warn them not it would be all the same to them, they believe not. God has sealed (*khatama*) their hearing and their hearts, and on their eyes there is a covering (*ghishāwah*). (II, 5–6/6–7)

> They [i.e. those who, on some specious excuse, do not go forth to fight 'in the way of God'] are pleased to be with those who tarry behind. God has sealed (*ṭabaʿa*) their hearts, so that they can understand nothing. (IX, 94/93)

Or it is expressed by saying that there are 'locks' on their hearts:

> Will they not meditate upon the Qurʾān, or is it that there are locks (*aqfāl*) upon their hearts? (XLVII, 26/24)

Or, again, by the image of rust covering up the heart little by little:

> Nay but what they used to do has corroded their hearts with rust (*rāna*, from *RYN* 'to cover with rust'). (LXXXIII, 14)

'Those who have a heart' (L, 36/37) must easily grasp the deep meaning of the signs sent down by God; upon them the revealed words of God should work as a real reminder (*dhikrá*). But, being veiled and obstructed in the way just described, the hearts of the Kāfirs cannot perceive the religious significance of anything. They remain blind and deaf to the divine signs. The imagery of blindness and deafness is among the most commonly used in the Qur'ān for describing the distinguishing features of the Kāfirs.

> We made for them hearing, and eyesight, and hearts, but their hearing, and their hearts availed them naught, seeing that they always denied the signs of God and they are now surrounded on all sides by what they used to mock at. (XLVI, 25/26)

This means that, physically, the Kāfirs are without defect; it is their hearts 'that are within the bosoms' that are defective. The following verses bring out this point in explicit terms:

> Have they not travelled in the land [the earth is full of divine signs] so that they have hearts wherewith to understand or ears wherewith to hear? Nay, it is not the eyes that are blind, but it is rather the hearts within the bosoms that are blind. (XXII, 45/46)

> O believers, obey God and His Apostle . . . and be not like those who say, 'We hear', while in fact they hear not.
> Verily, the worst of beasts in the sight of God are those who are deaf and dumb and do not understand. Had God recognized any good in them, He would have made them hear. But had He made them hear, they would have turned back and gone aside. (VIII, 20–23)

All efforts to induce them to believe are sure to end in a sheer waste of labor. We often see God advising Muḥammad to stop extending his apostolic enthusiasm towards these people, for it is almost certain that it is impossible for them to be converted.

> Dost thou think that most of them hear or understand? They are but as the cattle. Nay, they are farther astray from the way. (XXV, 46/44)

> Verily, thou canst not make the dead to hear, nor canst thou make the deaf to hear the call when they turn their backs to thee. Neither canst thou guide the blind out of their straying. Thou canst make none to hear save those who believe in Our signs and surrender [unto Us]. (XXVII, 82–83/80–81)

> Of them there are some who give ear to thee. But canst thou make the deaf to hear when they understand naught? And of them there are some who look towards thee. But canst thou guide the blind when they see naught? (X, 43–44/42–43)

Having a veiled heart, a Kāfir cannot apprehend the signs of God as they are, even though he gives ear to the recitation of the Qurʾān and looks towards the Apostle. To him, the divine signs are just the fairy tales of old folks.

> Of them there are some who give ear to thee, but as We have placed a veil upon their hearts, they apprehend it [i.e. the deep meaning of God's words] not. And in their ears [We have put] deafness. And even if they see any sign, they do not believe in it, so that when they come to thee they start an argument with thee, these Kāfirs, saying 'This is naught but old folks' tales.' (VI, 25)

Thus he who attempts to convert the Kāfirs is likened to a drover shouting to his cattle. The cattle only hear his voice; they never apprehend what his words mean.

> The likeness of [one who calls to *īmān*] those who disbelieve (*kafarū*) is as the likeness of him who shouts to that which can hear naught else but a shouting voice. Deaf, dumb, and blind, they apprehend naught. (II, 166/171)

## *Kufr* and *Shirk*

Since *kufr* in both of its main aspects, 'thanklessness' and 'disbelief', cannot but end in denying the absolute Oneness of God, there is naturally a respect in which it can fairly be equated with polytheism. Polytheism in ancient Arabia consisted in the worship of idols, and a number of minor deities that were called sometimes the daughters of God, or more simply 'companions' or 'associates' of God. The most usual term for this kind of polytheism is *shirk*; and for the idolater *mushrik*, literally, 'one who associates', that is, one who ascribes partners to God.

First I shall quote some passages where *kufr* is talked of expressly in terms of 'associating'.

> Praise be to God who created the heavens and the earth, and put in order the darkness and the light. Yet the Kāfirs (*alladhīna kafarū*) ascribe equals unto their Lord. (VI, 1)

> They ascribe unto God associates (*shurakāʾ*). Say, 'Name them.' Is it that you would tell Him what He knows not in the earth? Or are they but empty names? Nay, but their contrivance appears fair to the Kāfirs, and thus they are kept away from [God's] way. (XIII, 33)

> Whenever God alone was invoked, you disbelieved (*kafartum*), but if others were associated [with Him], you believed. (XL, 12)

In the next quotation, the semantic content of the word *mushrik* is chiefly determined—by implication—by two factors: *not* following Revelation, and *not* acknowledging the absolute Oneness of God.

> Follow thou that which is revealed to thee from thy Lord. There is no God but He. Turn away from the *mushrik*. (VI, 106)

It will be worth noting that from the standpoint of the thoroughgoing monotheism of Islām, the Christian doctrine of Trinity constitutes a representative example of polytheism. And so also the deification of Jesus Christ. In the following, be it remarked, these central tenets of Christianity are treated invariably as acts of the Kāfirs. Semantically, this should be understood in this way: these belong to the category of *kufr* by being cases of *shirk*. This point comes out explicitly in the text.

> They surely are Kāfirs who say, 'God is the Messiah, son of Mary.' For the Messiah [himself] said, 'O children of Israel, worship God [alone], my Lord and your Lord.' Verily, whoso ascribes unto God associates, God has surely forbidden Paradise unto him, and his final abode shall be the Fire. For the wrong-doers there shall be no helpers. They surely are Kāfirs who say, 'God is the third of Three.' Nay, there is no god save One God. If they desist not from saying so, there shall befall those of them that commit such an act of *kufr* a painful chastisement. (V, 76–77/72–73)

Seen from still another angle, *shirk* is neither more nor less than forgery, that 'forging against God a lie', *iftirāʾ ʿalá Allāh al-kadhib*, which we have discussed in connection with the moral value of 'truthfulness', *ṣidq*, in Chapter VI. For, obviously, idolatry of polytheism consists in creating 'out of caprice' beings that are in reality mere names and nothing else. And via this route, too, *shirk* connects ultimately with *kufr*, as the following passage shows clearly.

> They say, 'God has taken to Himself a son.' Glorified be He! He is the Self-sufficient. His is all that is in the heavens and all that is in the earth. You have no authority for this. Will you say about God what you do not know? Tell them. 'Verily, those who forge against God a lie shall not end well.' . . . We shall make them taste the harsh chastisement for that they were Kāfirs. (X, 69–71/68–70)

The Kāfir in this sense—i.e. *kāfir* = *mushrik*—is compared to a man who stretches forth his hands in vain towards the mirage of water in the desert.

> To Him alone is the prayer of truth, whilst those unto whom they pray apart from God answer them naught. It may be compared to

> a man who stretches forth his hands to water that it may come unto his mouth, and it reaches it not. The prayer of the Kāfirs is sure to go astray. (XIII, 15/14)

> As for the Kāfirs, their deeds are like a mirage in the desert; the thirsty man takes it for water, till when he comes unto it he finds it naught, but he finds God instead, and He pays him his account. For swift indeed is God at reckoning. (XXIV, 39)

There follows this last-quoted passage another comparison which pictures a *kāfir-mushrik* as a man covered by thick layers of darkness on a vast, abysmal sea.

> Or like darkness upon an abysmal sea, covered by a wave above which is a wave, overspread with clouds, darkness upon darkness. When he stretches forth his hand, scarce can he see it. To whomsoever God has given no light, for him there can be no light. (XXIV, 40)

Here is another simile used for emphasizing the essential vanity of the deeds of the *mushrik*:

> Whoso associates (*yushrik*, verbal form corresponding to the participial-adjectival *mushrik*) with God partners, it is as though he has fallen from the sky and the birds snatch him away, or the wind blows him away to a far-off place. (XXII, 32/31)

Concerning *kufr-shirk* there remains one more important point to be noticed. The Qurʾān attributes *shirk* ultimately to the working of the mental faculty of *ẓann* 'thinking', a word which is used as a general rule in contrast to *ʿilm* 'knowledge (established unshakably on the basis of reality)', and denotes accordingly a groundless, unwarranted type of thinking, uncertain or doubtful knowledge, unreliable opinion, or mere conjecture.[6] Thus it comes about that in the Qurʾanic contexts this term behaves as a negative value, just as *ʿilm*, its contrary, has acquired the status of a positive value. Both *ẓann* and *ʿilm* are value words in the Qurʾān.

> Dost thou not see that to God belongs whosoever in the heavens and whosoever in the earth? What, then, do those follow who call upon associates (*shurakāʾ*) besides God? They follow naught but *ẓann*, verily they are merely conjecturing (*yakhruṣūna*). (X, 67/66)

This last word, *yakhruṣūna*, comes from the root *KH-R-Ṣ* having also the meaning of 'doing or saying something by uncertain—and

[6] For more details about *ʿilm* and *ẓann*, see my *God and Man in the Koran*, pp. 59–62.



(zann) thinking = unreliable doubtful groundless
vs
(ʿilm) knowledge = established on basis of reality

mostly false—opinion', and is opposed to *ᶜilm*. In Sūrah LI, we have an example of the use of this root under the emphatic form, *kharrāṣ*, one who indulges in conjecturing. It is significant that the commentator al-Bayḍāwī explains this word in this passage by *kadhdhāb*, 'a big liar', showing how easily the concept of 'conjecturing' could shade into that of 'telling a lie' in the semantic consciousness of the old Arabs.

> Accursed be the *kharrāṣūn* (pl.), who are heedless [of the warnings of God] in the abyss [of *kufr*]! 'When is the Day of Judgment?' they ask [sarcastically]. (LI. 10–12)

The following passage shows very clearly that, in the Qurʾanic conception, *ẓann* is basically opposed to *ᶜilm* and that the false deities whom the polytheists worship are nothing but products of *ẓann*.

> Verily, those who believe not in the Hereafter name the angels with female names. But in reality they have no knowledge (*ᶜilm*) thereof: they only follow *ẓann*. *Ẓann*, however, can never replace the truth. (LIII, 28–29/27–28; see also X, 37/36)

A few verses earlier in the same Sūrah, we find the three ancient goddesses of Mecca, Allāt, al-ᶜUzzá, and Manāt, declared to be empty names and mere products of groundless conjecture.

> Have you considered Allāt and al-ᶜUzzá, and in the third place Manāt? What, will you attribute to Him females [referring to the fact that these goddesses were known as 'Daughters of Allāh'] while you [desire only] male offspring? That were indeed an unfair division. Nay, these are but names which you have named, you and your fathers. God has sent down no warrant for them. They [here the subject changes abruptly] do but follow *ẓann* according to the dictates of their souls' desire. (LIII, 19–23)

## *Kufr* in the Sense of 'Going Astray'

As we shall see later in Chapter IX, the Qurʾān defines 'belief', *īmān*, in terms of a number of key concepts. One of them—and certainly one of the most important—is the concept of *ihtidāʾ*. Viewed from this point of view, 'to believe' is to 'be rightly guided' or 'to accept the guidance [of God]'. And if *īmān* is thus to be understood as *ihtidāʾ*, then its opposite, *kufr*, would obviously mean 'going astray from the right way'. The typical word used in the Qurʾān for this meaning is the verb *ḍalla* (nom. *ḍalālah* or *ḍalāl*).

We shall begin by remarking that this verb, as one of the most common words in Arabic, may be used at various levels of discourse. It may be used, in the first place, in a concrete sense, i.e. 'to lose one's way while travelling in the desert'. It may also be used in a metaphorical sense. And in this latter case, we may distinguish between two different levels of discourse: religious and non-religious or secular.

Of the non-religious use of this word, the Qur'ān itself (the Chapter of Joseph) furnishes us with two examples. One of them refers to the excessive and 'partial' love Jacob shows to Joseph in preference to all his other sons. The point of view here is, needless to say, that of Joseph's brothers.

> They [Joseph's brothers] said, 'Verily, Joseph and his brother [the youngest one, Benjamin] are dearer to our father than we, though we are so many. Verily, our father is in manifest *ḍalāl.*' (XII, 8)

The other refers to the aberrant passion for young Joseph, which he has inflamed in the heart of the wife of the Egyptian Governor.

> Some women in the city said, 'The wife of the Governor desires to entice his page to lie with her. He has smitten her heart with love. Verily, we see her in manifest *ḍalāl.*' (XII, 30)

It will be clear that in both cases the term *ḍalāl* implies that the action in question is something which is felt to go against the normal moral sense. But, of course, the basic meaning is in this case, too, 'going astray from the right path'.

Far more usual in the Qur'ān is, however, the religious usage of the word. In fact we find the basic conceptual opposition of *ihtadá* and *ḍalla* expressed everywhere in the Qur'ān in the most emphatic way. Out of a huge number of examples, I give here a few typical ones.

> Whoso is guided (or 'accepts guidance,' *ihtadá*), is guided only to his own benefit, and whoso strays (*ḍalla*), strays only to his own loss. Nobody shall bear the burden of another on top of his own burden. (XVII, 16/15)

> Verily, thy Lord knows best who goes astray (*yaḍillu*) from His way, and He knows best the rightly guided (*muhtadīn*). (VI, 117)

> In the following example *ḍalālah* is opposed to *hudá*, 'guidance':

> Those are they who have purchased *ḍalālah* (straying) at the price of *hudá* (guidance), and chastisement at the price of pardon. (II, 170/175)

It is noteworthy that here 'straying' is paired with 'chastisement', *ʿadhāb*, and 'guidance' with 'pardon', *maghfirah*. This alone will be enough to show that the 'straying' here in question is another name of *kufr*. In the next example, 'straying' and 'chastisement' appear in combination.

> Nay, but those who believe not in the Hereafter are in *ʿadhāb* and far *ḍalāl*. (XXXIV, 8)

We must remark in this connection that the stage in which man lives in complete ignorance of Revelation is sometimes designated in the Qurʾān by the same word, the stage, that is, that precedes all revelational activity on the part of God, and where, therefore, the problem of *kufr* in the strict sense of the word cannot properly arise yet.

> Verily, God showed mercy on the believers when He sent amongst them an Apostle of their own, to recite unto them His signs and to purify them, and to teach them the Scripture and wisdom, although they were before that in manifest *ḍalāl*. (III, 158/164)

It is interesting to notice that the following verse suggests that the cattle are naturally in the state of *ḍalāl*. But the Kāfirs, it declares, are 'further astray' from the right path:

> Dost thou [Muḥammad] think that most of them hear or understand? They are but as the cattle. Nay, they are farther astray (*aḍallu*) from the way. (XXV, 46/44)

If, as we have just seen, the state *before* Revelation is to be classified in the category of *ḍalāl*, still more must this be true of the state of those who reject Revelation knowingly. The Qurʾān furnishes numerous examples of this.

> Verily those who disbelieve (*kafarū*) and obstruct the way of God; they have strayed (*ḍallū*) far astray (*ḍalālan baʿīdan*). (IV, 165/167)

> The likeness of those who disbelieve (*kafarū*) in their Lord—their deeds are like ashes whereon the fierce wind blows on a day of tempest. They have no control at all over that which they have earned. That is indeed the far *ḍalāl*. (XIV, 21/18)

It should be remarked that this equivalence, *kufr* = *ḍalāl*, obtains only from the standpoint of the believers. Viewed from the standpoint of the Kāfirs themselves, it is of course the position of the believers that is *ḍalāl*. Whenever a warner comes to them, the Kāfirs call him a liar and say,

> God has sent down naught. You [believers] are but in great *ḍalāl*. (LXVII, 9)

On this, Muḥammad is urged to retort, saying,

> He is the Merciful. In Him we believe and in Him we put our trust. You will soon know who it is that is in manifest *ḍalāl*. (LXVII, 29)

The same is true of the following passage:

> We sent Noah unto his people, and he said, 'O my people, worship God! You have no other God than He. Verily, I fear for you the chastisement of an awful day. The chiefs of his people said, 'Verily, we see thee in manifest *ḍalāl*'. He said, 'O my people, there is no *ḍalālah* in me, but I am an Apostle from the Lord of all beings.' (VII, 57–59/59–61)

Since *shirk*, 'associating', i.e. polytheism, is, in the Qurʾanic conception, nothing but one of the most typical manifestations of *kufr*, it is not at all surprising that it should be counted as a case of *ḍalāl*. A few examples will suffice.

> He [an idol-worshipper] calls, beside God, upon that which neither hurts him nor profits him [i.e. idols that are completely powerless]. That is indeed the far *ḍalāl*. (XXII, 12)

> When Abraham said to his father Azar, 'Takest thou idols for gods? Verily, I see thee and thy people in manifest *ḍalāl*.' (VI, 74)

> Shall I take, beside Him, gods who, if the Merciful [God] should wish me any calamity, will never be able to intercede effectively for me, and who will never deliver me? Then surely I should be in manifest *ḍalāl*. (XXXVI, 22–23/23–24)

Indeed, *kufr* in all its forms is *ḍalāl*. Those, for instance, who 'cry lies' (*takdhīb*) to Revelation are 'those who stray'.

> 'Then lo! you who go astray (*ḍāllūn*, part. pl.) and cry lies [to the Day of Judgment], you shall eat of a tree of Zaqqūm [the infernal tree].' (LVI, 51–52)

> We sent among every nation an Apostle, 'Worship you God, and shun idols!' Some of them God guided, but some of them there were who were predisposed to *ḍalālah*. Travel in the land and see how was the fate of those who cried lies (*mukadhdhibīn*). (XVI, 38/36)

Those 'whose hearts are hard' (*qasat qulūbuhum*)—a phenomenon which we examined above—are also in *ḍalāl*.

> Woe to those whose hearts are hard against the remembrance of God! Those are in manifest *ḍalāl*. (XXXIX, 23/22)

*Ẓulm* 'wrong-doing' is in the Qurʾanic context a particular aspect of *kufr* as we shall see in the following chapter. So it is but natural that a 'wrongdoer' (*ẓālim*) is described as 'erring' away from the right path.

> Woe to those who disbelieve (*kafarū*) for the assembly of an awful day! . . . The wrong-doers (*ẓālimūn*) are today in manifest *ḍalāl.* (XIX, 38–39/37–38; see also XXXI, 10/11)

Even those who are 'in doubt' concerning the Truth are already in far *ḍalāl.* Likewise, those who, because of their lack of 'patience', despair of God's mercy.

> Those who believe are in fear (*mushfiqūn*) of it [i.e. the Last Hour], being well aware that it is the Truth. Ay, indeed, those who are in doubt (*yumārūna*) concerning the Hour are in far *ḍalāl.* (XLII, 17/18)

> Who would despair of the mercy of his Lord save those who are erring (*ḍāllūna*)? (XV, 56)

The verb *ḍalla* has a number of synonyms in the Qurʾān that are used more or less in the same sense in the same sort of contexts. The verb *ghawiya* or *ghawá* is one of the most important, meaning 'to go astray from the right course'. In the following passage, *ghāwī*, which is the participial form of this verb, meaning 'one who goes astray', is opposed, first of all, to *muttaqī*, which as we know means 'godfearing', and then, after a few verses, is definitely shown to be synonymous with *ḍāll.*

> And Paradise shall be brought nigh unto the *muttaqīn* (pl.) while Hell shall be brought forward for the *ghāwīn* (pl.). . . . They [the Kāfirs in the Fire] shall say, while quarrelling therein, 'By God, we were surely in manifest *ḍalāl* when we made you [idols] equal with the Lord of all beings. The truth is that the sinners (*mujrimūn*) led us astray (*aḍalla*).' (XXVI, 90–91, 96–99)

That the verb *ghawá* is a synonym of *ḍalla* in its religious sense may be proved by another fact: namely, that it is sometimes used in the Qurʾān to denote the reverse of *ihtidāʾ*, 'being guided'.

> Adam disobeyed (*ʿaṣá*) his Lord [in reference to the fact that he ate of the Tree of Eternity in the Garden], and so he went astray (*ghawá*). Afterwards, however, his Lord chose him, turned again towards him, and guided (*hadá*) him [i.e. brought him back to the right path.] (XX, 119–120/121–122)

Another important synonym is *zāgha* (nom. *zaygh*), meaning to 'swerve aside, or deviate from the right course'. Here is a typical example of its use:

> He it is who has sent down upon thee the Scripture, of which some verses are clear . . . and others ambiguous. As for those in whose hearts is *zaygh* ('swerving inclination', so to speak), they cling to the ambiguous part, seeking to cause dissension. . . .
> Yet those who are firmly rooted in the knowledge (*rāsikhūn fī al-ᶜilm*) say, 'We believe in it. All is from our Lord. . . . Our Lord, cause not our hearts to swerve (*tuzigh*, causative form of *zaygh*) after that Thou hast guided (*hadayta*) us.' (III, 5–6/7–8)

Likewise the verb *ᶜamiha*, or *ᶜamaha*, meaning roughly 'to wander astray blindly, being utterly perplexed as to which way to go'. The verb, as is clear, is particularly fit for describing the state of the Kāfirs going to and fro in this world, without ever finding the right direction.

> Verily, as for those who believe not in the Hereafter, We have made their deeds look fair unto them so that they wander astray (*yaᶜmahūna*). (XXVII, 4)

Very similar to *ḍalāl* in the close relationship it bears to guidance is *ghaflah* which literally means 'heedlessness' or 'carelessness'. Nothing brings out better the basic meaning of this word than a 'secular' use of it. The Qurʾān itself furnishes an interesting example. The passage is found in the Chapter of Joseph; it is put in the mouth of Jacob, who is extremely anxious about his beloved child, Joseph, whom his brothers are going to take out to make him play in the open air.

> Verily, it grieves me that you should take him out with you; I fear lest the wolf devour him [Joseph] while you are heedless (*ghāfilūn*) of him. (XII, 13)

While *ḍalāl* in its religious use consists in swerving from the path of guidance, *ghaflah* means to remain utterly heedless of it. It is highly interesting to note that, just as *ḍalāl*, as we have seen above, can denote the state before Revelation, so *ghaflah*, too, can be used in reference to the pre-revelational conditions of man. In Sūrah XXV, 46/44 we saw the Kāfirs compared to the cattle in regard to the state of *ḍalāl* in which they find themselves. Exactly the same is true of them in regard to the property of heedlessness which characterizes them.

> Whomsoever God guides (*yahdi*), he is guided (*muhtadī*), while whomsoever He leads astray (*yuḍlil*), such are the losers. We have created for Gehenna a huge number of jinn and men who, having hearts, understand not therewith. They are like the cattle. Nay, they are further astray (*aḍallu*). They are the heedless (*ghāfilūn*, part. pl.). (VII, 177–178/178–179)

The Revelation of the Mighty, the Merciful, that thou [Muḥammad] mayest warn a people whose fathers were never warned, and who are, consequently, heedless. (XXXVI, 4–5/5–6)

It is noteworthy that Muḥammad himself is described as having been in the state of *ghaflah* before he began to receive Revelation.

We narrate to thee the best of stories in that We have revealed to thee this Qurʾān, although thou wast aforetime of the heedless. (XII, 3)

The following example brings 'heedlessness' into a close relationship with *kufr*, *ẓulm*, and *shirk*.

When the true promise [i.e. the chastisement of Hell] draws nigh, lo, how fixedly open they are, the eyes of the Kāfirs! [They say], 'Alas for us! We were in heedlessness (*ghaflah*) of this. Nay, we were wrongdoers (*ẓālimīn*).' 'Verily, you and what you used worship beside God, are all fuel for Gehenna. You are now going to enter it.' (XXI, 97–98)

Next I give two examples that would bring to light the semantic equivalence between *kufr* and *ghaflah*.

... God guides not the Kāfirs. They are those upon whose hearts and ears and eyes God has set a seal. Those are the heedless (*ghāfilūn*). (XVI, 109–110/107–108)

Give thou [Muḥammad] warning to them of the day of grief, when the matter shall be decided [ultimately], while they are in heedlessness (*ghaflah*) and unbelieving (*lā yuʾminūn*). (XIX, 40/39)

## *Hawá* as the Immediate Cause of *Ḍalāl*

The Qurʾān mentions *hawá* (pl. *ahwāʾ*) as the principal and immediate cause of *ḍalāl*. He who follows his *hawá* in matters that concern religious faith is sure to stray from the right path. And those who follow the person who pursues his *hawá* will inevitably be misled far from God's way.

Say, 'I am forbidden to worship those [idols] you call upon beside God.' Say, 'I will not follow your *ahwāʾ* (pl. of *hawá*), for then I would go astray (*ḍalaltu*) and would not be of the guided (*muhtadīn*).' (VI, 56)

Who is further astray (*aḍall*, comparative) than he who follows his own *hawá* without guidance from God? Verily God guides not *ẓālim* people. (XXVIII, 50)

> Follow not the *ahwāʾ* of people who went astray (*ḍallū*) of old and led astray (*aḍallū*) many, and [now] have gone astray (*ḍallū*) from the level road. (V, 81/77)

It is highly significant that later in theology the heretics come to be called the 'people of *ahwāʾ*' (*ahl al-ahwāʾ*).[7] It is one of the key terms of Islamic thought. Already in Jāhilīyah it used to play an important role. Only, at that time the word carried good as well as bad connotations. As an example of the former we may quote Taʾabbaṭah Sharran's famous verse:

*Qalīl al-tashakkī lil-mulimm yuṣībuhu* *
*kathīr al-hawá shattá al-nawá wa-al-masālik*

> [He is a man who] seldom complains of whatever calamity befalls him, but has plenty of desires (*hawá*), many different directions to move in and ways to go.[8]

Likewise the following verse by an anonymous poet, in which he urges his tribesmen to reflect and to awake before it is too late, i.e. before the tribe is completely disintegrated:

*Afīqū Banī Ḥazn wa-ahwāʾunā maᶜan* *
*wa-arḥāmunā mawṣūlat lam taqaḍḍab*

> Awake [from your *ghaflah* before the war breaks out]! Awake, while our hearts' desires (*ahwāʾ*) are still united, and our blood relationship still kept intact without being cut asunder.[9]

As an example of the use of the word in a bad sense, I shall give the following hemistich by ᶜAntarah:

* *lā utbiᶜu al-nafs al-lajūj hawāhā*

> I do not allow my obstinate soul to follow her own *hawá*. [i.e. I never lose self-control; whenever my soul desires to do something which I know will endanger my position, I restrain myself.][10]

The word *hawá* may be said to mean, roughly, the natural inclination of the human soul, born of lusts and animal appetites. In the Qurʾanic context it means invariably an evil inclination which is liable to mislead man from the right way. Thus in the Qurʾān *hawá*

7 In theology *hawá* (*ahwāʾ*) is a technical term used always in a disparaging sense. For instance, al-Ashᶜarī says, 'The Muᶜtazilites and the Qadarites who have gone astray (*zaygh*) from the Truth have been led by their own *ahwāʾ* to imitate blindly their leaders and forefathers and to interpret the Koran in quite an arbitrary way.' *Kitāb al-Ibānah*, 2nd pr. (Hyderabad-Dn., 1948), p. 3.
8 Abū Tammām, *Ḥamāsah*, I, 47.
9 *Ibid.*, 164.
10 ᶜAntarah, *Dīwān*, ed. ᶜAbd al-Raʾūf (Cairo, n.d.), p. 186, v. 1.

forms the opposite of *ʿilm*, 'knowledge', i.e. the revealed knowledge of the Truth.

> If thou [Muḥammad] shouldst follow their *ahwāʾ* after the knowledge (*ʿilm*) that has come to thee, then surely thou wilt be of the wrong-doers (*ẓālimīn*). (II, 140/145)

> Nay, but those who do wrong (*ẓalamū*) follow their own *ahwāʾ* in place of knowledge (*ʿilm*). Who shall guide (*yahdī*) him whom God has led astray (*aḍalla*)? They have no helpers. (XXX, 28/29)

> The Jews will not be satisfied with thee [Muḥammad], nor yet the Christians, until thou followest their creed. Say, 'God's guidance (*hudá*) is the guidance.' If thou followest their *ahwāʾ* after the knowledge that has come to thee, thou shalt have then against God no protector nor helper. (II, 114/120)

It will be evident from the foregoing that the act of following one's own *hawá* as opposed to 'knowledge' is, in ultimate analysis, nothing other than forming wild conjectures concerning God and His Revelation. So we see sometimes *hawá* being replaced by some such expressions as *ẓann*, to take the most conspicuous case.[11]

> If thou obeyest most people on earth they would lead thee astray (*yuḍillū*) from God's way, for they follow naught but mere conjecture (*ẓann*); they speak only by opinion (*yakhruṣūna*). (VI, 116)

It goes without saying that 'knowledge', *ʿilm*, in its turn, may be replaced by 'truth', *ḥaqq*, for, as we have seen earlier, they are but two different aspects of one and the same thing: Revelation.

> Judge thou between them in accordance with what God has sent down, and follow not their *ahwāʾ* to turn away from the Truth (*ḥaqq*) that has come to thee. (V, 52/48)

It is interesting to note that the attitude of those who follow their own *hawá* in place of Guidance is sometimes designated in the Qurʾān by a very significant expression; 'taking one's own *hawá* for one's god'.

> Hast thou seen him who has taken his *hawá* for his god, and God has led him astray (*aḍalla*) knowingly, and has set a seal upon his hearing and his heart, and has placed a covering upon his eyesight? Who shall, then, guide him after God? (XLV, 22/23; see also XXV, 45/43)

[11] We have already examined the basic opposition of *ẓann* and *ʿilm* above in connection with the problem of *shirk*, 'polytheism' (see pp. 130–133).

Of less importance is a synonym of *hawá*, *shahwah*, a word meaning 'desire', 'appetite', or 'lust'. It may, in certain contexts, replace *hawá* without causing any noticeable change in meaning.

> God wishes to turn towards you, but those who follow their *shahawāt* (pl. of *shahwah*) wish that you should swerve away [from the Truth] with great swerving. (IV, 32/27)
>
> There succeeded them [i.e. the great Prophets such as Abraham, Moses, Ishmael, etc.] a generation who abandoned the prayer and followed the *shahawāt*. (XIX, 60/59)

## The Attitude of Haughtiness

Another important element in the semantic structure of the concept of *kufr* is 'haughtiness' or 'arrogance'. We should remark that in the Qur'anic conception the inborn arrogance of the mind is not simply one of the various features of *kufr*. The Qur'ān never tires of laying special emphasis on this element in the structure of *kufr*, so much so that in many cases it is made to represent the most typical characteristic of a Kāfir. A Kāfir is an arrogant, haughty man in a religious sense. Even a cursory examination of the Scripture will convince anyone that it looks at the phenomenon of *kufr* mainly from this angle. In the Qur'ān the insolent boaster walks around as the central figure in the province of negative properties.

> Then said the chiefs of his [i.e. the Apostle Ṣāliḥ's] people [i.e. the people of Thamūd), who grew arrogant (*istakbarū*), unto those that were despised [i.e. the menials of the people], 'Do you know for certain that Ṣāliḥ is one sent from his Lord?' They said, 'In that which [i.e. the divine message] he has been sent with, verily, we do believe.' Those, however, who grew arrogant (*istakbarū*) said, 'We, on our part, in that which you believe do disbelieve (*kāfirūn*).' (VII, 73–74/75–76)
>
> Yea, My signs did come to thee [this is said to an infidel in the Hell Fire], but thou didst cry them lies, and wert arrogant (*istakbarta*). Thou hast become of those who disbelieved (*kāfirīn*). (XXXIX, 60/59)

This of course implies that 'haughtiness', on its positive side, is definitely opposed to 'belief' (*īmān*). Those who are 'haughty' cannot accept 'belief', and, conversely, those who do not believe in the divine 'signs' are simply 'behaving haughtily'.

> Moses said, 'I seek refuge in my Lord and your Lord from every man puffed up with pride (*mutakabbir*) who believes not in the Day of Reckoning.' (XL, 28/27)

As for those who believe and do good deeds, He will not only pay them in full their wages, but give them more than they merit, out of His bounty. But as for those who show only disdain and scorn (*istankafū*, from *NKF* meaning 'to refuse scornfully') and behave haughtily (*istakbarū*), He will punish them with a painful chastisement. (IV, 172/173)

They [Pharaoh and his ministers] said [to Moses], 'Whatever sign thou dost bring unto us to bewitch us therewith, we shall never believe in thee.' So We sent upon them the flood, the locusts, the lice, the frogs, and the blood, all manifest signs, but [every time] they only behaved arrogantly (*istakbarū*), for they were naturally a sinful people. (VII, 129–130/132–133)

It may be worth recalling in this connection what we said above about the nomadic virtue of *murūwah*. The concept, as we saw, is based on an exceedingly high opinion of human power. It was considered most natural in Jāhilīyah that he who was conscious of the inherence of power in his soul should manifest it in all his behavior, that he should act with pride and haughtiness. Even idolatry, the only authentic religion in Jāhilīyah, was kept within narrow bounds so that it could not hurt the pride of such persons. From the standpoint of Islām, however, such an attitude of man was nothing less than a titanic rebellion against the supreme authority of God. I have already pointed out that even in the daily relations of life, Islām stresses the importance of keeping to the virtue of *ḥilm*. And in effect, there is in the Qurʾān constant denunciation of those who 'walk about haughtily in the earth', puffed up with unreasonable pride, bellowing in the most disagreeable voice, and oppressing the poor and weak in their blind contumely.

Distort not thy cheek, turning proudly away from men, nor swagger about in the earth. For God loves not any man haughty and boastful. But be modest in thy gait, and lower thy voice. Verily, the most detestable of all voices is the voice of the ass. (XXXI, 17–18/18–19)

Such an attitude, which, even in the domain of man-to-man relationship, is sure to incur God's displeasure, attains the highest degree of sinfulness when taken towards God and His Apostle and Revelation. In order to understand this point we have only to recall that the name itself of Islām means nothing but 'humble submission'. Here are some of the passages which describe in vividly concrete terms the reaction of this type produced by God's 'signs' in the Kāfirs.

May he be accursed—how he estimated [Our signs]! Again, may he be accursed—how he estimated! He cast a look, then he frowned and grimaced, then he stepped back and grew big with pride (*istakbara*), and said, 'Ha, this is naught but magic transmitted. This is naught but man-made speech!' (LXXXIV, 19–25)

It will be noticed that the most usual term for this kind of arrogance is *istakbara* which, as we saw in an earlier chapter, is a derivation from the root *KBR* with the basic meaning of 'big', and means literally 'to become big, puffed up with pride'.

Verily, when it is said to them, 'There is no god but God', they become big with pride (*yastakbirūna*) and say, 'What, shall we abandon our gods to follow a poet possessed?' (XXXVII, 34–35/35–36)

Then We sent Moses and his brother Aaron with Our signs and a manifest authority unto Pharaoh and his ministers. But they grew big with pride (*istakbarū*)—for they were a haughty (*ʿālī*) people—and said, 'What, shall we believe two mortals like ourselves, when their people are but our servants?' (XXIII, 47–49/45–47)

Here, be it remarked, the Qurʾanic text uses two different words, *istakbara* and *ʿālī*, so as to express the two different aspects of the same state of affairs. The first, which is a verb, denotes the arrogance, as it were, as a dynamic phenomenon of the moment, that is, as a sudden outbreak of the violent emotion of scornful anger, while the second term, which is an adjective meaning 'high', refers obviously to the inborn quality of haughtiness which is always there, at the bottom of the mind, ready to break out at any moment at the slightest instigation. The next example will make this point still clearer.

When thy Lord said to the angels, 'Lo, I am about to create a mortal out of clay. When I have shaped him, and breathed into him of My spirit, fall you down before him in adoration.' So the angels fell in adoration all together, except Iblis [i.e. Satan] who became big with pride and proved to be a Kāfir. He [God] said, 'Hast thou become proud (*istakbarta*) [that is, on the spur of the moment] or art thou [naturally] a haughty one (*ʿālī*)?' (XXXVIII, 71–76/71–75)

Sometimes the word *ʿālī* appears in the nominal form *ʿulūw*, the meaning expressed being exactly the same:

When Our signs came to them, plain to see, they said, 'This is mere sorcery.' Thus they denied them, though acknowledging them at bottom, wrongfully and through arrogance (*ʿulūwan*). (XXVII, 13–14)

There is another closely related word *takabbara*—another verbal form derived from the root *KBR*—which is also very often used in the same sort of contexts. As far as we can judge from its actual use in the Qur'ān, this word, particularly in its participial form *mutakabbir*, seems to be used to denote arrogance as a permanent attribute of the Kāfir rather than to describe the momentary outburst of the emotion. It will be worthy of notice that al-Bayḍāwī, commenting on the passage in question explains *ʿālī* by *mutakabbir*.

> I will turn away from My signs those who are puffed up with pride (*yatakabbarūna*, from *takabbara*) in the earth with no right. If they see any sign they believe not therein; and if they see the path of rectitude they take it not for [their] path; but if they see the path of error they take it for [their] path. All this is because they cry lies to Our signs and are ever heedless of them. (VII, 143–144/146)

The next one is particularly important for our purpose because it brings to light the fundamental relationship that joins *shirk*, *kufr*, and *takabbur* into a semantic nexus.

> Chains shall be put on their necks, and fetters, and they shall be dragged into the boiling water, then in the Fire they shall roast. Then it is said to them, 'Where are all those [gods] that you used to associate (*tushrikūna*), besides God?' They shall say, 'They have disappeared. Nay, but [it is clear now that] it was "nothing" that we used to pray to.' Thus does God lead astray the Kāfirs. 'All this is because you exulted (*tafraḥūna*) in the earth without right, and were self-complacent (*tamraḥūna*). Enter the gates of Gehenna, therein to dwell forever.' Evil indeed is the last abode of the arrogant (*mutakabbir*) ones. (XL, 73–76/71–76)

In a similar way, the next quotation discloses the relation of semantic equivalence that exists between the forging of lies (*iftirāʾ al-kadhib*) against God and the attitude of *takabbur* (the forgery of impious lies = arrogance.) And to this, further, is opposed very significantly the 'fear (*taqwá*) of God'.

> On the Day of Resurrection thou shalt see those who lied (*kadhabū*) against God, with their faces all blackened. Is there not in Gehenna final abode for the arrogant (*mutakabbir*) ones? But God shall rescue those who were god-fearing (*ittaqaw*) into a safe refuge, where evil shall not befall them, nor shall they be grieved. (XXXIX, 61–62/60–61)

The same thought may be expressed by an analytic periphrasis containing the semanteme of *KBR* in a purely non-temporal form: *kibr*. Here is an instance of it, which, by the way, interprets the 'wrangling' (*JDL*) about God—to be discussed presently—in terms of 'arrogance' in the heart:

> Those who wrangle (*yujādilūna*) concerning the signs of God without any authority given them, verily, there is in their breasts naught but arrogance (*kibr*). (XL, 58/56)

It goes without saying that *istakbara* is not the only word for the impious haughtiness which has formed the subject matter of the preceding discussion. We have, in effect, already seen instances of such terms in the adjective *ʿālī* and the verb *istankafa*. In old Arabic there are a number of other words that are more or less approximately synonymous with *istakbara* (or *takabbara*). Some of them do appear in the Qurʾān with considerable frequency and serve to spotlight, each in its way, this or that aspect of the phenomenon of human arrogance towards God.

1. *Baghá*. Presumptuousness must of necessity induce one to pass beyond the proper bounds of one's sphere in social life. The verb *baghá* appears to mean basically 'to act unlawfully and unjustly against others' out of an excess of self-conceit. Ibn Isḥāq, referring to the most vehement persecution of the early Muslims by the Meccan idolaters, uses this word in the description of the situation. 'Quraysh grew arrogant (*ʿatā*)[12] towards God, rejected His grace, cried lies to His Prophet, persecuted and exiled those who worshipped Him proclaiming His Oneness, who believed in His Prophet and kept to His religion. So He gave permission to His Apostle to fight and to defend himself against those who did wrong (*ẓalama*) to them and *baghá* against them.'[13] The following are some of the examples of its use in the Qurʾān.

> If God were to spread [i.e. give without measure] His provision to His servants, they would surely become insolent (*baghaw*) in the earth. But He sends down within measure whatever He pleases. (XLII, 26/27)

'They would *baghá*,' that is, to quote the words of al-Bayḍāwī, 'they would become big with pride (*takabbarū*) and work great corruption (*afsadū*) out of insolence (*baṭar*).' This last word will be explained presently. Here we are merely concerned to point out the fact the the famous commentator explains *baghá* by *takabbara*. This interpretation finds a strong confirmation in the following passage:

> Qārūn [i.e. Korah] was of Moses' folk. But he *baghá* against them. because We had given him so much of the treasures that even the

12 For the meaning of this word, see below, pp. 148–149.

13 Ibn Isḥāq, I, 313.

> keys thereof were a burden too heavy for a troop of strong men. When His folk said unto him, 'Do not exult (*tafraḥ*), for, verily, God loves not those who exult. . . . Do good (*aḥsin*), just as God did good to thee. And crave not to work corruption (*fasād*) in the earth, for, verily, God loves not those who work corruption.' He replied, 'What I have been given I owe wholly to my own knowledge.' (XXVIII, 76–78)

Here we see the word *baghá* given, as it were, a contextual interpretation. It is, in the first place, equated with another verb *fariḥa* ('Do not exult', *lā tafraḥ*), meaning 'to be overjoyed at something'. From this it becomes clear that *baghá* refers in particular to the fact of Korah's being exultant in his wealth, being intoxicated with his worldly power. Then, *fasād* 'corruption' is mentioned as a concrete manifestation in behavior of the inner state denoted by *baghá*; the meaning of *fasād* itself is contextually defined in part by being contrasted with *iḥsān* 'doing good', that is, doing works of kindness and charity. In the following verse, the word is applied in its nominal form *baghī* to the conduct of Pharaoh, pursuing Moses and the Israelites.

> Thus We brought the children of Israel across the sea [the Red Sea], and Pharaoh and his hosts came pursuing them in *baghī* and *ᶜadw*, till, when he was about to be drowned, he said, 'I do believe that there is no god but He in whom believe the children of Israel. I am a pious believer [lit. one of those who have surrendered].' 'Now at last? Before this thou hast ever rebelled against [Me], and hast done much corruption.' (X, 90–91; see also VI, 146/145)

The word *ᶜadw* in the text, which appears often in combination with *baghī* roughly means 'to pass beyond one's limit' and thence 'to act wrongfully'. It may be remarked that again the element of *fasād* is introduced into the context. The phrase, 'thou hast ever rebelled' (*ᶜaṣayta*) brings out another shade of meaning contained in *baghī*.

The element of 'violence' or 'outrage' may be best perceived in the following quotation:

> Whoso helps himself after having suffered any wrong (*ẓulm*)[14] [i.e. he who finds himself constrained to have recourse to violence

[14] The fact that *ẓulm* 'wrong-doing' and *baghī* were from the beginning roughly synonymous will best be seen in the following verse of the famous pre-Islamic poet ᶜAntarah: *Udhakkiru qawmī ẓulmahum lī wa-baghyahum * waiq-llat insāfī ᶜalá al-qurb wa-l-buᶜ d* (*Dīwān*, p. 62, v. 5). Here the poet refers to the behavior of his tribesmen who, having been helped so much in the past by ᶜAntarah's sword, insult him by calling him a 'black fellow'. He says: 'I will remind my tribesmen of their *ẓulm* and *baghī* against me, and of the fact that they have treated me so unjustly on all occasions.'

zulm = wronging someone else; oppression

as the means of self-defense]—against such, there is no way [of blame]. The way [of blame] is only against those who do wrong [i.e. who take the initiative in wronging others] and behave insolently (*yabghūna*, from *baghá*) in the earth. For such there is a painful torment. (XLII, 39–40/41–42)

2. *Baṭira.* In the quotation from al-Bayḍāwī, we have just met with this word in its nominal form, *baṭar*. The verb means, roughly, 'to exult (in one's own wealth, for instance) excessively'; it suggests that one exults so excessively that one comes to behave insolently, with boastfulness. The Qurʾān itself does not afford much information about the semantic structure of this word. But the following example will serve to elucidate an important aspect of its meaning:

> How many a city have We destroyed that exulted excessively (*baṭirat*) in its opulence! Look, those are their dwellings, that have been left uninhabited after them, save indeed a little; We Ourselves have inherited them. (XXVIII, 58)

This passage may profitably be compared with that which will be given below as the second of the examples of *ᶜatā* (LXV, 8). It should also be remembered that the expression: 'how many a city have We destroyed that . . .' is almost a cliché for describing the miserable end of the Kāfirs. This shows that we are still in the domain of *kufr*.

3. *ᶜAtā.* This word is one of the synonyms of the *istakbara*, and means approximately 'to be immoderately proud', 'to behave very haughtily', and with the preposition *ᶜan* denoting the movement of turning away 'from' something, means 'to turn away disdainfully from something commanded', 'to revolt against an ordinance'. Judging from many instances of its actual usage, we might perhaps say that *ᶜatā* tends to refer to the concrete, outward manifestations, whether in conduct or expression, of haughtiness, while *istakbara* seems to refer rather to the inner state of haughtiness itself. The first of the following quotations from the Qurʾān would appear to confirm this interpretation.

> Those who expect not the meeting with Us [on the Day of Judgment] say, 'Why is it that the angels are not sent down upon us, or why do we not see our Lord [i.e. if Muḥammad were really God's Apostle]?' How haughty they have grown (*istakbarū*) within themselves, and with what an immoderate arrogance (*ᶜutūwan*, a nominal form derived from the same root as *ᶜatā*) they behave! (XXV, 23/21)

How many a city turned away disdainfully (*ᶜatat*, from *ᶜatā*) from (*ᶜan*) the commandment of its Lord and His Apostles and We settled accounts severely with it and punished it with an unwonted chastisement. (LXV, 8)

But when they turned away disdainfully (*ᶜataw*) from (*ᶜan*) what they had been forbidden, We said to them, 'Be you apes, repelled far away!' (VII, 166)

4. *Ṭaghá.* This verb is another synonym of *istakbara*, which plays an important role in the Qurʾān. Starting from the image of water rising so high as to exceed the bounds and overflow the banks, it came to mean, as a metaphor, the attitude of contumely or rebellious pride. Thus, according to Professor Montgomery Watt, he who *ṭaghá* is a 'man who presses on regardless of obstacles, and especially regardless of moral and religious considerations, who allows nothing to stop him and has unbounded confidence in his own powers', and in the specific contexts of the Qurʾān it denotes 'the absence of a sense of creatureliness, . . . linked with disregard or denial of the Creator.'[15] The Arab philologist, al-Bayḍāwī, in his commentary on Sūrah XXIII, 77 says that *ṭughyān* (nominal form) implies 'an excess in *kufr*, man's being too puffed up with pride (*istikbār*) to accept the Truth, and an open hostility against the Apostle and the believers.'

*Ṭughān* is often used in combination with *kufr*, showing that the two words are almost synonymous:

That which has been sent down unto thee [Muḥammad] is sure to increase many of them [i.e. the Jews] in *ṭughyān* and *kufr*. (V, 69/64; see also 72/68)

As for the boy [killed], his parents were believers and we feared lest he [the boy, who was not 'pure', i.e. irreligious, and was always 'rude' to his parents—cf. verse 80] should impose on them *ṭughyān* and *kufr*. (XVIII, 79/80)

Sometimes *ṭughyān* is given as the immediate cause of *takdhīb*. Note that in the following quotation the word appears in a slightly different form: *ṭaghwá*. The meaning is exactly the same.

[The people of] Thamūd cried lies [to their Apostle] in their *ṭaghwá*, when the most wretched of them rose up [as God's Apostle]. (XCI, 11–12)

*Ṭughyān* is sometimes used in place of *nifāq*, the attitude of those who, when they meet the believers, say, 'We are with you; we believe in God and the Last Day', but, when they are alone 'with their

[15] Watt, p. 67.

Satans', say, 'How shall we believe, as fools do? We have only been mocking.' (II, 13/14) The Qur'ān uses the word *ṭughyān* very aptly to describe this type of malicious conduct.

> God mocks them [i.e. the truth is that it is not they, but God that is mocking], and leaves them to wander blindly in their *ṭughyān*. (II, 14/15)

It is to be noted that 'to wander blindly' (*ʿamaha*) is a verb that appears very frequently in combination with *ṭughyān*, forming thus one of the most usual set phrases in use in the Qur'ān. The precise implication of this set phrase, 'to wander blindly in *ṭughyān*, is brought out more clearly when it is employed to describe the state of those who, well-pleased with the life of the present world, remain utterly heedless of God's signs.

> Verily, those who expect not the meeting with Us and are well-pleased with the life of the present world and are comfortably at home therein, and those who are heedless of Our signs—their dwelling shall be the Fire. . . . But [for the time being] We shall leave those who expect not the meeting with Us wandering blindly in their *ṭughyān*. (X, 7–8, 12/7–8, 11)

In the following passage, 'he who *ṭaghá* and remains attached to the enjoyments of the present life' is directly contrasted with 'him who fears God and restrains his soul from worldly desires'.

> As for him who *ṭaghá* and preferred the life of this world, verily, Hell shall be his dwelling-place. But as for him who lived in fear and awe of the majesty of his Lord and restrained his soul from lust, verily, Paradise shall be his dwelling-place. (LXXIX, 37–41)

In the last-quoted passage reference was made incidentally to the 'fear of God' as an opposite of *ṭughyān*. The word actually used was *khāfa* which literally means 'to be afraid of' and is often used in the Qur'ān synonymously with *taqwá* (or more exactly, with the corresponding verb from the same root, *ittaqá*.) This last word is also sometimes employed actually in the text in such a way as to make a formal contrast to *taghá*. Here is an instance of it:

> For the godfearing (*muttaqīn*, participial form of *ittaqá*) there is prepared a good dwelling-place, Gardens of Eden, the doors whereof are open to them. . . . But, verily, for the *ṭaghīn* (part. pl. of *ṭaghá*) there is prepared an evil dwelling-place, Gehenna, wherein they shall roast. (XXXVIII, 49–50, 55–56)

5. *Istaghná.* Closely related to *ṭaghá* in meaning is the verb *istaghná* which is also used to denote an excess of self-confidence in man.

But of course there is also a considerable difference in semantic structure between the two. In the case of *taghá* the underlying image is, as I noted above, that of water overflowing the banks. *Istaghná* suggests the basic meaning of being rich or wealthy, the root being *GH-N-Y*.

Every reader of the Qur'ān must know that it constantly emphasizes the idea of God being 'rich', *ghanī*, in the sense that He is rich enough to stand all alone, i.e. that He is absolutely independent and self-sufficient. Now in the case of man, the assumption of such self-sufficiency betrays the lack of a sense of creatureliness; it is nothing but presumptuousness and arrogance, involving as it does the denial of God as the Creator. *Istaghná* is the word for this kind of presumptuousness. It literally means 'to consider one's self rich', and consequently 'to put unbounded confidence in one's own power'. It is interesting to note that in the following passage which purports to describe the constitution of human nature in general, these two words appear side by side as almost synonymous:

> Nay, verily, man proves himself to be insolent (*yaṭghá*, from *ṭaghá*), [by the fact] that he regards himself as self-sufficing (*istaghná*). (XCVI, 6–7)

In the next passage from XCII, the parallelism of construction puts this verb *istaghná* in opposition to *ittaqá*, 'to fear God'.

> As for him who gives alms and is godfearing (*Man aʿṭá wa-(i)ttaqá*) and believes as true the best reward to be given him on the Last Day, We shall surely make his way easy to the comfort. But as for him who grudges and regards himself as self-sufficing (*Man bakhila wa-(i)staghná*), and cries lies to the best reward, We shall make his way easy to the Distress. (XCII, 5–11)

The antithetic relationship which is clearly observable here between 'fear of God' with the accompanying attribute of 'open-handedness (in God's way)' and *istaghná* with the accompanying attribute of 'stinginess', would give, particularly in the light of what was said in Chapter V, a very instructive glimpse into the semantic structure of the word *istaghná*.

6. *Jabbār*. He who magnifies himself to such a degree that he considers himself 'rich' enough to stand alone tends naturally to be domineering over his fellows in all affairs, and desires to wield an unlimited tyrannical power over them. *Jabbār* is the word for such a man. In the first example that follows the word qualifies 'heart', not man, but the reference is evidently to the Kāfirs in general. It is

noteworthy that the word appears alongside *mutakabbir*, showing that the two are almost identical in meaning.

> Thus does God put a seal on every insolent (*mutakabbir*) and *jabbār* heart. (XL, 37/35)

In the next example, an important sidelight is thrown on the meaning of *jabbār* by the fact that, besides being reinforced by an adjective meaning 'rebellious', it is contrasted sharply with words implying loving-kindness and piety.

> And We gave him [John, son of Zachariah] discretion when yet a little boy, and grace from Us, and purity; and he was godfearing (*taqī*) and pious (*barr*) towards his parents, and was not insolent (*jabbār*), rebellious (*ʿaṣī*). (XIX, 13–14/12–14)

The following passage furnishes another good example of *jabbār* used in a precisely similar sort of situation. These words are put in the mouth of Jesus.

> He [God] has enjoined upon me prayer and almsgiving so long as I live, and piety towards my mother. He has not made me insolent (*jabbār*), miserable. (XIX, 32–33/31–32)

## Mocking at Revelation

The attitude of 'arrogance' and 'haughtiness', which has been described in the preceding section as typical of those who refuse to believe, may appear in a number of different forms. In fact, all the distinguishable aspects of the phenomenon of *kufr* are nothing but so many manifestations of this basic attitude. Of all of them, however, two concepts stand out in the Qurʾān as most directly connected with the 'arrogance' of the Kāfirs. One is mocking at whatever the Prophet has brought, and the other is contentiousness.

The Qurʾān describes repeatedly the Kāfirs sneering at God and all that He sends down. This mocking attitude is pointed out as most characteristic of them. We have already seen that the people of Jāhilīyah as they are mirrored in the Qurʾān, were characterized by jovial levity and foolish carelessness. We know also already that this carelessness originated in their worldly-mindedness. For those who saw nothing beyond the present earthly life, a religion preaching the eternal future life could in any way be no more than a laughing-stock. The most usual expressions for the mocking attitude of this sort in the Qurʾān are *ittakhadha huzuʾan* ('to take for mockery') and *istahzaʾa* ('to mock at') both deriving from the root *HZʾ*. The quotations that follow are, semantically, of special importance in that they bring out, each in its own way, the close relationship that exists between *shirk-kufr* and *istahzaʾa.*

> Proclaim loudly whatever thou art commanded, and pay no attention to those who 'associate' (*mushrik*). Verily, We defend thee from the mockers (*mustahziʾīn*, participial form of *istahzaʾa*), from those who set up with God other gods. (XV, 94–96)

> Whenever the Kāfirs behold thee, they make a mockery of thee, [saying] 'Is this the fellow who talks [disparagingly] of your gods?' Thus they deny utterly the Reminder of the Merciful God. (XXI, 37/36)

> Such is their recompense: Gehenna, because they acted [in the world] as Kāfirs, making a mockery of My signs and My Apostles. (XVIII, 106)

*Sakhira*, or *istaskhara* (root *S-KH-R*) is another word meaning the same thing as *istahzaʾa*, and is used in the Qurʾān in exactly the same kind of contexts. Just as the connotation of *istahzá* may be 'transposed' analytically by a periphrasis consisting of a verb and a noun: *ittakhadha huzuʾan*, so *sakhira* or *istaskhara* may be analytically replaced by *ittakhahda sikhrīyan*, the latter half of this phrase being a noun derived from the same root *S-KH-R*. The synonymic relationship between *istahzaʾa* and *sakhira* is best recognizable in the first of the following quotations.

> Apostles have been mocked at (*ustuhziʾa*, passive construction) before thee [Muḥammad], those that mocked (*sakhira*) at them [i.e. the Apostles] ended by being surrounded on all sides by that which they used to mock at (*yastahziʾūna*). (VI, 10; see also XXI, 42/41)

> Thou [Muḥammad] art filled with wonder [at God's omnipotence], but they [do nothing but] mock (*yaskharūna*, from *S-KH-R*). When they are reminded, they remember not, and when they see a sign, they mock at it (*yastaskhirūna*), and say, 'This is obviously naught but sorcery.' (XXXVII, 12–15)

> [God will say, on the Day of Judgment, to the Kāfirs in Gehenna], 'Verily, there was a party of My servants who used to say, 'Our Lord, we believe, so forgive us, and have mercy upon us, for Thou art the best of the merciful ones.' You, however, took them for mockery (*ittakhadhtumūhum sikhrīyan*), and in laughing at them you were led to forget My remembrance. (XXIII, 111–112/109–110)

## Contentiousness

The 'haughtiness' of the Kāfirs may take a different, more serious, course in manifesting itself concretely: contentiousness. As we saw above, the Kāfirs are born sceptics and rationalists. They do not surrender easily to the commandments of God transmitted by the Prophet, if they perceive in the revealed words anything discordant with what their Reason acknowledges as true. The theory of the unicity of God, for example, or that of resurrection after death is, to their sceptical minds, simply absurd and unacceptable. Hence their tendency to 'plunge into disputes' concerning God and the prophetic mission of Muḥammad.

The Qurʾān mentions as one of the most characteristic traits of the sceptically minded to be always putting embarrassing questions to the Prophet concerning his mission and wrangling among themselves about the divine Truth.

> Would you go on questioning your Apostle just as Moses was questioned aforetime? But whoso chooses disbelief (*kufr*) instead of belief (*īmān*) has surely gone astray from the right way. (II, 102/108)

Vain arguing or wrangling about God and Revelation is a typical manifestation of *kufr*. The root *JDL*, whose primary meaning is that of 'twisting (things like ropes) tight and firm', presents the fit image for this kind of vehement altercation.

> None wrangle (*yujādilu*, from *JDL*) concerning the signs of God save those who disbelieve (*kafarū*). So let not their bustling in the land deceive thee. The people of Noah before them also used to cry lies, and all the parties thereafter. Every nation wished to seize their Apostle, and wrangled (*jādalū*) with vain discourse, that they might refute thereby the Truth. (XL, 4–5)

> We send not the Apostles save as bearers of good tidings and as warners. But those who disbelieve wrangle with vain discourse, that they might refute thereby the Truth. They take My signs and the warnings given them in mockery. (XVIII, 54/56)

> Amongst men there are those who wrangle (*yujādilu*) concerning God without knowledge, without guidance, and without an illuminating Scripture, turning away to seduce [others] out of the way of God. For such men is ignominy in the present world, and on the Day of Resurrection, We shall make them taste the chastisement of burning. (XXII, 8–9; see also XXXI, 19/20)

Although there is no explicit reference to *kufr* in this quotation, the contextual situation makes it beyond any doubt clear that 'those who wrangle' are no other than typical Kāfirs. The same is true of the following examples, the first of which is of particular interest semantically in that it sees this sort of altercation in its relation to the haughtiness and arrogance of the mind.

> Those who wrangle (*yujādilūna*) concerning the signs of God, without any warrant given them—this is greatly hateful in the sight of God and those who believe. Thus does God put a seal on every insolent and arrogant heart. (XL, 37/35)

> When the son of Mary [Jesus] is mentioned as an example, lo! thy folk turn away from it and say, 'Are our gods better, or is he?' They mention him not to thee, save for wrangling (*jadal*). Nay, but they are an extremely contentious people [the word here rendered as 'extremely contentious' is ***khaṣim*** from *KH-Ṣ-M* meaning one who is particularly fond of wrangling, and tends to be very vehement in dispute]. (XLIII, 57–58)

From innumerable cases of this sort God Himself draws the conclusion that man is the most contentious of all creatures.

> We have verily displayed for men in this Qur'ān all manner of similitudes, and yet [most of them stubbornly refuse to believe]; man is indeed the most contentious of all things (*akthar shay' jadalan*). (XVIII, 52/54)

# VIII. The Semantic Field of *Kufr*

In the preceding chapter I endeavoured to analyze the inner structure of the concept of *kufr* itself. The picture will not be complete, however, unless we consider analytically the other key terms that surround this major concept. The conceptual network formed by these closely related words is what we call the semantic field of *kufr*.

As a matter of fact, *kufr* is not only the most comprehensive term for all negative ethico-religious values recognized as such in the Qurʾān, but it functions as the very center of the whole sytem of 'negative' properties. This would seem to imply that we grasp the real nature of *kufr* only when we know the nature of the elements that go to form the whole system itself. The purpose of the present chapter is to analyze semantically these elements. The key words that will be dealt with are five: (1) *fisq or fusūq* (adj.-nom. *fāsiq*), (2) *fajr* or *fujūr* (adj.-nom. *fājir*), (3) *ẓulm* (adj.-nom. *ẓālim*), (4) *iᶜtidāʾ* (adj.-nom. *muᶜtadī*), and (5) *isrāf* (adj.-nom. *musrif*).

## *Fāsiq* p159 1-6 = elements of a fāsiq

This word is of particular importance from the standpoint of Islamic thought, for, unlike the remaining four, it is destined to play an exceedingly significant role later in theology, as a key technical term having a definite meaning of ***murtakib kabīrah*** 'one who has committed a grave sin'. At the Qurʾanic stage, however, the word has as yet no such technical meaning. This point must be kept in mind when we try to analyze its semantic structure within the Qurʾanic context.

*Fāsiq as a synonym of kāfir*. *Fāsiq*—and, for that matter, the other four terms as well—has much in common in semantic structure with ***kāfir***, so much so that in many cases it proves extremely difficult to make a distinction between them. I shall begin by giving a typical example of ***fāsiq*** used synonymously with ***kāfir***. Thus it is related concerning Abū ʿĀmir, who was a well-known ascetic in Jāhilīyah and had won the by-name of ***rāhib*** 'monk', and who was socially a very influential man in Medina about the time of Hijrah, that he stubbornly refused to the last to believe in Muḥammad's God although most of his tribe accepted the faith of Islām, and even positively abandoned them and went over to Mecca with a few of those who remained faithful to him. Upon this, Muḥammad is said to have remarked, 'Don't call him henceforward the "monk", but call him the *fāsiq*.'[1] Muḥammad might well have used the word ***kāfir*** instead of *fāsiq*. Indeed, this little piece of tradition gives us an important clue as to what type of conduct deserves the use of this word from the standpoint of Islām, but as to the distinction to be drawn between ***kufr*** and ***fisq*** it furnishes practically no information, except perhaps that it suggests that the distinction, if there be any, must be one of degree rather than of quality. It would appear, in other words, that ***kufr***, when it exceeds a certain degree, turns into ***fisq***: that is, ***fisq*** is a higher degree of ***kufr***, and *fāsiq*—one who is characterized by the quality of ***fisq***—is a very stubborn kind of ***kāfir***, as al-Bayḍāwī remarks in his commentary.

The most commonly accepted view is that ***fisq*** means ***khurūj ʿan al-ṭāʿah***, lit. 'going out of obedience', i.e. 'disobeying God's commands', and that, therefore, *fāsiq* is a term of wider application than ***kāfir***; anybody who disobeys God in any sense may be called *fāsiq*, while ***kāfir*** has a much more restricted sense. This may be true, but it tells almost nothing concrete about the semantic structure of ***fisq*** as it is actually used in the Qurʾān.

In any case, all we can say at this stage of analysis is that *fāsiq* is synonymous with ***kāfir***. Before turning to more concrete conditions of its use, I should like to quote here a verse in which ***kufr*** and ***fisq*** are almost completely equated with each other.

[1] Ibn Isḥāq, I, 411.

Verily, We have sent down upon thee (Muḥammad] signs, tokens manifest, and none will disbelieve (*yakfuru*) therein save the *fāsiqūn* (pl. of *fāsiq*). (II, 93/99)

*Discordance between words and deeds.* Apparently, the next example throws no further light on this problem, for it is obvious that it does nothing but confirm the equivalence between *fisq* and *kufr*.

Verily, they disbelieved (*kafarū*) in God and His Apostle, and died as *fāsiqūn*. (IX, 85/84)

What is implied here is that *fisq* is a state resulting from one's having acted in a *kāfir* way towards God and the Prophet. When, however, we give somewhat closer attention to this quotation by placing it back in the concrete context from which it has been taken, it becomes clear at once that it refers to those who, though usually making a great show of religious zeal as 'good Muslims', betray their real selves by declining on some pretext or other to take part in the common cause of *jihād*, the Holy War, being averse to stake their life and possessions on such a precarious matter. This principle of 'all talk and no action', the lip devotion followed by downright betrayal by behavior, would seem to be the element which plays a decisive role in the Qurʾanic verses in determining the characteristic trait of a *fāsiq*. The following words that are put in the mouth of Moses present a further example of the use of this term in an exactly similar sort of situation:

He said, 'My Lord, I have verily no command except over myself and my brother [Aaron]. Therefore do divide between us and these *fāsiq* people.' (V, 28/25)

This he says to God when his people, who have hitherto followed him, suddenly declare that they refuse to fight against enormous odds in spite of his encouraging words, 'Enter the gate against them! If you enter it, you are sure to win the battle. Put your trust in God, if you are really believers!' In the last analysis, this, too, is doubtless a manifestation of *kufr*, but there is added to it a special nuance, so to speak, which makes it semantically rather closer to *nifāq* 'religious hypocrisy' than pure *kufr*. And, in effect, we have an instance affirming formally and openly that the 'hypocrites' are people of *fisq*.

Verily, the hypocrites are *fāsiq* people. (IX, 68/67)

The passage that follows also concerns the rich who pay lip-service to Muḥammad to please him, but, when it comes to endangering their lives and possessions, turn their back on him and do not participate in the Holy War.

> They will swear to you so that you may be pleased with them. But even if you are pleased with them, God will never be pleased with the *fāsiq* people. (IX, 97/96)

The same is true of the following example which is taken from the same Sūrah. I give it here because it enumerates in detail those elements that are liable to drive the wavering believers from the way of faith into the vice of *fisq*.

> If your fathers, your sons, your brothers, your wives, your tribe, and the wealth you have accumulated, and the trade for which you fear depression, and the dwellings you are so contented with—if [these things] are dearer to you than God and His Apostle and fighting in His way, then wait till God brings His command to pass. God will never guide the *fāsiq* people. (IX, 24)

Again in the same Sūrah (49–60), we have a still more detailed description of the main traits of the *fāsiq*. Instead of quoting the lengthy passage here, I shall content myself with summarizing the *fāsiq*-making characteristics that can be gathered from the text.

1. The *fāsiq* swear by God that they are on the side of the believers. This they only do because they are afraid of the military power of the Muslims.
2. At bottom they are disbelievers (*kāfir*), and they will continue being such until their souls depart in the state of *kufr*.
3. Their *kufr*-nature is betrayed by their conduct: they come to worship only idly, and they do not expend of their wealth in the way of God save reluctantly. Concerning this point, Muḥammad is commanded to declare to them, 'Whether you expend willingly or unwillingly, it shall not be accepted from you, for you are surely a *fāsiq* people!'
4. When pressed to behave more piously, they say, 'Leave me alone and do not tempt me.'
5. If some good fortune befalls Muḥammad, they get annoyed, but if some evil befalls him, they rejoice and leave him exultantly.
6. They are always grumbling about the way alms are divided; if they are given a share they are satisfied, if not, they get angry. They forget or ignore that the alms are collected to be used in aid of the poor and needy and that they, being of the wealthier class, have no claim to any share.

As far as we can gather from this description, a *fāsiq* is not a downright *kāfir*, for, nominally at least, he is in the camp of the Muslims. Only, he is a wavering, very unreliable kind of a Muslim who tends to reveal his *nifāq*-nature on every occasion.

So a fāsiq performs actions of a nifaq-nature and leaves the world in a state of kufr??

*Disloyalty or treachery.* The *nifāq*-nature of these people comes out prominently in matters involving faithfulness to any bond or treaty they happen to have made. The first of the following examples discloses particularly well this relationship between their readiness to say whatever may please Muḥammad and his followers and their absolute disregard for all duty of loyalty.

> If they chance to have the upper hand of you, they will not observe towards you any pact or bond. They try to satisfy you with their mouths, while their hearts refuse, for most of them are but *fāsiqūn*. (IX, 8)

> We found no [loyalty to a] covenant in most of them. Nay, we found most of them *fāsiqūn*. (VII, 100/102)

> Then whosoever after this [i.e. after having made a solemn covenant with God to bear His load whatever might happen] turns away—these are the *fāsiqūn*. (III, 76/82)

> The *fāsiqūn* who break the covenant of God after having entered into it, and sever what God has commanded to be joined, and work corruption in the earth—these shall be the losers. (II, 25/27)

In Sūrah XLIII, 45–55/46–55, we find *fisq* predicated of the Pharaoh and his people. The reason for this is as follows. God sent Moses with His clear signs to them and let him declare, 'I am the Apostle of the Lord of the worlds.' They only laughed at the divine signs. When, however, God seized them with the painful torment, they addressed Moses saying, 'O thou wizard, entreat for us thy Lord by the covenant He has made with thee. We promise, we will surely turn to the right way.' But when God removed from them the torment, they broke their word without the slightest compunction. Pharaoh, moreover, proclaimed among his people, 'O my people, am I not the lord of Egypt, with these rivers flowing under me? Can you not see? I am better than this contemptible fellow who can hardly make himself understood.' And thus he made his people waver, and finally they obeyed him. The conclusion drawn from this is:

> Verily they were a *fāsiq* people (v. 54)

*Acting against God's Will.* To act against God's Will, whether in the sense of violating a ban or in that of not carrying out a command given, is often denounced in the Qurʾān as *fisq* worthy of the most severe punishment. Sometimes this goes a step further and then *fisq* appears to denote the object of divine abhorrence itself.

> When We ordered the angels, 'Bow in reverence to Adam', they all bowed, save Iblis, who was one of the jinn. He *fasaqa* against (i.e. committed *fisq* against, or, disobeyed) the command of his Lord. (XVIII, 48/50)

This example makes it undeniably clear that *fisq* in certain contexts denotes nonperformance of what has been commanded by God. The following one concerns precisely the contrary case: doing what has been prohibited.

> When you traffic with each other, you should have witnesses. Let not either scribe or witness be compelled [to do anything wrong]. If you do this, it is *fusūq* (=*fisq*) in you. You should fear God. (II, 282)

'What God has prohibited' means naturally what He has found abominable, detestable. Hence *fisq* appears sometimes to come very near the meaning of 'an abomination (in the eyes of God)'. In the Qurʾān the game of *maysir* (a kind of gambling by divining arrows), eating what has been hallowed to other than God, sodomy, slandering and the like, are all called *fisq*.

> Eat not of that whereon God's name has not been pronounced at the time of slaughtering. Verily, it is an abominable act (*fisq*). (VI, 121)

> Verily, We are about to send down upon the people of this city [Sodom] wrath from heaven because of that they have committed *fisq* [meaning sodomy]. (XXIX, 33/34)

> Those who accuse [of fornication] virtuous women but bring not four witnesses . . . those are *fāsiqūn*. (XXIV, 4)

*Fisq as opposed to īmān.* Speaking more generally, all acts that point to the underlying *kufr* as opposed to *īmān* (belief or faith) may be called *fisq*. Thus in the two following examples we see *fāsiq* directly opposed to the believer.

> If they [people of the Scripture] had really believed in God and the Prophet and that which has been revealed to him, they would not have taken these [idolaters] for their friends. But [the truth is that] many of them are *fāsiqūn*. (V, 84/81)

Here, it is clear, the 'people of the Scripture', in this case the Jews, are called *fāsiqūn* because 'they do not really believe in God and Revelation', the undeniable evidence of that being the fact that 'they are on friendly terms with the idolaters.'

*people of the Scripture = Jews*

Had the people of the Scripture believed, it would have been better for them. True, there are a few believers among them, but most of them are *fāsiqūn*. (III, 106/110)

The same state of affairs is described in somewhat different terms in the next passage. Note that the expression 'their hearts have hardened' is, as we saw earlier, a standing phrase for the stubbornness peculiar to the Kāfirs, while 'humbleness of heart' is one of the distinguishing marks of a true believer.

Is it not high time that the hearts of those who believe should become humble to the remembrance of God and what Truth He has sent down, and that they should no longer be like those who were given the Scripture formerly? They became impatient of delay, and their hearts have grown hard, so that many of them are *fāsiqūn*. (LVII, 15/16)

As *īmān* means to follow the guidance of God and thus to go the right way, he who does not do so is a *fāsiq*.

We sent Noah and Abraham [as Our Apostles] and put the Prophethood and Revelation among their seed. And of them there are some who are well-guided (*muhtadī*), but many of them are *fāsiqūn*. (LVII, 26)

For a similar reason, 'to forget God' is to commit *fisq*. It will be noteworthy that the following verse accounts for this matter in this way: him who forgets God, God in His turn induces to forget his own soul so that he may become a *fāsiq*.

Be you not like those who forgot God, and whom He caused to forget their own souls. These are the *fāsiqūn*. (LIX, 19)

We might add that in Sūrah X, 34/33, the phrase *alladhīna fasaqū*, i.e. those who commit *fisq*, is applied to the idolaters (*mushrikūn*) who 'associate other gods' with God. Thus it is clear that *shirk* also is a case of *fisq*.

*So fisq encompasses acts of kufr???*

## Fājir

*What's the relationship kufr/fisq/shirk (etc)*

Unlike *fāsiq*, which we have been considering, the word *fājir* (*fajr*, *fujūr*) does not become later a technical term in Islamic theology. In this particular sense, it has no post-Qur'anic history. But, of course, as an ordinary, non-technical moral term, it continues to play in post-Qur'anic literature the same important role as it used to do in Jāhilīyah. And sometimes in theology, we find the word used to designate the 'negative' category within the concept of *mu'min*, 'believer', as opposed to the 'positive' category which is designated by the word *barr*. Here, *fājir* refers to a believer who conducts himself badly, who, for instance, commits the sin of drinking wine.

In *al-Fiqh al-Akbar* attributed to Abū Ḥanīfah, for example, we read: *al-ṣalāt khalfa kull barr wa-fājir min al-muʾminīn jāʾizah*, which means 'Prayer behind a "believer" *muʾmin* is permissible, whether he be "of good conduct" *barr* or "of bad conduct" *fājir*.'[2] Here, as is evident, *fājir* is a 'man of bad conduct', and yet he is still counted as a member of the Muslim community. In the Qurʾān there is as yet no such definite semantic delimitation.

In fact, the Qurʾān does not furnish much information concerning this word except perhaps that it is roughly synonymous with *kāfir*. The underlying meaning is said to be that of 'deviating'; thence it comes to mean metaphorically 'to depart from the (right) way' and then, 'to do an immoral deed'. It is interesting to note in this connection that in one passage the verb *fajara* seems even to do precisely the job which is usually assigned to *kafara*: that of denoting refusal to believe in the eschatological teaching of Islām about Resurrection.

> Eh, does man think that We shall not be able to assemble his bones? Yea, We are able to reshape even his finger tips. Nay, but man desires to disbelieve (*yafjura*) in what lies so far ahead, asking 'When will be that Day of Resurrection?' (LXXV, 3–6)

There is, indeed, some uncertainty as to whether the above interpretation of the phrase, *yafjura amāmahu* be right. If it *is* right—and it is possible that it *is*—then *amāmahu* (lit. 'what is before him') would refer to the occurrence of Resurrection, and this would be quite of a piece with the context. Another passage may well be cited as affording a striking confirmation of the view here taken. In it we see *takdhīb* of the Day of Judgment mentioned as the characteristic mark of all *fājirs*.

> Nay, indeed, the record of the *fujjār* (pl. of *fājir*) is in *Sijjīn*. . . . Woe upon that day [i.e. on the Day of Judgment] unto those who cry lies to the Day of Judgment! None cries lies to it save every sinful *muʿtadī*.[3] (LXXXIII, 7–12)

In the following verse *fujūr* (nominal form of *fajara*) is formally contrasted with *taqwá* 'the fear of God' with which we are by now quite familiar:

> By the soul, and Him who fashioned it, and inspired into it *fujūr* or *taqwá*. (XCI, 7–8)

[2] As given in *Shuruḥ al-Fiqh al=Akbar*, comm. no. 1 wrongly attributed to al Māturīdī, 2nd pr., Hyderabad-Dn., 1365, p. 53; also A. J. Wensinck, *The Muslim Creed* (Cambridge, 1932), p. 192, Art. 13.

[3] For this word see below, pp. 172–174.

This verse asserts that God, in creating each human soul, inspires into it either the spirit of pious fear or its contrary, *fujūr*. This alone tells us a great deal about the semantic structure of the latter word: at least it strongly suggests that the meaning of *fujūr* has much to do with that aspect of *kufr* which is directly opposed to the fear of God. In fact, the word *fājir* appears sometimes alongside of *kāfir* in the Qur'ān.

> Noah said, 'My Lord, leave not upon the earth the *kāfir*, not even one of them! If thou shouldst leave them, they will mislead Thy servants, and will beget only *fājir-kaffār* (emphatic form of *kāfir*).' (LXXI, 27–28/26–27)

> Some faces on that day [i.e. the Day of Resurrection] shall be illumined, laughing, beaming with joy. And some faces on that day, covered with dust, overspread with darkness—these are the *kafarah* (pl. of *kāfir*)-*fajarah* (pl. of *fājir*). (LXXX, 38–42)

Finally, I shall quote a passage in which *fājir* is opposed to *bārr*. The same conceptual opposition of *fājir* and *bārr* (or *barr*) we already met with above in the quotation from *al-Fiqhal-Akbar*. There we translated *fājir* 'of bad conduct' and *barr* 'of good conduct'. Within the Qur'anic context, however, *bārr* has a more complex semantic structure. We shall deal with it in Chapter XI. For the time being we may be content with saying that the word describes the characteristic quality of a man who is particularly obedient to God, who, moreover, manifests his pious nature by behaving with extraordinary kindness and affection towards all his neighbors, whether kindred or strangers. The men of this type naturally go to Paradise. The *fujjār*, who represent the opposite type, go to Hell.

barr

> Verily, the *abrār* (pl. of *bārr*) shall be in [Heavenly] bliss, while the *fujjār* (another pl. form of *fājir*) shall be in the Fire, to roast therein on the Day of Judgment, nor shall they ever be removed therefrom. (LXXXII, 13–16)

## *Ẓālim*

The word *ẓālim*, as we have often seen, is generally translated in English as 'wrong-doer' or 'evil-doer', and the corresponding nominal form *ẓulm* variously as 'wrong', 'evil', 'injustice', and 'tyranny'. The root plays an exceedingly important role in the Qur'ān. It is not too much to say that it is one of the most important negative value words in the Qur'ān. Indeed, we encounter the root on almost every page of the Scripture under a variety of forms.

The primary meaning of *ZLM* is, in the opinion of many of the authoritative lexicographers, that of 'putting in a wrong place'. In the sphere of ethics it seems to mean primarily 'to act in such a way as to transgress the proper limit and encroach upon the right of some other person.' Briefly and generally speaking, *ẓulm* is to do injustice in the sense of going beyond one's own bounds and doing what one has no right to. It is very interesting to note in this connection that the Qurʾān repeats everywhere that God does not wrong (*yaẓlim*, a verb form of *ẓulm*) anyone 'even by the weight of an ant' or 'by a single date-thread'.[4] In one passage God Himself declares that He will never wrong the believers.

> I do absolutely no wrong [lit: I am not a *ẓallām*, an emphatic form of *ẓālim*] to My servants! (L, 28/29)

The 'wrong', in the case of God, refers mostly to the Last Judgment; in other words, and in more concrete terms, it consists in God's paying every soul in full according to its deeds on earth. A good deed He will double, a bad deed He will punish; in any case man will never be wronged.

> Today [this is said on the very Day of Judgment] each soul shall be rewarded according to that which it has earned. There shall be no wrong (*ẓulm*) on this day. (XL, 17)

> Fear a day in which you will be brought back to God. Then, each soul shall be paid in full that which it has earned, and they shall not be wronged (*yuẓlamūna*, pass. construction). (II, 281)

> If only thou couldst see when the angels bring to death the Kāfirs, beating them on their faces and their backs, 'Taste you the chastisement of burning. All this is on account of what your hands have sent on before. You see, God is no *ẓallām* towards His servants.' (VIII, 52–53/50–51)

God's punishment may visit a community of men even before the Day of Judgment, in this very world. The numerous ruins of cities that flourished in ancient times are regarded as visible 'signs' of the dreadful wrath of God. But in such cases, too, God is said to have destroyed the cities only when their inhabitants fully deserved it, and that only after He had repeatedly given them warnings through His Apostles. For if He had punished men while they were doing right, or—in the case of the wrong-doers—without warning, He would have acted unjustly (*bi-ẓulm*, lit. 'with *ẓulm*')

> Thy Lord would never destroy towns with *ẓulm*, while their people were doing good deeds (*muṣliḥūn*).[5] (XI, 119/117)

[4] See for instance IV, 44/40; 52/49.

[5] From the root *ṢLḤ*; see below, Chapter XI, pp. 204–207.

> Thy Lord would never destroy towns with *ẓulm*, while their people were heedless [i.e. without giving warnings beforehand]. (VI, 131)

Thus men are made to bear the consequences of their own deeds. Even the torment of the Fire which all evil-doers are to suffer will after all be of their own making. Hence the concept of *ẓulm al-nafs* (lit. 'wronging of the soul', i.e. 'doing wrong to one's own soul, or one's self') which we find expressed very frequently in the Qurʾān in connection with that of the divine chastisement of evil-doers. 'God wrongs nobody; man wrongs himself.'

> Whoso does that [i.e. transgresses the limits set by God] has wronged his soul [or himself] (*ẓalama nafsahu*). (II, 231)

> As for the Kāfirs, their wealth shall be of no avail at all, nor their children, against God. They are the fellows of the Fire, dwelling therein forever. The likeness of what they spend in this life of the world is as the likeness of wind, ice-cold, that smites the tilth of a people who have wronged themselves, and damages it. God wrongs them not, but they wrong themselves. (III, 112–113/116–117)

Coming down now from the sphere of God's activity to that of human conduct, we may remark, to begin with, that the occurrence of *ẓulm* is possible in two different directions: (1) from man to God, and (2) from man to man. In the first direction, *ẓulm* consists in man's transgressing the limits of human conduct imposed by God Himself, while in the second, it is to go beyond the bounds of proper conduct in social life, recognized as such by the society, though, as a matter of actual fact, it proves extremely difficult or even impossible to distinguish between the two directions, for God in the Qurʾanic conception interferes in the minutest details of human affairs. Thus in Sūrah XII, the Chapter of Joseph, 75, the committing of a theft is assessed in purely human terms, as a case of *ẓulm*.

> 'This shall be the penalty. He in whose bag the goblet is found shall be the penalty [i.e. he shall pay the penalty by allowing himself to be detained]. We [Egyptians] are accustomed to requite the *ẓālim* in this way.' (XII, 75)

But in Sūrah V, 43/38, we find the same sort of act talked of as a case of *ẓulm* committed against God.

> But whoso repents after his wrong-doing (*ẓulm*) [which means here contextually the act of stealing], and makes amends, verily, God will turn towards him [i.e. forgive his sin]. Lo, God is forgiving, merciful.

In the Qur'ān, the rules of human conduct in society as established by God and imposed upon men, are called 'the bounds of God' *ḥudūd Allāh*. He who remains all his life within the God-made bounds will be allowed to enter, on the Day of Judgment, Gardens beneath which rivers flow, while he who transgresses His bounds (*yataʿadda ḥudūdahu*) will be thrown into the Fire, to dwell therein forever. (IV, 17/13)

> These [i.e. all the minute rules regulating divorce] are the bounds of God. Transgress them not. All those who transgress the bounds of God—they are the *ẓālimūn*. (II, 229)

The same thing may also be expressed in terms of *ẓulm al-nafs* to which reference has been made.

> These are the bounds of God, and whoso transgresses the bounds of God has wronged himself. (LXV, 1)

God's Will is unfathomably deep, and it is not for the human mind to probe it to its depths and to understand how and why it works as it does. So it comes about very frequently that the reason for a particular 'bound' remains an unsolvable mystery to men. A 'bound' is there simply because God has so decreed. Such is, for instance, the case with the Biblical image of the Tree in the Garden: We said, 'O Adam, dwell thou, and thy wife, in the Garden, and eat freely thereof wherever you like. But draw not nigh this Tree; if you do, you will be of the *ẓālim*.' (II, 33/35)

There are, however, many cases in which the setting of a 'bound' is understandable in terms of the social welfare; this occurs when the particular 'bound' is clearly calculated to produce some direct benefit to the life of people in a community. Thus God decrees in the Qur'ān that there should be no usury, and He designates usury by the name of *ẓulm*: 'without wronging (*lā taẓlimūna*), and without being wronged (*lā tuẓlamūna*)'. (II, 279). In Sūrah IV, after a description in full detail of the rules concerning inheritance (vv. 12–16/11–12), it is declared: 'These are the bounds of God. Whoso obeys God and His Apostle, He will admit him into gardens beneath which rivers flow . . . but whoso disobeys God and His Apostle and transgresses His bounds, He will admit him into a Fire, to dwell therein forever.' (vv. 17–18/13–14) The rules concerning divorce, which I have just referred to, may be taken as another example.

> O Prophet, when you divorce women, divorce them after they have reached the determined term. Calculate the term, and fear God your Lord. Do not drive them out of their houses, nor let them go unless they commit a manifest indecency. These are the

> bounds of God, and whoso transgresses the bounds of God has wronged himself. (LXV, 1)

It will be easy to see that the 'bounds' of this kind are destined to develop later into the Law of Islām.

But 'bounds' may be understood in a much wider sense. Then the word *ẓulm*, as 'transgression of a bound', would denote, as suggested at the outset, any kind of human act that goes beyond the proper limit and encroaches on the right of others. It is extremely interesting to remark here that *ẓulm* in this sense may very well represent the point of view of the idolaters; in one passage, namely, the violence done by the believers to idols is described, from the standpoint of idol-worshippers, as a flagrant case of *ẓulm*.

> Then he [Abraham] broke them [the idols] into pieces. . . . They said, 'Who dared to do this with our gods? Surely he is a *ẓālim*.' (XXI, 59–60/58–59)

Thus to practice an act of *ẓulm* is to hurt someone seriously without any conceivable reason. So in the last analysis *ẓulm* is essentially relative to the standpoint one takes from which to look at the matter. In the passage just quoted the destruction of the idols constitutes a piece of *ẓulm* because, viewed from the angle of the polytheists, there is no reason at all why this should be done, while from that of the believers the same act would be amply justifiable. In similar fashion, the expulsion of Muslims from their homes by the Kāfirs only because they, i.e. the Muslims, say, 'Our Lord is God', is, for them, an undeniable act of *ẓulm*, being justified by no conceivable reason. From the standpoint of the Kāfirs, however, the Islamic belief in One God provides abundant reason for their behaving towards the believers in that way.

> Sanction is given to those who take up arms because they have been wronged (*ẓulimū*) . . . who have been expelled from their homes without any legitimate reason (*bi-ghayr ḥaqq*) only because they say, 'Our Lord is God.' (XXII, 40–41/39–40)

In the same way, Muslims would be wrong-doers (*ẓālim*) if they should repulse the poor brethren for the sole reason that they are poor, because that does not in any way constitute a reason.

> Drive not away those [poor believers] who call upon their Lord at morn and evening, desiring His countenance. No responsibility for them is upon thee, and no responsibility for thee is upon them, that thou shouldst drive them away and become one of the *ẓālim*. (VI, 52)

In another passage, the Muslims are admonished against doing wrong (*ẓulm*) by 'devouring' without a justifiable reason the property of orphans entrusted to their care.

> Verily, those who devour the property of orphans wrongfully (*ẓulman*), they do but devour fire in their bellies; they shall be exposed to burning flames. (IV, 11/10)

Chiefly, however, the word is employed in the Qurʾān from the standpoint of the Muslims, and naturally, it has most to do there with the characteristic conduct of the Kāfirs towards God and the believers.

Let us begin with the case in which *ẓulm* is used almost synonymously with *kufr*. We may point out in passing that al-Bayḍāwī, commenting on the word *ẓālim* that occurs in Sūrah VI, 136/135 in the place of *kāfir*, remarks that the former is 'more general and more comprehensive in meaning' than the latter.

> How shall God guide a people who disbelieved (*kafarū*) after having once believed and testified to the truth of the Apostle, to whom clear signs came? God guides not *ẓālim* people. (III, 80/86)

We often find some of the most characteristic traits of *kufr* classified in the category of *ẓulm*. Thus, he who only listens to Revelation mockingly and calls the Apostle a magician or poet is sometimes labeled *ẓālim* instead of *kāfir*.

> There never comes unto them a new reminder [i.e. Revelation] from their Lord but they listen to it while playing, with their hearts distracted. They confer secretly, those wrong-doers (*alladhīna ẓalamū*), saying, 'Is [not] this aught but a mortal like yourselves? What, will you go to magic when you can see?' . . .
>
> They say, 'A jumble of nightmares! Nay, he has forged it. Nay, he is a poet.' (XXI, 2–3, 5)
>
> Who is more *ẓālim* than he who, being reminded of the signs of his Lord, turns away therefrom and forgets what his own hands have sent forward [to the Day of Judgment]? (XVIII, 55/57)

*Takdhīb*, or 'crying lies to God's signs', which we discussed above as one of the most characteristic aspects of *kufr*, belongs naturally to the sphere of *ẓulm*. One example may suffice.

> Evil is the likeness of the people who have cried lies to the signs of God, for God guides not the *ẓālim* people. (LXII, 5)

The same is true also of the vice of *iftirāʾ* 'forging a lie (against God)' which has already been discussed in detail. *Takdhīb* is to call the

Truth brought by somebody else a lie, while *iftirā*ʾ is to invent a lie. In some cases, the two appear side by side in one and the same verse and are labeled altogether as *ẓulm*.

> Who is more *ẓālim* than he who forges a lie against God or cries lies to His signs? Verily, the *ẓālim* shall not prosper. (VI, 21)

> Who is more *ẓālim* than he who forges a lie against God and cries lies to the Truth, when it reaches him? (XXXIX, 33/32)

The following quotation furnishes an ideal example describing with a touch of realism the characteristic conduct of such 'forgers'.

> Who is more *ẓālim* than he who forges a lie against God, or says, 'I have received a divine revelation', when naught has been revealed to him, and he who says, 'I will reveal the like of that which God has revealed?' If only thou couldst see when these *ẓālimūn* (pl.) are in the throes of death. (VI, 93)

*Ẓālim* also are those who 'plunge deeply into God's signs', a cliché for religious scepticism which brings into the domain of pure faith vain arguing or wrangling about God and His Revelation. That this type of scepticism is usually called *kufr* I have already explained in detail.[6] In the following passage those people are called *ẓālim*.

> When thou [Muḥammad] seest those who plunge into [cavilling at] Our signs, turn away from them until they begin to plunge into some other subject. Or if Satan should make thee forget, sit not, after thou hast remembered, with the *ẓālim* people. (VI, 67/68)

Similarly, 'he whose heart is hardened' is, we have seen, a standing phrase for a Kāfir. In Sūrah XXII 52/53, such men, too, are called *ẓālim*.

We know also that the malignant policy of obstructing the path of God is highly characteristic of the Kāfirs. All acts of intriguing against the Prophet and his followers belong in the category of *ẓulm* as it does in the category of *kufr*.

> Who is more *ẓālim* than he who obstructs the places of worship of God, that His name be not mentioned therein, and endeavors to destroy them? (II, 108/114)

Sometimes we find the two concepts occurring side by side in one and the same passage:

6 See above, Chapter VII, 'Contentiousness', pp. 154–155.

The curse of God is surely on the *ẓālimīn* who debar [men] from the way of God and desire to make it crooked, while in the Hereafter they do disbelieve (*kāfirūn*). (XI, 21–22/18–19; see also VII, 42–43/44–45)

Verily, those who disbelieve (*kafarū*) and obstruct the way of God; they have strayed far astray. Verily, those who disbelieve and do wrong (*ẓalamū*), God will not forgive them. (IV, 165–166/167–168)

Concerning the Golden Calf of Moses' people, to which reference has been made more than once, it is written:

'Moses came unto you [children of Israel] with manifest signs, but you worshipped the Calf in his absence, and you were *ẓālim*.' . . . They were made to drink deep the [spirit of the] Calf into their hearts because of their *kufr*. (II, 86–87/92–93)

It is not only those who are Kāfirs themselves that are accused of *ẓulm*, but even those who take Kāfirs for friends—and that even if they be their own fathers or brothers—are denounced as *ẓālim*. Note that this attitude implies the most radical break with the social pattern of Jāhilīyah based on the natural bond of kinship by blood.

O believers, take not your fathers nor your brothers for friends if they prefer disbelief (*kufr*) to belief (*īmān*). Whoso of you take such ones for friends, those are the *ẓālimūn* (pl.). (IX, 23)

If, as we have just seen, *kufr* in all its aspects may be classified under *ẓulm*, it is quite natural that we find *shirk* 'polytheism' in the Qurʾān often mentioned as a case of *ẓulm*. Thus in one passage, Loqman the Wise says to his son, admonishing him:

'O my son, associate none with God. Verily, association (*shirk*) is a great *ẓulm*.' (XXXI, 12/13)

Here we find *ẓulm* directly predicated of idolatry. The next example is semantically no less important in that it brings out the triple relationship between *kufr*, *shirk*, and *ẓulm*.

They surely are Kāfirs who say, 'God is the Messiah, son of Mary.' For the Messiah [himself] said, 'O children of Israel, worship God [alone], my Lord and your Lord.' Verily, whoso ascribes unto God associates, God has surely forbidden Paradise unto him, and his final abode shall be the Fire. For the *ẓālimīn* there shall be no helpers. (V, 76/72)

Of men there are such as take unto themselves rivals to God, and love them with a love [which is suitable only for God. . . . Ah if only those who do wrong (*ẓalamū*) saw, in the face of the chastisement, that the supreme power belongs entirely to God. (II, 160/165)

We have seen above that the folk of Moses who made out of their ornaments the Golden Calf as an object of worship—which is nothing but *shirk*—are accused of having committed a *ẓulm*.

They took it [i.e. the Calf] and they became *ẓālim*. (VII, 147/148)

Similarly, *fisq*, which constituted the topic of the first section of the present chapter, appears in a parallel expression to that of *ẓulm*. Mention is made of Moses' folk who dared to distort a revealed saying in order to ridicule it and changed it into something which, though similar in outward form, is essentially different from the original. Those who did this are said to have *yaẓlimūn* 'done wrong' (VII, 162). In the next verse people who broke the Sabbath are labeled *fisq*-doers (VII, 163).

## *Muᶜtadī*

*Muᶜtadī* is a participial form of the verb *iᶜtadá* which means approximately 'to pass beyond one's proper limit', and thence 'to act aggressively and unjustly against someone.' It will be easy to see that this word and the preceding one, *ẓulm*, have large common areas of meaning. Indeed, in many important cases, the word *muᶜtadī* behaves as a perfect synonym of *ẓālim*. Take, for instance, the following verse:

Fight in the way of God with those who fight with you, but transgress (*taᶜtadū*, from *iᶜtadá*) not. Verily, God loves not the transgressors (*muᶜtadīn*, pl.). (II, 186/190)

The words 'transgress not', put in a more concrete way, would mean, 'Do not challenge your enemy to a fight from your side.' Substantially the same thought might very well have been expressed in terms of *ẓulm* (as in Sūrah XXII, 40/39–40, cited above).

This close semantic relationship between *ẓulm* and *iᶜtadá* is more directly brought to light by another example. In the formula of testimony which we find given in Sūrah V, 106/107, to be used by those who attend in the capacity of legal witnesses to the bequeathing of property, it is stated most clearly that one's being a *ẓālim* is an immediate result of one's having 'transgressed'. The passage runs as follows:

Let them swear by God, 'Our testimony is more reliable than their testimony. We never transgress (*iᶜtadaynā*), for then we should surely be of the *ẓālim*.'

It may profitably be recalled here that an important aspect of *ẓulm* consists in transgressing 'the bounds of God'. The word *iʿtadá*, too, is used in this sense in exactly similar situations. The following are some of the examples.

> You know of those among you who transgressed (*iʿtadaw*) the Sabbath so that We said unto them 'Be ye apes, driven away!' (II, 61/65)

Commenting on a similar phrase—'they transgress, or break, (*yaʿdūna*) the Sabbath'—that occurs in Sūrah VII, 163 al-Bayḍāwī remarks that it means: they go beyond the bounds of God by catching fish on the day of Sabbath. Of the same kind are the following two instances.

> God has forgiven what is past [i.e. what was done in the pre-Islamic days when God's 'bounds' were not known yet], but whoso transgresses (*iʿtadá*) after this [i.e. after the promulgation of God's 'bounds' regulating the minute details of right conduct during the period of pilgrimage], for him there shall be a painful chastisement. (V, 96/95)

> O believers, do not make unlawful the good things which God has made lawful for you; transgress (*taʿtadū*) not; verily God loves not the transgressors (*muʿtadīn*, pl.). (V, 89/87)

'Lawful' (*ḥalāl*) and 'unlawful' (*ḥarām*) are two important terms, belonging to the older layer of taboo-language, that play an important part in the Qurʾān as semi-legal terms and are later integrated into the system of Islamic jurisprudence. But with these two we shall have to deal at length in Chapter XI. Suffice it to note for the moment that, at the Qurʾanic stage, they represent part of the 'bounds' of God, and that any attempt at introducing a change into the revealed system of *ḥalāl—ḥarām* is regarded as a genuine case of 'transgression'.

It may be noted in this connection that the practice of sodomy is sometimes regarded as an act of 'transgression'. In such a case, the notion of the 'transgression of the bounds of God' approaches remarkably close to that of an 'abomination', that is, more concretely, any object to which God's abhorrence is directed. This view is confirmed by the fact that sodomy is most usually described as *fāḥishah* which is the very word for an 'abominable thing'.[7]

> What, do you approach the males out of all beings, and leave your wives that your Lord has created for you? Nay, but you are people who transgress (*ʿādūna* from the same root as *iʿtadá*). (XXVI, 165–166)

[7] For this word see below Chapter XI, pp. 233–234.

It will be clear from what precedes that the meaning of *iʿtadá* comes very near that of *ʿaṣá* 'to be rebellious', 'to disobey (the commands of) someone'. In fact, these two verbs often appear side by side in the Qurʾān. I give here an example that is semantically of particular interest. The passage concerns the 'children of Israel' who followed Moses out of Egypt and indulged in all sorts of ungodliness. It will be noticed that 'rebellion' and 'transgression' are interpreted in terms of *kufr*.

> So there befell them humiliation and poverty, and they drew upon themselves wrath from God. All this was because they used to act in a characteristically *kāfir* way (*yakfurūna*) towards the signs of God and slew the Prophets without right; all this was because they disobeyed (*ʿaṣaw*, from *ʿaṣá*) and always transgressed (*yaʿtadūna*). (II, 58/61)

In the following passage, the *takdhīb*, which I have repeatedly referred to as one of the most characteristic features of *kufr*, is put in a close semantic relation with the act of transgression:

> Woe that day [i.e. the Day of Judgment] unto those who always cry lies (*mukadhdhibīn*, pl. of *mukadhdhib*), those who cry lies to the Day of Judgment! None cries it lies save every sinful (*athīm*) transgressor (*muʿtadī*). (LXXXIII, 10–12)

## *Musrif*

We have seen above that both *ẓālim* and *muʿtadī* contain the notion of 'transgressing the bound' as the core of their meaning structure. In *musrif* we have another word with a very similar semantic constitution. It comes from the verb *asrafa* (*isrāf*), the so-called 'fourth' derivative verbal form of *SRF*, and means basically 'to exceed, or, transgress the right measure'. But, unlike *ẓulm* and *iʿtidāʾ*—and this is particularly obvious in the former—which carry an unmistakable implication of enmity, aggressiveness, or encroachment upon another's rights, *isrāf* seems to mean primarily 'to go beyond the due limits' without any such implication; 'to behave too extravagantly' and thence, 'to be immoderate', 'to commit excesses'. Thus in the following two examples, the quality of *isrāf* is attributed to the act of eating and drinking immoderately: the act in itself is by no means wrong, but it becomes morally wrong when it is carried to an absurd extreme. This it is that is called *isrāf* and is declared to be the object of God's hatred:

> O children of Adam, take your adornment at every mosque, and eat and drink, but do not commit *isrāf* (*tusrifū*), for He [i.e. God] loves not the *musrif*. (VII, 29/31)

> He it is Who produces gardens trellised as well as untrellised, the date-palm, and crops of various taste, and olives and pomegranates, alike and unlike. Eat you of the fruit thereof when they fructify, and bring the due thereof upon the harvest day, but commit not *isrāf*. Verily He loves not the *musrif*. (VI, 142/141)

In the next passage the word is applied to the custom of sodomy among 'the people of Lot'.

> And Lot when he said to his people, 'What, do you commit such an abominable act as no one in all the world has ever committed before you? Lo, you approach men with lust instead of women. Indeed, you are a *musrif* people.' (VII, 78–79/80–81)

The following is a passage from the speech of the Prophet Ṣāliḥ, which he addresses to his people in order to admonish them for their godless way of life. Here the *musrif* is one who spreads nothing but corruption in the land and never does right.

> So fear God and obey me, and obey not the command of the *musrif* who do corruption( *yufsidūna*) in the earth and never do right (*yuṣliḥūna*). (XXVI, 150–152)

As regards the meaning of 'do corruption' and 'do right', which determine the inner structure of the concept of *musrif* in this passage, much will be said when we come to discuss the problem of 'good' and 'bad' in the Qur'ān.

Probably—though there is room for a little uncertainty about this point—the word *musrif* which occurs in the next passage, must be understood in a similar way. The contextual situation is as follows. When Pharaoh was about to kill Moses on the pretext that Moses, if left free and alive, 'would surely spread corruption (*fasād*, from the same root as *yufsidūna* which we have just encountered) until in the end he would corrupt even the traditional religion of the people', a believing man of Pharaoh's people who kept concealed his faith, tried to admonish him against taking a rash step. He said:

> 'What, will you kill a man only because he says, "My Lord is God", when he has brought you the manifest signs from your Lord? If he be a liar, his lying will be against himself, but if what he says be true, there will smite you some of that which he promises you. Verily, God guides not him who is *musrif*, *kadhdhāb*.' (XL, 29/28)

The word *kadhdhāb*, as we saw earlier, is the emphatic form of *kādhib*, meaning something like 'a big—or habitual—liar'. The *musrif* refers most probably to the point made by Pharaoh that Moses will surely go on spreading corruption in the land. If this interpretation be right, what this 'believing man' means by these words would amount to this: If, as Pharaoh asserts, Moses is really a great liar (*kadhdhāb*) and if he does nothing but spread corruption in the land (*musrif*), he will go to perdition of his own accord, for God will never guide a man qualified by such abominable properties.

It will be easy to see that the meaning of *musrif* in contexts of this kind comes remarkably near that of *kāfir* or *ẓālim*. In effect, a few verses down in the same passage we find the same word *musrif* employed in reference to those who entertain grave doubts as to the sincerity of the Apostle and indulge in vain disputes concerning the signs of God.

> Joseph brought you before the manifest signs, yet you never ceased being in doubt (*shakk*) concerning what he brought you . . . thus does God lead astray him who is *musrif*, *murtāb* ('doubter'). [This refers to] those who like to wrangle about God's signs without any authority given them. This is extremely hateful in the sight of God and in the sight of those who believe. Thus does God put a seal on every proud (*mutakabbir*) and insolent (*jabbār*) heart. (XL, 36–37/34–35)

Nothing will show more clearly that *isrāf* in certain contexts behaves almost synonymously with *kufr*. Grave doubts concerning God's revelations, vain disputes about God, hearts too proud and insolent to believe in Him, these are all well-known marks of the Kāfirs. This impression is confirmed further when we see the term *musrif* applied to 'those who ascribe partners' to God, that is, those who indulge in idolatry.

> You urge me to disbelieve (*akfura*) in God, and to associate (*ushrika*) with Him I know not what [i.e. idols of suspicious origin], while I urge you to come unto the Mighty Forgiver. There can be no doubt but that [the idols] unto which you call me have no claim in this world or in the world to come, that our [final] return will be unto God and that the *musrif* will be the inhabitants of the Fire. (XL, 45–46/42–43)

In the following verse, the word appears in a verbal form: *asrafa* lit. 'he transgressed the due bound'. It is contextually plain that the reference here is to a man who passed all his life in follies and merrymaking, utterly heedless of the signs of God that He sent down—'Our signs came unto thee, but thou wert heedless of them.' This, of course, is neither more nor less than genuine *kufr* as I have explained above in detail.

Thus We recompense him who *asrafa* in the world and believed not in the signs of his Lord. (XX, 127)

I shall bring this section to a close by quoting a passage in which the word *musrif* implies most clearly the act of committing excesses in revolt against an explicit prohibition of God.

Therefore we prescribed for the children of Israel that whoso kills a human being unless it be in retaliation for a man killed or some corruption done in the land, it shall be as if he had killed mankind altogether. . . . Already Our Apostles have come unto them with signs manifest, but many of them even thereafter continue to commit *isrāf* (*musrifūn*). (V, 35–36/32)

# IX. Religious Hypocrisy

THIS SHORT CHAPTER WILL BE CONCERNED WITH THE SEMANTICAL analysis of the concept of *nifāq*. The word is customarily translated 'hypocrisy' in English. We shall use this English word for the convenience of exposition, keeping in mind that what is most important is not the problem of semantic equivalence between the English 'hypocrisy' and the Arabic *nifāq*, but the structure of the latter itself. Roughly speaking, *nifāq* consists in professing faith with the tongue while secretly disbelieving in the heart. Thus it is obvious that the discordance between words and deeds in matters that concern religious faith, which is one of the characteristic features of *fisq*,[1] is the most basic element in the meaning of *nifāq*. I have cited an important verse in which it is even openly declared that 'the hypocrites are *fāsiq* people'. (Sūrah IX, 68/67) In similar fashion, we find in Sūrah LXIII, 6 the following remarkable words concerning those who show hypocrisy in religious matters: 'It will be all the same to them whether thou [Muḥammad] askest forgiveness for them or thou dost not ask forgiveness for them, for God will not forgive them in any case. God guides not a *fāsiq* people.' This, however, does not exhaust the whole story of this kind of religious hypocrisy. Far

[1] See above, Chapter VIII, p. 158.

from coinciding completely with *fisq*, the word *nifāq* has a very peculiar sort of semantic structure; indeed, so peculiar that some people have thought it necessary to treat *nifāq* as a distinct basic category which takes rank with *kufr* and *īmān* in dividing the entire domain of Islamic morals into three main regions.

According to this view, men are to be classified into three main categories: (1) *muʾmin* 'believer', (2) *kāfir* 'disbeliever', and (3) *munāfiq* 'hypocrite'. The most remarkable representative of this view in early Islām is Ḥasan al-Basrī.[2] Much later, Fakhr al-Dīn al-Rāzī writes in his 'Great Commentary' that the *muʾmin*, one who is qualified by *īmān*, is he whose heart and conscience are religiously clear and good; the *kāfir* is he whose distinguishing mark is stubborn perseverance in refusal to believe; while the *munāfiq* (grammatically, a participial form corresponding to *nifāq*) is he who pretends to believe but whose conscience is against it.[3]

There is no denying that *nifāq* has much in common with *kufr*, for, in the last resort, it is nothing but a particular type of disbelief. So it is hardly surprising that the Qurʾān itself should appear to make no essential distinction between the two. Thus in the first of the following examples, we see 'disbelievers' and 'hypocrites' lumped together as enemies of God:

> O Prophet! strive against the *kuffār* (pl. of *kāfir*) and the *munāfiqīn* (pl.), and be harsh with them. Gehenna shall be their final abode, an evil journey's end. (LXVI, 9)

This last point, that is, the decree of God that the final abode of the *munāfiq* should be the Hell Fire, is very significant in that it discloses the essential connection of *nifāq* with *kufr*, for the common punishment suggests that the two are equal in the degree and nature of sinfulness. In Sūrah IV, 144/145, we read: 'Verily, the *munāfiqīn* shall be in the very depths of the Fire, and thou shalt not find any helper for them.'

In the next quotation, which—although the word *munāfiq* is not actually mentioned—clearly refers to the 'hypocrites', *nifāq* happens to be more directly identified with *kufr*.

> O Apostle, let them not grieve thee who vie one with another in the *kufr*, those who pretend with their mouths, 'We believe', while their hearts believe not. (V, 45/41)

This being the case, it is most natural that some of the Arab philologists have come to count *nifāq* as one of the varieties of *kufr*,

[2] Ritter, *op. cit.*
[3] Fakhr al-Dīn al-Rāzī, *Tafsīr al-Kabīr*, comm. on Sūrah II, 7/8.

and called it *kufr al-nifāq*, that is, literally 'the *nifāq* kind of *kufr*'. And yet, in spite of this, there is a certain respect in which *nifāq* would appear to be more aptly treated as an independent semantic category standing between 'belief' and 'disbelief'.

Let me, first, give an example showing clearly this mid-way nature of *nifāq* wavering between the two extreme poles.

> The *munāfiq* seek to deceive God, when in fact it is God who deceives them. When they stand up to pray, they stand up languidly to be seen of men, and do not remember God save a little, wavering between this [and that], neither to these nor to those. (IV, 141–142/142–143)

The same is true of the example that follows. The passage refers to the famous battle of Uḥud in which things turned unfavorably for Muḥammad and his followers, a golden opportunity to distinguish true believers from those who had only paid lip service to the new religion.

> What befell you the day the two hosts met, it occurred by God's leave, that He might distinguish between those who [truly] believed and those who only pretended to be [believers] hypocritically (*nāfaqū*, a verbal form). When it was said to these latter, 'Come now, fight in God's way', or 'repel [the disbelievers]', they said, 'if we knew how to fight we would surely follow you.' They were that day nearer to *kufr* than to *īmān*, saying as they did with their mouths that which was not in their hearts. But God knows best what they hide. (III, 160–161/166–167)

This passage seems to show plainly that the semantic category of *nifāq* is in no way a water-tight compartment situated between *kufr* and *īmān*, but rather an extensive range of meaning with uncertain boundaries. It is, so to speak, a category of a conspicuously dynamic nature, that may extend with elasticity towards either direction to shade off almost imperceptibly into *kufr* or *īmān*.

In some cases, *nifāq* conveys the impression that it is born in the very midst of belief. When a believer does not act in accordance with his belief, a first step has already been taken towards *nifāq*; he is still a believer but his conduct is most hateful in the sight of God. This point is brought out by the following example.

> O you who believe, why say you that which you do not? Most hateful it is in the sight of God that you say that which you do not. (LXI, 2–3)

Note here the expression 'you who believe'; it shows clearly that God regards these people and addresses them as 'believers'. Such an attitude originates, according to the Qur'ān, in 'doubt', that presumptuous doubt as to the truth of God's Revelation, which gnaws at one's heart, even after one has accepted the faith of Islām.

On the Day of Judgment, we are told, all hypocrites, men as well as women (*munāfiqūn* and *munāfiqāt*) standing on the brink of the Fire, will cry out to the believers going to Paradise, 'Wait! Wait for us. Were we not with you in the earthly world?' To this the believers will reply: 'Yea indeed, but you fell into temptation; you hesitated and entertained doubts (*irtabtum*); vain hopes deluded you, until at last there came the final judgment of God. The Deceiver [i.e. Satan] deceived you concerning God.' (LVII, 13–14)

A step further towards *kufr*, and he who 'says what he does not' becomes a genuine *munāfiq*. The type just described was one who began to entertain doubts about God in the midst of Islām. The type which I am about to describe is represented by those who remain from beginning to end outside the faith of Islām, but, instead of declaring outright that they are disbelievers, accept Islām outwardly and use the faith as a cloak under which they work all sorts of evil. We find in the Qur'ān a number of very interesting descriptions of such typical 'hypocrites'. Here I give two of the instances that are particularly well-suited for elucidating the real nature of *nifāq*.

> When the hypocrites (*munāfiqūn*) come to thee [Muḥammad] they say, 'We bear witness that thou art surely the Apostle of God.' But God knows that thou art His Apostle, and God bears witness that the hypocrites are all liars (*kādhibūn*). Having made the faith (*īmān*) a covering, they try to bar from the way of God. Verily, evil is that which they have been doing. All this is because they accepted belief and then disbelieved (*kafarū*), wherefore their hearts are sealed so that they understand naught. When thou seest them, their bodily appearance may very well please thee, and when they speak thou listenest to what they say. But [in reality] they are like timbers propped up. They think every noise is directed against them. They are the [real] enemy, so beware of them. May God annihilate them. How perverted they are! And when it is said unto them, 'Come now, the Apostle of God will ask forgiveness for you!' they avert their heads, and thou seest them turning away, being too big with pride (*mustakbirūn*). (LXIII, 1–5)

The following passage contains no explicit mention of the word *nifāq* itself, but no one denies that it describes in concrete terms the most characteristic marks of the 'hypocrites'.

> They say, 'We believe in God and the Last Day', but in reality they are not believers (*muʾminīn*). They only try to deceive God. (II, 7–8/8–9)
>
> When they meet the believers, they say, 'We believe', but when they are alone with their Satans [i.e. their leaders], they say 'We are with you. We are only mocking them.' (v. 13/14)
>
> When it is said to them, 'Believe as other people do', they reply, 'Shall we believe as fools believe?' The truth is that they are the fools, but they do not know. (v. 12/13)
>
> They are the workers of corruption (*mufsid*), but they are not aware of it. When it is said to them, 'Do not work corruption in the land', they say, 'We are doing nothing but good.' (vv. 10–11/11–12)
>
> They are born with an incurable sickness in their hearts, which God has increased because of their bad conduct. (v. 9/10)

This metaphor of 'sickness' or 'disease' (*maraḍ*) in the heart is one of the most important elements in the semantic constitution of *nifāq*. In fact, we see the peculiar expression, 'those in whose hearts is a sickness' recurring incessantly in the Qurʾān to denote the 'hypocrites'.

> They are like a man who kindles a fire, and when it lights up around him God snatches it away to leave him in darkness. Deaf, dumb, and blind, he cannot return. (v. 16/17)
> God mocks them and leaves them to wander blindly in their insolence (*ṭughyān*). They have bought error (*ḍalālah*) at the price of divine guidance.[4] (vv. 14–15/15–16)

This passage, I believe, discloses better than any lengthy discussion both those features which *nifāq* shares in common with *kufr* and those that are quite peculiar to *nifāq*.

Originally the word *nifāq* (or *munāfiq*) seems to have been used to refer to some of the citizens of Medina, who joined the Prophet's camp after he migrated from Mecca to their city. Standing in sharp contrast to those Meccan believers who followed him with an unshakably firm faith in God and His Apostle, many of the Medinese believers were conspicuously lukewarm in belief and always 'wavering between this side and that'. Having accepted Islām without any deep-rooted belief in God, some of them remained opportunists. The slightest misfortune that happened to Muḥammad was enough

[4] We must recall that both *ṭughyān* and *ḍalālah* have been analyzed above in Chapter VII as characteristic features of *kufr*.

to raise doubts in their minds and to sway their belief in God. It was, it appears, to the Medinese of this type that the word *munāfiq* was applied at first. In the nature of the case, however, *nifāq* could not be restricted to these wavering Muslims of Medina. And in fact, in Sūrah IX, we find the conduct of some Bedouin described as being of a *nifāq* nature. It is declared there: 'The Bedouin are generally more stubborn in *kufr* and *nifāq* and less inclined towards accepting the bounds of God.' (v. 98/97). And again: 'Some of the Bedouin around you are *munāfiqūn*' (v. 102/101). All those, in a word, who harbor a gloomy doubt—'sickness'—in their hearts, and yet pretend to be faithful believers, fully deserved the name of *munāfiq*.

# X. The Believer

JUST AS *KUFR* CONSTITUTES, AS WE HAVE SEEN, THE PIVOTAL POINT round which turn all the qualities belonging to the sphere of reprehensible properties, so *īmān* 'belief' or 'faith', is the very center of the sphere of positive moral properties. 'Belief' is the real fountainhead of all Islamic virtues; it creates them all, and no virtue is thinkable in Islām, which is not based on the sincere faith in God and His revelations.

As for the semantic structure of 'belief' itself, it may be admitted that we know already all the essential points, for, by trying to analyze semantically the principal terms of negative valuation, we have also been describing the characteristic features of the true 'believer' in the Islamic sense from the reverse side, as it were. So our main task in this chapter will consist simply in re-examining briefly all that has been said about *kufr* and its various aspects from the opposite angle.

## The Ideal Believer

What sort of a man, in the Qur'anic view, is 'one who believes'? What are—or, should be—the characteristic features of 'belief'? How, in a word, is an ideal believer expected to behave socially as well as religiously? These are most important questions we must ask about *īmān*, and that not only generally but also from our specific point of view, for the answers to them will at once determine the semantic contents of the words meaning 'belief' and 'believer' in the Qur'anic context. Let us begin by taking up a passage in which 'belief' is considered exclusively in its religious aspects. This passage is of particular relevance to our research in that it furnishes an almost perfect verbal definition of the 'true believer'.

> Only those are [true] believers who, whenever God is mentioned, their hearts quiver, and when His signs are recited to them, they [i.e. the signs] increase them in belief, and upon their Lord they place reliance, those who attend divine service steadfastly, and expend [in alms] of what We have bestowed upon them. These are the believers in the true sense (*ḥaqqan*). (VIII, 2–4)

This verbal definition pictures 'the believer in the true sense of the word' as a genuinely pious man, in whose heart the very mention of God's name is enough to arouse an intense sense of awe, and whose whole life is determined by the basic mood of deep earnestness. The next quotation is more concerned with the outward manifestations of piety:

> [True believers are] those who go back repentant [to God], those who worship [Him], those who praise [Him], those who fast, those who bow down, those who fall prostrate [before Him], those who enjoin the good and forbid the evil, those who keep within God's bounds. Give thou good tidings to the believers (*mu'minīn*, pl.). (IX, 113/112)

The genuine faith must work as the most powerful motive that actuates men to good works; if not, the faith is not genuine. The fundamental attitude of contrition and awe before God, the unquestioning obedience to God's will, the heartfelt gratitude for divine benefits—all these elements that go to characterize the Islamic faith at its highest, must of necessity materialize in the officially recognized 'good works' (*ṣāliḥāt*) which we shall examine in the following chapter; they must, further, find expression almost in every action in the ordinary man-to-man relations of life. This basic connection of faith with good works assumes later in theology a remarkable importance when the Murji'ah raise the question in a more acute form by asserting that 'faith' is quite independent of deeds; whatever sins one commits do not affect in any way one's being a true 'believer' if only faith is present. We shall come back to this problem in the following chapter in which we shall deal with the concept of *ṣāliḥah* 'good work' together with other related concepts.

Here I give two quotations from the Qurʾān, which will shed light on this phase of the phenomenon of *īmān*. They enumerate those acts that are deemed particularly fitting to the true 'believers'.

> The servants of the Merciful [i.e. the true believers] are those who walk upon the earth with modesty and, when the *jāhil* address them, answer, 'Peace [be upon you]!'
> Those who pass the night before their Lord, prostrate and standing;
> Those who say, 'Our Lord, turn away from us the torment of Gehenna. Verily, the torment thereof is atrocious torture; how evil it is as an abode and a dwelling!';
> Those who, when they expend, neither act immoderately [the vice of *isrāf* as described above] nor yet grudge, but [take] a proper stand between the two [extremes];
> Those who call not upon any other god with God, nor kill any living being which God has forbidden save when it is justifiable, nor commit fornication;
> . . . . . . . . . . . . . . . . . . . . . .
> And those who testify not falsely, and, when they pass by idle talk, pass by honorably;
> Those who, whenever they are reminded of the signs of their Lord, fall not thereat deaf and blind;
> Those who say, 'Our Lord, give us enjoyment of our wives and offspring, and make us a model to all those who fear [God].' (XXV, 64–68/63–68; 72–74)

In summary we would say that, according to this passage, the characteristics that may reasonably be expected to be in an ideal believer are as follows: the basic attitude of *ḥilm*; constant devotional exercises; the fear of the Last Judgment; almsgiving as the most important of the works of genuine piety, without going, however, to the extreme of the impulsive and boastful generosity of Jāhilīyah; keeping away from the Jāhilī acts which God has sternly forbidden, such as polytheism, the slaying of a living being without right, fornication; avoidance of perjury and idle talk; a delicate sensitiveness to the deep import of the revealed words; and serene and restful happiness in the life of this present world, based on the expectation of the Hereafter.

The portrait which the next passage gives of the ideal believer is essentially similar. It runs as follows:

> Prosperous indeed will be the believers who are humble in their prayers, who turn away from idle talk, who are active in giving alms, who hold back their genitals save from their own wives and

> what their right hands possess [i.e. the slave-girls] . . . who keep faithfully their trusts and their covenant, who are assiduous in observing their prayers. These are the inheritors who will inherit Paradise, to dwell therein forever. (XXIII, 1–6, 8–11)

To this portrait we might add one more touch to complete it. What I have in mind here is a short passage in Sūrah XXXIII, in which absolute obedience to whatever God decrees is required of all believers as the *sine qua non* of the really genuine faith.

> It becomes not a believer, whether man or woman, when God and His Apostle have decided any affair, to have his or her own choice in the affair. Whoso disobeys God and His Apostle, he has indeed gone astray into error manifest. (XXXIII, 36)

Now that I have given a general picture of the ideal 'believer' in the Qurʾanic view, I shall proceed to a more detailed analysis of some of the personal properties on which the Qurʾān places special emphasis as being characteristic of the true believers.

## *Imān*, Belief, as Opposed to *Kufr*

That *kufr* is the exact antithesis of 'belief' is a point which requires no laboring. I think I have made it sufficiently clear that it is this basic antithesis between *īmān* and *kufr* that furnishes the ultimate yardstick by which all human qualities are divided, in Islamic outlook, into two radically opposed moral categories. This basic dichotomy is the very keynote of the whole ethical system of Islām. Everywhere in the Qurʾān this fundamental opposition is perceptible. I shall give here a few of the most typical examples.

> Verily, God will admit those who believe (*āmanū*) and do good works (*ṣāliḥāt*) into Gardens underneath which rivers flow, while Kāfirs take their enjoyment in the present world, eating as the cattle eat, but the Fire shall be their final dwelling-place. (XLVII, 13/12)

Here, it may be remarked, the radical contrast between *muʾmin* and *kāfir* is brought out in reference to two essential points: (1) what they do in this world—the believer is only concerned to do pious works, while the Kāfir passes his days in the pursuit of worldly pleasures; (2) what they obtain on the Day of Judgment—the believer will get the reward of Paradise, while the Kāfir goes to Hell. Substantially the same is true of the following quotation.

> As for those who believe and do good works, they shall rejoice in a meadow green but as for those who disbelieve and cry lies to Our

signs and the meeting of the Hereafter, in the torment of Hell they shall be placed. (XXX, 14–15/15–16)

In the example that follows, the same contrast is made to stand on the difference in the Way in which one fights.

Those who believe (*āmanū*) fight in the way of God, while those who disbelieve (*kafarū*) fight in the way of the idols. (IV, 78/76)

The following two examples describe *kufr* and *īmān* in terms of temporal succession, or to be more concrete, they suggest that *kufr* and *īmān* are two contradictory personal properties which a man may assume interchangeably, though in the nature of the case they cannot possibly reside in one person both at the same time. There is, in other words, constant danger of apostasy.

O you who believe (*āmanū*), if you obey a sect of those to whom has been given the Scripture, they will turn you back, after you have become believers (*ba*ᶜ*da īmānikum* lit. 'after your belief'), into disbelievers (*kāfirīna*). How can you disbelieve (*takfurūna*) when you hear the signs of God recited to you, and among you is His Apostle? (III, 95–96/100–101)

Whoso disbelieves (*kafara*) in God after he has become a believer—save him who [does so] under compulsion and whose heart remains unwavering in his belief (*īmān*)—but whoso finds satisfaction in disbelief (*kufr*), upon them shall be wrath from God, and theirs shall be a severe chastisement. (XVI, 108/106)

'To buy *kufr* at the price of *īmān*' is a very characteristic Qurʾanic phrase for apostatizing from Islām to idolatry.

Verily, those who purchase *kufr* at the price of *īmān*, they do not hurt God at all, and theirs shall be a painful chastisement. (III, 171/177)

If 'belief', in this way, is diametrically opposed to *kufr*, there is no reason at all for surprise if we find it opposed to other ethico-religious terms that are more or less synonymous with *kufr*.

Is he who is a believer (*muʾmin*) like unto him who is a *fāsiq*? They cannot be equal. (XXXII, 18)

Here *fāsiq*, which we considered in detail in Chapter IX, is made the antithesis of 'one who believes' in place of *kāfir*. In the next example, three vices, *kufr*, *fusūq*, and ᶜ*iṣyān* ('rebellion' or 'disobedience'), are tied up all in a bundle and opposed to *īmān*.

God has endeared *īmān* and has beautified it in your hearts, and He has made hateful to you *kufr* and *fusūq* and ᶜ*iṣyān*. (XLIX, 7)

## *Islām and Muslim*

As we saw in an earlier chapter, *islām* (from the verb *aslama*) means literally 'submission' or the act of surrendering one's self entirely to someone else's will, and *muslim*, which is grammatically the participial-adjectival form of *aslama*, is 'one who has surrendered'.[1] The supreme importance of these terms in Islamic religion is shown by the well-known fact that *Islām* is the very name of this religion, while *Muslim* is a member of the religious community established by Muḥammad, the Prophet.

The origin of these peculiar appelations can be traced back to a passage in the Qurʾān itself. The passage is important also for our specific purpose because its general context gives a very instructive glimpse into the meaning of the word *islām*.

> Say, 'We believe in God and that which has been sent down upon us, and that which was sent down upon Abraham and Ishmael, Isaac and Jacob, and the Tribes, and that which was given unto Moses, Jesus, and the Prophets from their Lord; we make no distinction whatsoever between them, surrendering as we do unto Him (*lahu muslimūn*).' And whoso desires to have other than the Surrender (*islām*) as religion, it will not be accepted of him, and he shall be among the losers in the Hereafter. (III, 78–79/84–85)

There is mentioned in the Qurʾān a very peculiar case in which, in reference to the nature of the desert Arabs, the act of *islām* is definitely distinguished from *īmān*. *Islām*, we are told, is but the very first step in the faith, a shallow belief which has not yet penetrated deep into the heart. So all 'believers' are naturally 'muslims', but the reverse is not always true.

> The Bedouin say, 'We believe (*āmannā*).' Say [Muḥammad,] unto them, 'You do not believe yet. Say rather, "We have surrendered (*aslamnā*)", for the belief (*īmān*) has not permeated your hearts'. . . . The [true] believers (*muʾminūn*) are those who believe in God and His Apostle, and afterwards never doubt, but struggle with their wealth and their lives in the way of God, these [only] are the faithful believers (*ṣādiq*). (XLIX, 14–15)

It must be borne in mind, however, that the *islām* here spoken of refers mainly to the formula, 'I have surrendered' *aslamtu*, used for the formal declaration of the faith. What is implied seems to be simply that the fact of someone having joined the community of Muslims does not guarantee that he has 'belief' in the true sense of

[1] For a more detailed analysis of the concept of *islām* itself, see my *God and Man in the Koran*, Chapter VIII.

the word. In the terminology of modern linguistic philosophy we might say that the expression *aslamtu* ('I have surrendered') is a 'performative' which is a self-involving use of language. In other words, by declaring *aslamtu*, the man commits himself to a particular type of future conduct or implies that he has a certain attitude or intention. But, as all 'performatives', the expression *aslamtu* may be insincere.[2]

This of course does not in any way detract from the supreme religious value of *islām* as an inner act of the complete surrendering of one's self to God's will. Taking this passage as the scriptural basis, al-Bukhāri distinguishes, quite rightly to my mind, between two kinds of *islām*: (1) the formal and superficial type of *islām* which is motivated by something not purely religious, the fear of being killed (by the Muslims) for example, and (2) the 'real *islām*' (*al-islām ʿalá al-ḥaqīqah*). According to him, Sūrah III, 17/19 refers to this latter kind of *islām: Inna al-dīn ʿinda Allāh al-islām* 'Verily, the religion in the sight of God is Islām.'[3]

In this sense, *islām* is no less an important element of this religion than *īmān*. Only, the semantic structure of the former is totally different from that of the latter, for *islām*, as its name itself suggests, is based on such ideas as humbleness, patience, reliance, lack of self-sufficiency, etc., which we discussed in detail in Chapter V.

Here is an illuminating example of the usage of this word showing the full significance of 'humble submission' in the Qurʾanic conception of religion.

> When Abraham, together with Ishmael, raised the foundations of the House, [he said], 'Our Lord, accept [this] from us. Verily, Thou art the Hearer, the Omniscient. Our Lord, makes us two submissive (*muslim*) unto Thee, and of our progeny a community submissive (*ummah muslimah*) unto Thee, and show us our sacred rites, and turn towards us [i.e. forgive our sins]. Verily, Thou art the Forgiving, the Merciful.' . . .
>
> When his Lord said unto him, 'Surrender (*aslim*, imperative form of *islām*),' he said, 'I have surrendered (*aslamtu*) to the Lord of all beings.' And Abraham admonished his sons to do the same, and Jacob likewise, saying, 'My sons, God has chosen for you the [true] religion. So you should never die save as men who have surrendered (*muslimūn*).' (II, 121–122, 125–126/127–128, 131–132)

In this important passage, the deep religious meaning of 'surrendering' comes out with utmost clarity. And, it should be remarked, the

[2] See an interesting study of this kind of language by Dr. Donald Evans, *The Logic of Self-involvement* (London, 1963), pp. 11–78.

[3] al-Bukhārī, *Ṣaḥīḥ* with Comm. of al-Kirmānī (Cairo, 1939), I, 128.

act of surrendering is immediately identified with 'the [true] religion'. We see that the Surrender, far from being, as is suggested by XLIX just quoted, a lukewarm and superficial sort of belief, or the first fumbling step in the faith, is the very foundation on which the whole religion of Islām is to be based.

In the following passage, *muslim* is contrasted with *qāsiṭ* which means 'one who deviates from the right course (and, consequently, acts unjustly)', with the implication that *islām* is the sole right course to take.

> Verily, of us some are *muslimūn* (pl.), and some are *qāsiṭūn* (pl.). Whoso has surrendered (*aslama*) they have taken the right course, but as for the *qāsiṭūn*, they have become fuel for Gehenna. (LXXII, 14–15)

Since the Surrender here means the surrendering of one's whole being to God, and to God alone, a *muslim* would flatly contradict himself if he should assume a conciliatory attitude towards idolatry.

In this sense *muslim* is the direct opposite of *mushrik*.

> I am commanded to be the first of those who surrender (*aslama*). [For God has said to me], 'Be not thou [Muḥammad] of those who associate [i.e. the idol-worshippers] (*mushrikīn*, pl.).' (VI, 14)

Most probably, the problematic word *ḥanīf* which begins to appear in the Qur'ān from the later Meccan period, has much to do with this conception of the exclusive—i.e. purely monotheistic—Surrender to God as the true, or right, religion. As far as we can judge from its actual usage in the Qur'ān, *ḥanīf*,[4] whatever its etymology, is a religious term whose semantic structure seems to comprise among other things the ideas of (1) the true religion deep-rooted in the natural disposition in every human soul to believe in the One God, (2) absolute submission to this One God, and (3) being the antithesis of idol-worshipping. It is highly significant in this conception that Abraham, who, as we have just seen, was the first 'surrenderer', is made the representative, or the ideal type of *ḥanīf*. The Qur'ān emphasizes repeatedly that Abraham was neither a Jew nor a Christian, much less an idol-worshipper, but a *ḥanīf* who discovered the vanity of polytheism by meditation and logical reasoning.[5] I shall give here a few examples that are most relevant to our subject.

> Verily, Abraham was a paragon of virtue (*ummah*)[6] submissive

[4] I have dealt with the problem of the pre-Islamic Ḥanīfitic movement in *God and Man*, Chapter IV, Section 5.

[5] *Cf.* Sūrah XXI, 51/50 ff.; VI, 74 ff.

[6] There is a good deal of disagreement among the commentators concerning the right interpretation of this word in this context. Some take it in the most ordinary

to God, a *ḥanīf* and not of the idol-worshippers (*mushrikīn*), ever thankful (*shākir*) for His favors—that He chose him and guided him to a straight path. . . . Then We revealed unto thee [Muḥammad], 'Follow the religion of Abraham, who was a *ḥanīf* and no idol-worshipper.' (XVI, 121–122, 124/120–121, 123)

In the following quotation, the conceptual opposition of *ḥanīf* and *mushrik* is particularly emphasized:

Set thy face steadfast towards the religion, as a *ḥanīf*, and be thou not of the idol-worshippers (*mushrikīn*), and call not, besides God, on what can neither profit nor harm thee [i.e. idols]. (X, 105–106)

The next two emphasize rather that the religion of the *ḥanīf* is the true 'upright' religion. The first of them, moreover, points out that the pure monotheism as represented by Abraham is the natural religion of mankind, to which all men would be led if only they followed the guidance of the God-given instinct in their souls.

Set thy face steadfast towards the religion as a *ḥanīf*, in accordance with the natural disposition upon which He created mankind. There can be no altering the creation of God. That is the upright [or 'right' *qayyim*] religion, though most men know it not. (XXX, 29/30)

They were commanded only to worship God, making the religion pure for Him, as *ḥunafāʾ* (pl. of *ḥanīf*), and to perform the prayer, and to give alms. That is the upright [community: the word *qayyimah* being interpreted as an epithet qualifying *ummah* which is here understood]. (XCVIII, 4/5)

The original words for 'making the religion pure for Him' in the passage just quoted are: *mukhliṣīn lahu al-dīn*.[7] The word *mukhliṣ* is the participial-adjectival form of the verb *akhlaṣa* meaning approximately 'to make (or keep) pure, free from all admixture'. It is sometimes translated, more or less rightly, 'sincere' in English. The root *KH-L-Ṣ*, under its various forms, is very frequently used in the Qurʾān to denote the type of the pure monotheistic faith that is suggested by the term *ḥanīf*, in contradistinction to all forms of *shirk*. The underlying idea is that, by 'associating' anything with God, man adulterates, as it were, his religion with foreign elements and makes it 'impure'.

---

sense of 'nation' or 'community', but this gives a very odd meaning. Here I follow another, more reasonable interpretation.

[7] The phrase 'making the religion pure for Him' has in some important places in the Qurʾān quite a different connotation—'temporary monotheism' as I would call it. For a detailed explanation of this phenomenon, see *God and Man*, Chapter IV, Section 2.

> We have sent down to thee the Scripture with Truth. So worship God, making thy religion pure for Him. Is not the pure (*khāliṣ*) religion for God alone? (XXXIX, 2–3)

In the following passage, the same act of 'keeping the religion unmixed' is mentioned in conjunction with the 'surrender' *islām*, showing the most intimate relationship between the two.

> Say, 'I am commanded to worship God, maintaining my religion pure for Him. And I am commanded to be the first of those who surrender (*muslimīn*).'
> Say, 'God do I worship, making my religion pure for Him. Worship you, then, what you will apart from Him!' (XXXIX, 14, 16–17/11–12, 14–15)

It may be remarked that the following quotation makes mention of Abraham as one of those who were made *mukhliṣ* by the hand of God Himself.

> Remember Our servants Abraham, Isaac, and Jacob, endowed with might and vision. Verily, We made them pure (*akhlaṣnā*) with something unmixed (*khāliṣah*), that is, the remembrance of the Abode of the Hereafter. (XXXVIII, 45–46)

## Divine Guidance

As I remarked earlier in connection with the concept of *ḍalāl* 'going astray', it is one of the most characteristic features of Qurʾanic thought that it conceives of 'religion' in terms of the 'guidance' of God. In this conception, the religion in the sense of *islām-īmān* is nothing other than *ihtidāʾ* (verb. *ihtadá*) which literally means 'to be rightly guided' or 'acceptance of guidance'. This is but a corollary of the basic fact that, in the Qurʾān, Revelation is regarded as essentially a merciful guidance (*hudá*) for those who are apt to believe. Indeed, even the casual reader of the Qurʾān would not fail to notice that through the whole of it there runs the fundamental thought that 'God guides whom He will', or—which would, logically, collide with the preceding—that God is absolutely fair in giving guidance graciously to all men, but some people accept it while others reject it of their own free will. In either case, the revealed 'signs' are divine Guidance.

> If there comes unto you guidance (*hudá*) from Me, then whoso follows My guidance shall never go astray nor fall into misery. But whoso turns away from My remembrance (*dhikr*), His shall be a strait life, and We shall raise him blind on the Day of Resurrection. (XX, 121–124/123–124)

It will be interesting to note that in the latter half of this passage the word *hudá* 'guidance' is replaced by *dhikr* 'remembrance', which is just one of the usual words in the Qurʾān denoting Revelation in the sense of what serves to recall God to one's mind. In the following passage a revealed Book as a whole is considered 'guidance'.

> Verily, We have brought to them a Scripture which we have expounded, based on [true] knowledge, a guidance (*hudá*) and a mercy for a people that believe. (VII, 50/52)

So, viewed from the human standpoint, 'belief' is neither more nor less than 'accepting the guidance' and to choose the right path, while *kufr* means 'turning away from the guidance' so as to go astray from the right path. Here is an example in which the human act of 'belief' appears explicitly connected with the idea of divine guidance:

> They were young men who believed (*āmanū*) in their Lord, and We increased them in guidance (*hudá*). (XVIII, 12–13)

Most evidently, the word 'guidance' here might very well be replaced by 'belief' without any essential change in the general meaning of the sentence. In the next quotation, also, 'belief' with all its characteristic features is semantically equated with the state of 'those who are guided'.

> It is not for the idol-worshippers (*mushrikīn* 'those who associate') to frequent the sanctuaries of God, witnessing as they do *kufr* against themselves.... Only he is allowed to frequent the sanctuaries of God who believes (*āmana*) in God and the Last Day, and performs the prayer, and gives the alms, and fears (*yakhsha*) none but God—such men may possibly be of the guided (*muhtadīn* part. pl.). (IX, 17–18)

He who is 'guided' takes, of course, the right way. This phase of the matter is usually denoted by another root *R-SH-D*. The root appears in the Qurʾān under several forms—verbal: *rashada*, nominal: *rashad*, *rushd*, *rashād*, *rashīd*. The first of the quotations that follow brings out most explicitly the intimate semantic relationship between 'guidance' and the concept of 'right direction'.

> We have heard a marvellous Qurʾān that guides (*yahdī*) to the right way (*rushd*). (LXXII, 1–2)

When, it is related in Sūrah XL, 29, a certain believer among Pharaoh's folk admonished his brethren against doing wrong to the people of Moses, and said, among other things, that 'God guides (*yahdī*) not him who is a *musrif*,[8] and a big liar (*kadhdhāb*), Pharaoh, offended at this, uttered the following words:

> I only let you see what I see! And I only guide (*ahdī*) you in the way of right direction (*rashād*)! (XL, 30/29)

In the following two passages, *rushd* is contextually identified with *īmān* and *islām* respectively.

> There should be no compulsion in religion. The right way (*rushd*) has come distinct from error (*ghayy*): whoso disbelieves (*yakfur*) in idols and believes (*yuʾmin*) in God, has got hold of the firm handle which will never break. (II, 257/256)

> Verily, of us some have surrendered (*muslimūn*) and some are unjust (*qāsiṭūn*). Whoso has surrendered (*aslama*), they have taken the right course (*rashad*). (LXXII, 14–15)

## The Fear of God

Turning now to the inner structure of the concept of *īmān* itself, we shall note in the first place the fact that in the Qurʾān it stands on two key concepts: *taqwá* 'fear of God' and *shukr* 'thankfulness'. In this section we shall deal with the first of them.

The Qurʾanic Revelation, particularly in the earlier period of the prophetic career of Muḥammad, abounds in most impressive eschatological visions. And the concept of *taqwá* is closely connected with this general atmosphere. In other words, *taqwá*, in this particular context, is an eschatological fear of the catastrophic Hour.

> O mankind, fear (*ittaqū*) your Lord! Verily the earthquake of the Hour will be a tremendous thing! (XXII, 1)

The fear of the Last Judgment and the Lord of the Day—that is the most fundamental motif of this new religion, that underlies all its aspects and determines its basic mood. To believe in God means, briefly, to fear Him as the Lord of the Day, the austere Judge who will punish the Kāfirs for their obstinate *kufr* with the eternal Hell Fire. The most concise possible formula of definition for 'believer' in the earlier Sūrahs is 'one who trembles in fear before God'.

It will be easy to understand now why in the Qurʾān 'belief' and 'fear' are very often used almost synonymously with each other. One example may suffice.

> The Kāfirs are lured by the beauty of the present world, and they laugh at those who believe, but those who fear God (*ittaqaw*, a

[8] See above, Chapter VIII, pp. 174–177.

verbal form of *taqwá*) [i.e. the believers] shall be placed above them on the Day of Resurrection. (II, 208/212)

The close relationship that exists between 'belief' and 'fear' may also express itself in the form of an implication: if A then B. Note that, as a matter of actual fact, B (that is, 'fear' in this case) mostly takes the form of an imperative sentence. 'Fear (*ittaqū*) God, if you are true believers.' (V, 62/57; see also 112, and passim).

If 'fear' forms in this way the central element of the conception of 'belief', it is only natural that *kufr* should represent its opposite. The *muttaqī* ('one who is characterized by *taqwá*') is in the Qurʾān, constantly contrasted with the *kāfir*. Here is a typical example:

The likeness of Paradise which is promised unto those who are god-fearing (*muttaqūn* pl.): rivers flowing underneath it, its food eternal, and also its shade. This is the reward of those who fear God (*ittaqaw*), while the reward of the disbelievers (*kāfirīn*) is the Fire. (XIII, 35)

Sometimes we find *ẓālim* behaving as the antonym of *muttaqī*.

Verily, the wrong-doers (*ẓālimīn* pl.) are friends of each other, while God is the friend of those who are god-fearing (*muttaqīn*). (XLV, 18/19)

As is obvious, *taqwá* is not in any way an ordinary kind of 'fear'.[9] And yet it *is*, originally at least, the emotion of fear. This is proved by the fact that the Qurʾān uses as synonyms of *taqwá* in several places some other words that are commonly used for the ordinary sort of 'fear'. The most important of them *khashyah*—the corresponding verb is *khashiya*—and *khawf*. I shall begin with a brief analysis of the meaning of the former.

The synonymity—at least within the bounds of the Qurʾanic language—of *khashyah* with *taqwá* is best shown by the following example in which the verb *khashiya* is used in an analytic phrase which is precisely designed to explain the word *muttaqī*.

The godfearing (*muttaqīn*) who fear (*yakhshawna* from *khashiya*) their Lord in the Unseen, being affected with the fear (*mushfiqūna*, another synonym) of the [Last] Hour. (XXI, 49–50/48–49)

The synonymity is also attested—though in a somewhat looser way——by the fact that *khashyah* and *taqwá* often appear together in one and the same sentence, with almost exactly the same meaning.

[9] For a more detailed philological discussion of the word *taqwá* as it is used in both *Jāhilīyah* poetry and the Qurʾān see *God and Man*, Chapter IX, Section 2.

> Whoso obeys God and His Apostle, and fears (*yakhsha*, from *khashiya*) God and fears (*yattaqi*, from *taqwá*) Him, such will be the ultimate gainers. (XXIV, 51/52)

We saw above that Paradise is promised to those who are characterized by the property of *taqwá*. Exactly the same is true of him 'who *khashiya* his Lord', another piece of evidence that there is, in such contexts, no notable difference between the words in question.

> Verily those who believe, and do good works, . . . their reward is with their Lord: Gardens of Eden underneath which rivers flow, therein to dwell forever. . . . Such [a reward] is for him who fears (*khashiya*) his Lord. (XCVIII, 7–8)

It may be remarked, further, that in the passage just quoted the phrase 'he who *khashiya* his Lord' is used evidently as a substitute for 'believer'.

The word *khashyah*, it appears, belongs to the class of words marked by semantic expressiveness. Judging by the actual usage in the Qurʾān, it describes an overwhelming emotion of violent terror that affects the senses. This facet of its meaning is best brought to light by the following example:

> God has sent down the best discourse in the form of a Scripture . . . whereat a chill creeps over the skins of those who fear (*yakhshawna*) their Lord, but after a while, their skins and their hearts soften at the remembrance of God. This is the guidance of God, whereby He guides whomsoever He likes. (XXXIX, 24/23)

The expressiveness of the word is brought out equally well by the following example. It is obvious that the *khashyah* of God is here being considered as charged with something like explosive energy.

> If We sent down this Qurʾān upon a mountain, thou [Muḥammad] wouldst see it humbled, rent asunder by the fear (*khashyah*) of God. (LIX, 21)

In so far as the Qurʾanic Arabic is concerned, the verb *khashiya* almost invariably takes God as its object. Sometimes, however, the 'fear' happens to go in the wrong direction. And then it is Man, not God, that is the object of the verb. The following passage is of particular interest in that it emphasizes explicitly that the proper object of *khashyah* should be God and not Man. The reference is to the occasion when the Prophet married Zaynab. Zaynab was the beloved wife of Zayd, the Prophet's freedman and adopted son, one of the most loyal of all the early Muslims. One day, in Zayd's absence, Muḥammad saw Zaynab and was visibly attracted by her superb beauty. She told her husband the impression she had made on the Prophet. Upon this, Zayd decided to divorce her so that Muḥammad might marry her. Muḥammad hesitated to accept this offer, because he was apprehensive of the scandal it would raise among the believers if it became known.

> Thou [Muḥammad] wast [when thou didst decline the offer] hiding in thy heart that which God was to bring to light [i.e. the desire to marry Zaynab]; thou didst fear (*takhshá*) men when it was rather God that thou shouldst fear. (XXXIII, 37)

Finally I shall give an example of the use of the word *khashiya* in a non-religious context. The 'object' of fear in this case is Pharaoh and his hosts, or rather the fact of being overtaken by them.

> We revealed unto Moses, 'Depart with My servants [i.e. the believers—here, the Israelites in Egypt] by night, and strike for them a dry path in the midst of the sea. Thou shouldst not fear (*takhāf*, from *khawf*) overtaking, neither shouldst thou be afraid (*takhshá*). (XX, 79–80/77)

Incidentally, the passage here quoted has brought to light the fact that *khashyah* may be replaced by another word, *khawf*, without occasioning any notable change in meaning. To this latter word we now turn.

Properly, the word *khawf* seems to denote the natural emotion of fear in general. It may naturally denote fear caused by some unusual, mysterious phenomenon. Thus in the Qurʾān the word is used repeatedly in reference to what Moses felt when he saw sticks and ropes miraculously changed into writhing snakes. Here I give two typical examples:

> 'Throw down thy staff' [this is said by God to Moses]. And when he saw it quivering as if it were a serpent, he turned back and took to his heels. 'Moses, fear (*takhaf*) not. The Messengers [of God] should not fear (*yakhāfu*) in My presence.' (XXVII, 10)

> They [i.e. the magicians of Egypt] said, 'Moses, either thou wilt throw, or we shall be the first to throw.' He said, 'Nay, you throw [first].' And lo, their ropes and staffs were made to appear, by their sorcery, to move about [as if they were snakes]. Thereupon Moses felt within himself a fear (*khīfah*, same as *khawf*). So We said unto him, 'Fear (*takhaf*) not. Thou shalt surely overcome [their sorcery].' (XX, 68–71/65–68)

It is quite natural that this emotion of *khawf* should be aroused by God's 'signs', particularly those that concern the punishment in Hell. God sends down these 'signs' precisely to cause fear (*khawwafa* or *takhwīf*) in the minds of the careless men.

> And We do not send [any Apostle] with signs save as a means of causing fear (*takhwīf*). . . . We will cause them to fear (*nukhawwifu*), but it only serves to increase them in great *ṭughyān*. (XVII, 61–62/59–60)

> Verily, I fear (*akhāfu*) for you the chastisement of an awful day. (XXVI, 135)

> All this is for him who fears (*khāfa*) My majesty and fears (*khāfa*) My threat. (XIV, 17/14)

A step further, and the object of *khawf* becomes God Himself—and, naturally, Satan in the case of the disbelievers.

> That is only Satan who would make his partisans fear (*yukhawwifu*). So fear (*takhāfū*) them not, but fear (*khāfū*) you Me, if you are believers. (III, 169/175)

That *khawf* in the last sentence, 'fear you Me, if you are believers', is a perfect synonym of *taqwá* will be self-evident if we compare it with another verse from another Sūrah, in which substantially the same meaning is conveyed precisely by the latter word.

> This [in reference to a description that precedes of the Fire] is wherewith God causes His servants to fear (*yukhawwifu*). 'O my servants, so fear (*ittaqū*) Me!' (XXXIX, 18/16)

This is corroborated further by the following sentence put in the mouth of the pious Abel when he refuses to stretch out his hand to kill his brother Cain even if the latter tries to kill him.

> I shall never stretch out my hand to kill thee. Verily, I fear (*akhāfu*) God, the Lord of the whole world. (V, 31/28)

Likewise, in the next verse we see the word *khawf* used in the sense of the fear of God's chastisement, that is, *taqwá* in the original Qurʾanic sense.

> Call upon Him in fear (*khawfan*) and craving (*ṭamaʿan*) [i.e. craving for His favor, or pardon]. (VII, 54/56)

And, we must note, in Sūrah V, 26/23, the pious believers are called 'those who fear' (*alladhīna yakhāfūn*).

In addition to *khashyah* and *khawf*, we may mention the verb *rahiba* which behaves usually as a synonym of *khawf*, and is in the particular context of the Qurʾān synonymous with *taqwá*. The synonymity is best illustrated in the following passage, in which the same meaning is expressed twice in succession by means of *rahiba* and *ittaqá*.

God says, 'Take not to yourselves two gods. God is surely only One God. So Me do you fear (*irhabū*, from *rahiba*).' His is indeed what is in the heavens and in the earth. His is the religion for ever. Other than God then will you fear (*tattaqūna* from *ittaqá*)? (XVI, 53–54/51–52)

In the next quotation, the 'hypocrites' are severely accused of being more fearful of powerful men than of God, the implication being that God is the only proper object of *rahbah* (nominal form of *rahiba*).

You [the Muslims in the ascendant] arouse stronger fear (*rahbah*) in their bosoms than God. This is because they are a people who understand naught. (LIX, 13)

We might add that the participial form of this verb, *rāhib*, lit. 'one who fears (God)' is the word in Old Arabic for the Christian monk devoted to religious exercises in his cell.

## Thankfulness

*Shukr* 'thankfulness' and *taqwá* represent the two proper types of human reaction to God's signs. Of the very remarkable place 'thankfulness' occupies in the whole system of Islamic ethics I have so often spoken that there should be no further need to labor the point here. Indeed, in an important sense 'thankfulness' is, in Islām, another name for 'belief'. To understand this, we have only to recall that in Chapter IX we interpreted the word *kufr* precisely in terms of 'lack' of thankfulness.

First of all, I shall give a few examples showing how *shukr* is essentially and fundamentally opposed to *kufr* in the Qur'anic outlook.

Said [Solomon when he saw a miracle], 'This is of my Lord's grace, that He may try me, whether I am thankful (*ashkuru*) or thankless (*akfuru*). Whoso is thankful (*shakara*) is only thankful for the good of his own soul, while whoso is thankless (*kafara*) [is so only to the hurt of his own soul].' (XXVII, 40)

If you are thankless (*takfurū*), God is quite independent of you: only He is not pleased to find ingratitude (*kufr*) in His servants. But if you are thankful (*tashkurū*), He will be pleased with it in you. (XXXIX, 9/7)

Your Lord proclaimed, 'If you are thankful (*shakartum*) I will surely give you more, but if you are thankless (*kafartum*), verily, My chastisement shall be terrible.' (XIV, 6–7)

In the following passage, *shirk*, or the 'ascribing of partners to God', takes the place of *kufr* and is opposed to *shukr*, as the most characteristic manifestation of 'thanklessness'.

> You call upon Him humbly and in secret, 'If only Thou deliverest us from this [danger], we shall surely be of the thankful (*shākirīn*).' Say, 'God delivers you from this and from every affliction, yet you associate partners (*tushrikūna*) with Him.' (VI, 63–64)

In the preceding section, I pointed out that God sends down His signs, especially those that concern Hell and the Fire, as a means of 'causing fear' (*takhwīf*) or 'threat' (*waʿīd*). The 'signs' of God are there also to arouse the feeling of deep gratitude in the minds of men; and this is particularly true of those that reveal Him as an infinitely gracious and merciful God. The Qurʾān never tires of emphasizing the benevolence which God bestows upon men. And in return for all the precious gifts He bestows upon him, man is expected to show Him deep gratitude.

Sometimes the 'sign' is nothing other than the marvellous creation of man.

> He began the creation of man from clay, then He made his progeny out of a jet of despised water, then He shaped him, and breathed into him of His spirit. And He created for you hearing, and sight, and hearts. Little thanks you give (*tashkurūna*)! (XXXII, 6–8/7–9)

Sometimes the 'sign' is the alternation of night and day (XXVIII, 73, and *passim*), or the sending of rain-clouds whereby God quickens the earth after death (XLV, 4/5; LVI, 68–69/69–70, etc.), or the cattle with which He has enriched man (XXXVI, 71–73), or again the ships like huge mountains that sail in the sea ('If God will, He may still the wind, and then they would have to remain motionless on the back thereof.' (XLII, 31/32–33); in short, everything that contributes in some way or other towards the maintenance and furtherance of human existence in this world. The Qurʾān constantly returns to these 'signs' of divine benevolence, and in the vast majority of cases the description ends with the complaint that man is ever ungrateful.

> Verily, God is gracious towards men, but most of them do not give thanks (*yashkurūna*). (X, 61/60, see also XXVIII, 73)

It would be highly interesting to observe that the 'thankfulness' in its perfect form is, in the Qurʾanic conception, not one-sided; it is reciprocal. If the duty of being thankful to God's favors devolves on man, God, on His part, is expected to respond to this act of thankfulness with thankfulness. Such mutual give and take of *shukr* is the ideal form of relationship between God and men. Besides, it could not be otherwise, since 'God is best aware of those who are really thankful for His benevolence.' (VI, 53).

> Whoso does good (*khayr*)[10] of his own accord, verily, God is thankful (*shākir*), He is aware of everything. (II, 153/158)

> Whoso desires the Hereafter and, being a believer (*mu'min*), strives after it persistently—those, their striving shall be received with thanks (*mashkūr*). (XVII, 20/19)

In Sūrah LXXVI, after a very detailed description of the everlasting enjoyments of Paradise, it is declared that all this is the well-merited reward for the 'striving' of the believers, which has been gratefully received by God.

> Verily, all this is a reward for you. Your striving has been received with thanks (*mashkūr*). (LXXVI, 22)

[10] See below, Chapter XI, pp. 217–221.

# XI. Good and Bad

THERE IS IN THE QURʾĀN NO FULLY DEVELOPED SYSTEM OF ABSTRACT concepts of good and evil. The formation of such a secondary-level moral language is the work of jurists in post-Qurʾanic ages. The Qurʾanic vocabulary contains a number of words that may be, and usually are, translated by 'good' and 'bad'; but many of them are primarily descriptive or indicative words. If we are justified in treating them as 'value' terms, it is because they invariably carry, in actual usage, a marked valuational import. They are descriptive as well as evaluative by implication. At the same time, there are, in the Qurʾān, a number of words for 'good' and 'bad' whose primary function is obviously evaluative rather than descriptive. There are also borderline cases in which it is difficult to tell whether a given term is mainly descriptive or mainly evaluative.

As I tried to explain in detail in Chapter VI, morality in Islām had its origin in religion and developed exclusively within its eschatological framework. Now this eschatological framework makes the ultimate destiny of man depend on what he does in the present world, with particular reference to whether his conduct furthers or hinders the cause of Islām. Thence comes the very specific nature of 'good' and 'bad' in the Qurʾanic outlook. Nothing shows this emphatically religious character of the conception of moral goodness in Islām better than the word *ṣāliḥ* which is one of the commonest words for ethico-religious excellence used in the Qurʾān.

## *Ṣāliḥ*

The word *ṣāliḥ* is most commonly translated in English 'righteous'; one may as well translate it by 'good'. Whether the translation is right or not is a matter of only secondary importance. What is really important is to isolate the concrete descriptive content of this word in the Qurʾanic context.

Let us remark, in the first place, that the strongest tie of semantic relationship binds *ṣāliḥ* and *īmān* together into an almost inseparable unit. Just as the shadow follows the form, wherever there is *īmān* there are *ṣāliḥāt* or, 'good works', so much so that we may almost feel justified defining the former in terms of the latter, and the latter in terms of the former. In brief, the *ṣāliḥāt* are 'belief' fully expressed in outward conduct. And so it comes about that the expression: *alladhīna āmanū wa-ʿamilū al-ṣāliḥāt*, 'those who believe and do *ṣāliḥ* deeds', is one of the most frequently used phrases in the Qurʾān. 'Those who believe' are not believers unless they manifest their inner faith in certain deeds that deserve the appellation of *ṣāliḥ*.

> Those who believe and do good works (*ṣāliḥāt*); such shall be the inhabitants of Paradise, to dwell therein forever. (II, 76/82)

As I have indicated earlier, this close relationship between 'faith' and 'good works' in the Qurʾanic conception raises later in theology a very serious problem. This is mainly due to the fact that the expression 'those who believe and perform good works' is capable of being interpreted in two diametrically opposed ways. It suggests, on the one hand, that these two elements are so inseparably tied together that 'faith' is inconceivable without 'good works'; 'faith', in other words, cannot be perfect if it is not accompanied by 'good works'. This is, in short, the doctrine of the Khawārij.

On the other hand, however, the very fact that the Qurʾān uses two different concepts, *īmān* and *ṣāliḥāt*, may be taken as an irrefutable evidence that these are in fact two different things. According to this latter view—which is that of the Murjiʾah—'faith' is an independent unit which, essentially, does not need any other element to be perfect. Why did God separate them from each other conceptually if they were an unanalyzable whole? However, this is not a Qurʾanic problem, and it does not concern us in the context of the present work.

We have to go back to the Qurʾān itself and ask: What are, then, these 'good works'? It is clear contextually that the 'good works' are those works of piety that have been enjoined by God upon all believers. As a matter of fact, the verse 77/83 which immediately follows the passage just quoted and which is given as the Covenant of God with the Israelites, may be taken as a summary description of the *ṣāliḥāt*. It enumerates the following five elements: to worship none save God; to be good (i.e. kind and benevolent, *iḥsān*) to parents, near kinsmen, orphans, and the needy; to speak kindly to everyone; to perform the prayer; and to pay the alms.

Of the two following examples, the first emphasizes the element of pure monotheism as 'a *ṣāliḥ* deed', and the second discusses prayer and alms.

> Say, 'I [Muḥammad] am only an [ordinary] man like you. It is revealed to me that your God is One God. Whoso hopes for the meeting with his Lord, let him do good (*ṣāliḥ*) work, and let him associate none else with the worship of his Lord.' (XVIII, 110)

> Verily, those who believe and do *ṣāliḥāt*, performing the prayer and paying the alms, their reward is with their Lord. There shall be no fear on them, nor shall they grieve. (II, 277)

In the next quotation, the attitude of arrogance and insolence which Noah's son takes up towards God's command is regarded as non-*ṣāliḥ* conduct.

> He [God] said, 'O Noah, he is no longer of thy family, for this is a deed that is not *ṣāliḥ*. So ask not of Me that whereof thou hast no knowledge [i.e. do not ask Me to deliver him from the Deluge].' (XI, 48/46)

The word *ṣāliḥ* does not always qualify human conduct; sometimes we find it also applied to men of a certain type. A brief examination of some of the examples falling under this head will prove of some help to us in analyzing the meaning content of this term. Here is, to begin with, a passage which we may consider almost a verbal definition of '*ṣāliḥ* man'.

> Some of the people of the Scripture are a nation upright (*qāʾimah*), who keep reciting God's signs throughout the night, falling prostrate [before God]. They believe in God and the Last Day, enjoin what is good (*maʿrūf*) and forbid what is bad (*munkar*), and vie one with the other in good works (*khayrāt*).[1] These are of the *ṣāliḥīn* (pl.) (III, 109–110/113–114).

[1] For an analysis of *maʿrūf*, *munkar*, and *khayrāt*, see pp. 213–221.

The following passage bears witness to the fact that the act of giving the alms is regarded as at least one of the characteristic marks of a *ṣāliḥ* man.

> Spend of what We have provided you before death comes unto anyone of you and makes him say, 'My Lord, if only thou wouldst allow me the grace of a little while, so that I might give alms and become one of the *ṣāliḥīn*. (LXIII, 10)

It is noteworthy that Jesus Christ is counted among the *ṣāliḥīn* 'He shall speak to people in the cradle, and grown up, he shall be of the *ṣāliḥīn*' (III, 41/46). A few verses before this in the same Sūrah we find John the Baptist also called a 'Prophet among the *ṣāliḥīn*. (v. 34/39)

We may also note that the 'believers' are sometimes called very characteristically the '*ṣāliḥ* servants' of God.

> Verily, We have written in the Psalms, after the remembrance, 'The earth shall my *ṣāliḥ* servants inherit.' (XXI, 105)

> [Solomon] said, 'My Lord, urge me to be thankful (*ashkura*) for Thy favor wherewith Thou hast favored me and my parents, and to do good work (*ṣāliḥ*) that shall be pleasing unto Thee; do Thou admit me by Thy mercy in the number of Thy *ṣāliḥ* servants.' (XXVII, 19)

The opposite of *ṣāliḥāt* is in the Qurʾān the word *sayyiʾāt* derived from the root *SWʾ*. This root itself will be analyzed later on. Here it must suffice to give some quotations in which *ṣāliḥ* is clearly opposed to some of the derivatives of this root. In the first example, we see the characteristic cliché of which I spoke above, 'those who believe and do *ṣāliḥāt*' opposed to 'those who commit *sayyiʾāt*'.

> Do those who commit *sayyiʾāt* think that we shall treat them in the same way as these who believe and do *ṣāliḥāt*, equal in life and death? How ill they judge. (XLV, 20/21)

In the next passage, *ṣāliḥ* is opposed to *sayyiʾah* (in the singular).

> Whoso does an evil deed (*sayyiʾah*) shall be repaid exactly the like thereof, but whoso does a good [deed] (*ṣāliḥ*), whether man or woman, being a believer—such shall enter Paradise and shall be supplied with food without reckoning. (XL, 43/40)

*Sayyiʾah* is a noun formed from the adjective *sayyiʾ*. Here is an example of the usage of this adjective itself, qualifying the noun *ʿamal* 'action' or 'deed', which is understood. It is, be it noted, used in contradistinction to *ʿamal ṣāliḥ*.

> Some of the Bedouin around you are 'hypocrites' . . . and others have confessed their sins (*dhunūb*) [i.e. they confessed that they had stayed behind from the Apostle in one of his raids on the Kāfirs]: they have mixed a good work (*ʿamal ṣāliḥ*) with another evil (*sayyiʾ*) work. It may be that God will forgive them. (IX, 102–103/101–102)

*Sūʾ* is another noun derived from the same root; this, too, may be used in opposition to *ṣāliḥ*, with exactly the same meaning as *sayyiʾah*. The following example must be compared with the verse from Sūrah XL, which we have just quoted. One will note that the general context is the same in both cases.

> Whoso does evil (*sūʾ*) shall be recompensed for it, and will not find for him beside God, a friend or a helper. Whoso does any of the *ṣāliḥāt*, whether man or woman, being a believer—such shall enter Paradise, and they shall not be wronged even a small spot on a date-stone. (IV, 122–123/123–124)

For all this, the proper antithesis of *sūʾ* or *sayyiʾ* is not *ṣāliḥ* but another word, *ḥasan*. So the meaning structure of the root *SWʾ*, will come up again for consideration at a later stage, when we shall deal with the root *ḤSN*.

## *Birr*

Very similar to *ṣāliḥ* in meaning—though not in form—is the word *birr*, which is perhaps among the most elusive of the Qurʾanic moral terms. In any case, an important clue to the basic semantic structure of this word may be gained if we compare it with *ṣāliḥ* which we have just examined. As we have seen, in the semantic constitution of *ṢLḤ* a very prominent place is given to factors relating to justice and love in human relations, so much so that—to take two representative elements—the act of rendering religious service to God and that of feeding the poor are made to stand there almost on the same footing. Nor, if we reflect, should this surprise us, for the Qurʾān as a whole gives an outstanding emphasis to justice and love in social life. Piety, in other words, cannot be piety unless it manifests itself in various works motivated by the will to practice justice and love towards others.

Now the word *birr* seems to lend further confirmation to this view. An extremely important passage from Sūrah II, which I quoted in Chapter II, furnishes a contextual definition of this word, at least within the general framework of the Qurʾanic thought.

> The *birr* does not consist in your turning your faces towards the East or the West, but [true] *birr* is this, that one believes in God,

and the Last Day, and the angels, and the Scripture, and the prophets; that one gives one's own wealth howsoever cherished it may be, to kinsfolk, orphans, the needy, the wayfarer, and beggars, and also for the sake of slaves; that one performs the ritual prayer, pays the alms. And those who keep their covenant when they have once covenanted and are patient in distress and hardship: these are they who are sincere; these are they who are godfearing. (II, 172/177)

A glance at the elements here enumerated as constituting true *birr* would make us understand at once that there is practically nothing to distinguish it from *ṣāliḥāt*, or true *īmān*. We see at the same time why this term has been so variously translated in English. It may very well be rendered as 'piety'; it may no less justifiably be rendered as 'righteousness' or 'kindness'. But any of these translations taken alone, cannot possibly do justice to the original word which includes all these and perhaps still others in its complex meaning. Other examples culled from the Qur'ān serve only to bring out this or that aspect of this complex meaning of *birr*.

*Birr and taqwá.* In the last sentence of the passage just cited, we see *birr* brought into the most explicit connection with 'fear of God' (*taqwá*). It is emphatically stated there that those who fulfil all the duties, social as well as religious, included under the name of *birr*, are alone worthy to be called 'sincere, or true, believers' (*alladhīna ṣadaqū*) and truly 'godfearing' (*muttaqūn*). In a similar way the passage declares that true *birr* does not consist in the keeping of the meaningless taboos but in 'fearing' God.

It is not *birr* that you should enter your houses from the backs of them.[2] But *birr* is to fear [God]. So enter your houses by the doors and fear God. (II, 185/189)

*Birr and almsgiving:*

You attain not to *birr* until you expend of what you love. And whatever you expend, God is aware of it. (III, 86/92)

Probably *birr* in the next quotation also refers to almsgiving:

Will you enjoin *birr* upon others while you yourselves forget? And yet you always read the Scripture! Have you no sense? (II, 41/44)

[2] Obviously this refers to a taboo-custom that was prevalent in Jāhilīyah. Several explanations have been offered. According to one of them, for instance, an Arab, when he went out in search of something and came back without it, used to enter his house or tent from the back entrance in order to avert from himself the effect of the evil omen (Sharīf al-Murtaḍá, *Amālī*, I, 377).

*Birr and piety to parents:*

> He [John, son of Zachariah] was godfearing (*taqī*, adj.) and pious (*barr*, adj. from the same root as *birr*) towards his parents. (XIX, 14/13–14)

> He [God] has enjoined upon me prayer and almsgiving so long as I live, and *birr* towards my mother. He has not made me a miserable, insolent fellow. (XIX, 32–33/31–32)

*Birr and qisṭ* (equity and justice in conduct):

> As to those who have not fought you on account of religion nor driven you out from your homes, God forbids you not that you should show *birr* (*tabarrū*, verb) to them and act equitably (*tuqsiṭū*, verb) towards them. Verily, God loves those who act equitably (*muqsiṭīn*, part, pl.). (LX, 8)

In the passage which I have just quoted, we see *qisṭ* behaving almost synonymously with *birr*. But while *birr*, as we saw, is a comprehensive name for all actions motivated by love and righteousness, and stimulated by the religious experience of 'fear', *qisṭ*, has a much more limited application, being used chiefly as a forensic term for justice, or impartiality in dealing with others. As such, the word is most often applied to the verdict in a trial.

> If they [i.e. the Jews hostile to Islām] come to thee [Muḥammad], judge thou between them, or simply turn away from them. . . . But in case thou judgest, then judge between them with justice (*qisṭ*). Verily, God loves those who practice justice (*muqsiṭīn*, part, pl.). (V, 46/42)

> Every nation has its own Apostle. So when their Apostle comes [on the Day of Judgment] it will be judged between them with justice (*qisṭ*), and they will not be wronged (*yuẓlamūna*). (X, 48/47)

It should be noticed that 'being judged with *qisṭ*' is here made equivalent to 'not suffering any wrong (*ẓulm*)'. In other words, *qisṭ* in such contexts is clearly opposed to *ẓulm*, a fact which may greatly aid us in understanding the meaning of both *qisṭ* and *ẓulm*.

As we might expect, the final yardstick of justice in such cases is, according to the Qurʾanic view, furnished by God's will. Revelation, in short, is the ultimate basis of *qisṭ*. The point comes out with utmost clarity in verses like the following:

> Whoso judges not by what God has sent down: such are *kāfirūn*. . . . Whoso judges not by what God sent down: such are wrong-doers (*ẓālimūn*). (V, 48–49/44–45)

More concretely, *qisṭ* may refer to various cases involving equity or justice. Thus, to take a typical instance, he who takes the witness stand should act with perfect impartiality and not allow himself to be swayed by his own personal likes and dislikes.

> O believers, be upright before God as witnesses with *qisṭ*. Let not your ill-will towards a people tempt you into the sin of not acting equitably (*taᶜdilū*). Act equitably (*iᶜdilū*); that is nearer to *taqwá*. Fear God, for God is aware of what you do. (V, 11/8)

The concrete meaning of the phrase 'with *qisṭ*' is made clear by what follows it in the verse. Essentially the same is true of the next example.

> O believers, be upright before God as witnesses with *qisṭ*, even though it be against yourselves, or your parents, or your kinsmen, whether [the accused] be rich or poor. (IV, 134/135)

The next passage concerns the legal way of dealing on credit.

> O believers, when you deal on credit one with another for a definite term, write it down, and let a writer write it between you with *ᶜadl* (= *qisṭ*). . . . Be not averse to writing it down, be [the amount] small or great, with its date of payment. That is more equitable (*aqsaṭ*, comp.) in God's sight. (II, 282)

The word is also used in reference to the standards and obligations in commerce. In the Qurʾān there are frequent exhortations to 'give full measure and full weight, in justice'. An example may suffice:

> O my people, give full measure and full weight with *qisṭ*, and do not defraud men of their things. (XI, 86/85)

There exists in Arabic another word which is almost a technical term for the occurrence of non-*qisṭ* in the specific field of measure and weight: *ṭaffafa* (root *ṬF*), which conveys precisely the meaning of 'giving short measure of weight'. This, too, appears in the Qurʾān in a very important passage. The context itself furnishes, as it were, a verbal definition of the word:

> Woe unto the defrauders (*muṭaffifīn*, part. pl.) who, when they measure against others, take full measure, but, when they measure or weigh for others, give short measure. (LXXXIII, 1–3)[3]

[3] It is interesting to observe that this concept of justice in measure is extended to the heavenly Balance—the 'just' Balance, as it is called—which is to be employed on the Day of Judgment.

> We shall set up the Balance of *qisṭ* for the Day of Resurrection, so that no soul shall be wronged in aught. Even if it be of the weight of a grain of mustard seed, We shall bring it out, for We are an absolute reckoner. (XXI, 48/47).

In Sūrah II, 282 that has been quoted above, we met with a synonym of *qisṭ*, namely the word *ᶜadl*. Here I shall give two further examples which will confirm the close relationship between the two words. The first passage contains *qisṭ* in its first half while in the second half approximately the same idea is expressed by *ᶜadl*.

> In case you fear that you cannot act justly (*tuqsiṭū*, verb) towards the orphans [in your charge], marry of the women, who seem good to you two, three, or four. But if you fear you cannot act equitably (*taᶜdilū*) [towards so many wives], then only one, or what your right hands possess [i.e. slave-girls]. Thus it is more likely that you will not be partial. (IV, 3)

> If two parties of the believers combat one with another, try to make peace between them. Then, if one of the parties acts wrongfully out of insolence (*baghat*, from *baghá* which we considered earlier, in Chapter X), fight the party that acts wrongfully until it returns to God's commandment. If it returns, make peace between them with *ᶜadl*, and act equitably (*aqsiṭū*, from *qisṭ*). Verily, God loves those who act equitably (*muqsiṭīn*, part. pl.). (XLIX, 9)

The next example is of particular significance in that it brings to light the focal point of the meaning of *ᶜadl* by contrasting it with *mayl* 'partiality', or favoritism.

> You will not be able to act equitably (*taᶜdilū*, verb) to all your wives, however eagerly you may wish to do so. But yet do not be altogether partial (*lā tamīlū kull al-mayl*) so as to leave one as in suspense. (IV, 128/129)

## *Fasād*

That the word *fasād* (or the corresponding verb *afsada*) is a very comprehensive word which is capable of denoting all kinds of evil-doing is clear from an examination of its behavior in non-religious contexts. Even within the limits of the Qurʾān, we find a few examples of such non-religious use of the word. Thus, for instance, in the Chapter of Joseph the act of stealing is called by this name.

> 'By God', they said, 'well you know that we came not here to do evil (*nufsida*, from *afsada*) in the land. We are not thieves.' (XII, 73)

This is said by Joseph's brothers who have fallen under suspicion of having stolen the king's goblet. In the following passage the reference is to the acts of atrocious violence committed by Gog and Magog everywhere on the earth:

> They said, 'O Two-Horned [i.e. Alexander the Great], look, Gog and Magog are doing evil (*mufsidūn*, part. of *afsada*) in the earth. Wilt thou set up a rampart between us and them, if we pay thee tribute?' (XVIII, 93/94)

In another passage, which, by the way, should be regarded as a 'religious' context from the point of view of the Qurʾān, the same word is used to mean the odious habit for which Sodom was notorious.

> Lot said to his people, 'Verily, you commit an abomination (*fāḥishah*)[4] such as none in all the world has ever committed before you. What, do you approach men, and cut the way [robbing way-farers], and commit in your assembly things disapproved (*munkar*)?'[5]

> But the only answer of his people was, 'Bring us God's chastise-ment, if what thou speakest is true!' He said, 'My Lord, help me against this people who do evil (*mufsidīn*).' (XXIX, 27–29/28–30)

The word is also applied to the conduct of Pharaoh, violently oppressing the Israelites without any justifiable reason:

> Verily, Pharaoh exalted himself in the land and divided the people thereof into sects; he oppressed one party of them [i.e. the Israelites], slaughtering their sons and sparing their women. Verily, he did evil [lit. he was one of the *mufsidīn*]. (XXVIII, 3/4)

In another place, the word is applied to the Egyptian sorcerers in the service of the Court. The reference is to the well-known scene of the magic tournament in the presence of Pharaoh.

> Moses said, 'That which you have shown is sorcery. God will surely bring it to naught, for God will never set right (*yuṣliḥu*, from *aṣlaḥa*) the work of those who do evil (*mufsidīn*).' (X, 81)

In properly religious contexts, however, the word very often, if not invariably, has the restricted meaning of *kufr*. Here I give a few typical examples, of which the first applies the word *mufsid* to the 'dis-believers' in particular reference to their *takdhīb*. This is clear from the general context from which the passage has been taken.

> Of them some believe therein [i.e. in the Qurʾān], and some believe not therein. But thy Lord knows well who are the evil-doers (*mufsidīn*). (X, 41/40)

> Those who disbelieve (*kafarū*) and bar from the way of God—We shall inflict upon them punishment after punishment, for that they were doing evil (*yufsidūna*). (XVI, 90/88)

[4] For an explanation of this concept see pp. 233–234.
[5] See the following section, pp. 213–217.

There is no god but God. . . . But if they turn away, verily God knows those who do evil (*mufsidīn*). (III, 55–56/62–63)

It is interesting to note that in a passage the same word is applied to the monotheists from the standpoint of the Kāfirs. Here the spread of the monotheistic movement causing irreparable damage to the traditional idolatrous customs is regarded as 'working corruption in the land'.

The chiefs of Pharaoh's people said, 'Wilt thou [Pharaoh] leave Moses and his people to do evil (*yufsidū*) in the land and to abandon thee and thy gods?' (VII, 124/127)

## *Maᶜrūf* and *Munkar*

*Maᶜrūf*. Among the various terms that may be regarded as constituting partial or near Arabic equivalents for the English 'good', *maᶜrūf* occupies a special place, because it seems to represent an idea that goes back to a remote past. In the Muslim exegeses of later ages we see the word *maᶜrūf* defined very often as 'what is acknowledged and approved by Divine Law'.[6] But this is of course but a reflection of the state of affairs peculiar to the classical age of Islām, and conceals rather than reveals the real nature of the word. The concept is far older than *sharᶜ*. It belongs to, and is based on the tribal type of morality that was peculiar to Jāhilīyah. As Professor Reuben Levy has remarked very pertinently, the use of this word—with its opposite, *munkar*—in the Qurᵓān for good (and evil), shows that the Qurᵓān adopted the tribal moral terminology and made it an integral part of the new system of ethics. *Maᶜrūf* means literally 'known', i.e. what is regarded as known and familiar, and, therefore, also socially approved. Its antithesis *munkar* means what is disapproved precisely because it is unknown and foreign. 'Tribal societies in a state of civilization parallel to that of the Arab tribes of the *Jāhilīya*, would, in the same way as they did, regard the known and familiar as the good and the strange as the evil.'[7] Here I give, as an example, a verse by a Jāhilī poet, Musāfiᶜ al-ᶜAbsī, in which he laments the death of the Banū ᶜAmr tribe and extols them as ideal people.

*Ulāka banū khayr wa-sharr kilayhimā* *
*jamīᶜan wa-maᶜrūf alamma wa-munkar*

Those were people of both good (*khayr*) [for their friends] and evil (*sharr*) [for their enemies] at the same time, they used to be [the

[6] See, for example, al-Bayḍāwī, comm. on Sūrah II, 232.
[7] Reuben Levy: *The Social Structure of Islam* (Cambridge, 1957), p. 194.

> cause] of *maʿrūf* [for their friends] that befell the latter and of *munkar* [for their enemies].[8]

But the word *maʿrūf*, whatever its origin, is actually used in the Qurʾān in a rather more restricted sense than this. We might perhaps do best to examine, first of all, an example which will give us an important clue as to what the Qurʾān itself meant when it used this word. The passage in question is contained in the admonition which God gives especially to the wives of Muḥammad.

> O wives of the Prophet, you are not as ordinary women. If you [truly] fear [God], be not too tender in your speech [in talking to men other than your husband], lest he in whose heart is sickness should become lustful. But always speak *maʿrūf* words. (XXXIII, 32)

It is clear contextually that the phrase 'words that are *maʿrūf*' here denotes the manner of speech which is really suitable to the Prophet's wife; a manner of talking, that is, which is honorable enough, dignified enough to give 'those in whose hearts is sickness' (i.e. men full of sensual desires) no chance of getting excited lustfully.

The next example throws further illuminating light on the meaning content of *maʿrūf* by contrasting it with the way of doing which is not *maʿrūf*.

> When you have divorced women, and they have reached their prescribed term, then retain them with *maʿrūf*, or else release them with *maʿrūf*; but do not retain them by force (*ḍirāran*) so that you transgress. Whoso does that has wronged his soul [or himself]. (II, 231)

'To retain the divorced women with *maʿrūf*' is here contrasted with 'to retain them by force', which suggests that 'with *maʿrūf*' must mean something like 'in the right way'. The 'right' here would, in Jāhiliyah, mean nothing but 'traditionally known (and approved)'; in the Qurʾanic conception, however, the source of rightness lies not in tradition, but in the will of God. This is clear from the fact that, in this passage, 'behaving not in the *maʿrūf* way' is declared to be a case of 'transgression', and 'doing wrong to one's own soul'—expressions that are, as we saw earlier, commonly used to describe precisely the conduct of the Kāfirs.

Incidentally, the passage I have just quoted is a legal provision for the divorced wife. Now it is another characteristic feature of the word *maʿrūf* that it tends to be used most appropriately in the legislative portions of the Book, particularly where regulations concerning

[8] Abū Tammām *Ḥamāsah*, III, 24.

moral duties in family relations, between husband and wife, parents and children, or among near kinsfolk, are in question. The following are some of the examples from Sūrah II and others.

> When you have divorced women and they have reached the prescribed term, prevent them not from marrying their [new] husbands, when they have agreed with each other with *maᶜrūf*. (II, 232)

The phrase 'with *maᶜrūf*' in this passage would seem to be equivalent almost to 'through due formalities'. Bayḍāwī paraphrases it thus: 'in compliance with the legal provision and according to what is acknowledged by the law of humanity'.

> Mothers shall suckle their children for the period of two whole years, provided they desire to complete the suckling. [During that period] the father of the child must fulfil the duty of feeding and clothing them [i.e. the mothers] with *maᶜrūf*. ('honestly' 'respectably' or 'in due form', one might say). (II, 233)

> But if you prefer to place your children under the care of a wet nurse, it is no sin (*junāḥ*) for you, provided you pay with *maᶜrūf* what you have to give. (II, 233)

> O you who believe, it is not lawful (*lā yaḥillu*) for you to inherit women against their will, nor to hinder them from remarrying so as to take back part of what you have given them, unless they commit a flagrant abomination [i.e. fornication]. Treat them with *maᶜrūf*. (IV, 23/19)

> Be grateful to Me and to thy parents. . . . But in case they attempt at inducing thee to associate with Me that which thou hast no knowledge of [i.e. idols], then obey them not. But keep company with them in this world in a *maᶜrūf* way (*maᶜrūfan*). (XXXI, 13–14/14–15)

*Munkar*. *Maᶜrūf* stands formally opposed to *munkar*, which, as we have seen, literally means 'unknown', 'foreign', and—precisely because of that—'disapproved' or 'bad'. The Qurʾān exhorts the Prophet and the believing community again and again, with strong emphasis, to 'enjoin the *maᶜrūf* and forbid the *munkar*'. And in the form of this combination, both terms seem to stand for very general and comprehensive ideas of '[religiously] good' and '[religiously] bad', *maᶜrūf* meaning any acts arising from, and in consonance with, the true belief, and *munkar* any acts that would conflict with God's commandments.

The believers, both men and women, are friends one of another. They enjoin the *ma<sup>c</sup>rūf* and forbid the *munkar*, and they perform the prayer and pay the alms, and they obey God and His Apostle. (IX, 72/71)

It is noteworthy that al-Bayḍāwī writes that the *ma[c]rūf* here means *īmān* 'belief' and *ṭā[c]ah* 'obedience', while *munkar* is equivalent to *kufr* and *ma[c]āṣī* 'disobedience'.

Let there be one community of you, all inviting men to good (*khayr*), enjoining the *ma[c]rūf* and forbidding the *munkar*. Those shall be the [ultimate] winners. (III, 100/104)

You are the best community that has ever been brought forth unto men. You enjoin the *ma[c]rūf* and forbid the *munkar*, believing in God. (III, 106/110)

It is to be noted that in the same passage it is affirmed that the *ṣāliḥ* people are those who believe in God and the Last Day, and devote themselves to pious works, 'enjoining the *ma[c]rūf* and forbidding the *munkar*'. (v. 110/114)

It is perhaps of more interest to observe that the 'hypocrites' are accused of doing the exact reverse of this: they enjoin the *munkar* and forbid the *ma[c]rūf*.

The *munāfiq*, both men and women, are all one; they enjoin the *munkar* and forbid the *ma[c]rūf*. . . . They have forgotten God, and He has forgotten them. Verily, the *munāfiq* are *fāsiq* people. (IX, 68/67)

Next I shall give a few examples showing the use of the term *munkar* disjoined from its usual companion, *munāfiq*. The first is of particular significance because the context in which the word is found is, if not definitely non-religious, rather of a secular nature in that it has nothing to do directly with belief and *kufr*. Note that the word here appears in the form of *nukr* (from the same root as *munkar*); the meaning remains exactly the same.[9]

So the two [i.e. Moses (as a legendary figure) and the Mysterious Man commonly known as Khaḍir] journeyed on until, when they met a boy, he [i.e. Khaḍir] slew him. Moses said, 'What, hast thou slain a pure [i.e. innocent] soul guilty of no murder? Verily thou hast done a hideous (*nukr*) thing.' (XVIII, 73/74)

9 In just the same way, *ma[c]rūf* can be replaced by *[c]urf*. And *[c]urf* and *nukr* form a pair just as *ma[c]rūf* and *munkar* go together. I give here an example from old poetry: *Ahl al-ḥulūm idhā al-ḥulūmhafat * wa-al-[c]urf fī al-aqwām wa-al-nukr* (by Ḥarrān b. [c]Amr b. [c]Abd Manāt, in Abū Tammām, *Ḥamāsah*, III, 34) 'People of sound judgment are they, even when other people lose their judgment (lit. when reason gets on a slippery road); they are also men of *[c]urf* [toward their friends] among all tribes, [while against their enemies, they are] men of *nukr*'.

The next example relates to the conduct of the disbelievers among the Israelites:

> Cursed were those of the children of Israel who became Kāfirs . . . because they disobeyed (*ᶜaṣaw*) and were always transgressing (*yaᶜtadūna*). They never forbade one another any ***munkar*** that they used to do. Verily evil was that which they used to do. (V, 82–83/78–79)

In the passage which I quote next, the word ***munkar*** is applied to the formula of divorce—'Thou art as my mother's back'—with which men in Jāhilīyah used to divorce their wives.

> Those of you who divorce their wives by the formula of 'mother's back', though they [i.e. wives] are not their mothers—their mothers being only those who gave them birth—verily, they utter an abominable thing (***munkar***) and a falsehood. (LVIII, 2)

That in this and other places ***munkar*** has semantically much in common with 'abomination' or 'indecency' is explicitly shown by the fact that the word sometimes appears in combination with *faḥshāʾ* which, as we shall presently see, is the very word for such a concept.

## *Khayr* and *Sharr*

Probably ***khayr*** represents the nearest Arabic equivalent of the English 'good'. It is a very comprehensive term, meaning as it does almost anything that may be considered in any respect valuable, beneficial, useful, and desirable. And even within the bounds of the Qurʾanic context, its semantic scope covers both the field of worldly affairs and that of religious belief. Let me begin with a brief examination of some examples falling under the former class. The first relates to the legend of Solomon: one day, it is related, he was so lost in admiration of his beautiful horses that he forgot the duty of the evening prayer; when he came to himself a bitter remorse seized him, and he uttered the following words:

> Verily, I have loved the love of good things (***khayr***) better than the remembrance of my Lord, until the sun sank behind the veil. (XXXVIII, 31/32)

But the most representative use of ***khayr*** in the field of worldly affairs is, without doubt, seen in those very numerous cases where the word behaves as a genuine synonym of *māl* 'wealth'.

> It is prescribed for you; when death visits any of you, if he leaves some wealth (***khayr***), he should bequeath in the *maᶜrūf* way unto his parents and near relatives. (II, 176/180)

Particularly important is the following passage in which we see the word *khayr* actually replaced by *māl* in the end, showing with utmost clarity that the two terms are interchangeable in contexts of this sort.

> Whatever good (*khayr*) you expend, it shall be for yourselves, for in that case you expend only because you seek God's countenance, and whatever good (*khayr*) you expend, it shall be repaid you in full, and you will never be wronged. . . . And whatever good (*khayr*) you expend, verily, God is aware of it. Those who expend their wealth (*amwāl*, pl. of *māl*) night and day, secretly and openly, verily, their reward is with their Lord. (II, 274–275/272–274)

No less important is the next verse in which the same word *khayr* clearly fulfils a double function: it means 'wealth' in the first sentence, and, in the second, 'pious work'. It should be observed that *khayr* in this sense is, as we shall presently see, almost synonymous with *ṣāliḥ* which we discussed earlier.

> They will ask thee [Muḥammad] concerning what they should expend [in alms]; say, 'Whatever good (*khayr*) you expend must go to parents and kinsmen, orphans, the needy, and the wayfarer. Whatever good (*khayr*) you do, verily, God is aware of it.' (II, 211/215)

Wealth represents the earthly good. Since, in actual fact, there can be an infinite variety of earthly goods or worldly values, *khayr* proves to be a word of extremely wide application in this field. We shall confine ourselves, however, to the analysis of the semantic content of *khayr* in contexts that are immediately related to religion and faith.

In this field too, the meaning of *khayr* is exceedingly wide in scope, for, as one might expect, anything religiously valuable or beneficial to man can be the denotatum of this word. And this shows that the word is fully entitled to be considered a 'secondary level' ethical term.

*God's bounty:*

> O God, owner of the Kingdom, . . . Thou makest whom Thou wilt rich and powerful, and Thou humblest whom Thou wilt. In Thy hand is the good (*khayr*). (III, 25/26)

The context itself suggests clearly that the 'good' here denotes the limitless bounty of God. Further confirmation of this view is afforded by vv. 66–67/73–74 of the same Sūrah, where we read: 'Verily, in God's hand is bounty (*faḍl*). . . . He specially favors with

His mercy (*raḥmah*) whom He will, for God is Lord of great bounty (*faḍl*).'

*God's special favor (Revelation):*

Those who disbelieve among the people of the Scripture and the idol-worshippers love not that there should be sent down upon you anything good (*khayr*) from your Lord. But God specially favors with His mercy whom He will, for God is Lord of mighty bounty. (II, 99/105)

It shall be said [on the Day of Resurrection] to those who fear [i.e. the pious believers], 'What has your Lord sent down?' They will answer, '[He has sent down upon us] good (*khayr*).' (XVI, 32/30)

He [God] gives the Wisdom unto whom He will, and whoso is given the Wisdom, has been given much good (*khayr*). (II, 272/269)

*Belief and genuine faith:*

O Prophet, say unto the captives who are in your hands, 'If God knows any good (*khayr*) in your hearts, He will give you better than that which has been taken from you, and will forgive you'. (VIII, 71/70)

*Positive effect of the faith:*

On the day when one of the signs of thy Lord [i.e. a portent of the approach of the Last Hour] does appear, its belief shall be of no avail to a soul which did not believe before, nor earned some good (*khayr*) by its faith. (VI, 159/158)

*Pious work (ṣāliḥāt):*

Perform you the prayer steadfastly, and pay the alms. Whatever good (*khayr*) you send forward for the sake of your own souls, you shall find it with God. Verily, God sees everything you do. (II, 104/110)

Be you emulous in good works (*khayrāt* pl.). (V, 53/48)

Verily, they vied one with another in good works (*khayrāt*), and called upon Us yearningly, yet with fear, and were humble before Us. (XXI, 90)

*Excellent believer:*

[Abraham, Isaac, and Jacob], verily, We made them pure with genuine sincerity, [that is,] the thought of the [Last] Abode. Thus in Our sight they were, verily, of the chosen, the good (*akhyār*, pl.). (XXXVIII, 46–47)

A glance at the examples given will make it clear that the denotata of the word *khayr* in the field of religious matters fall roughly into two classes: one is the 'good', the source of which lies in God, and the other is the 'good' produced by man. In either case, the basic connotatum remains the same: it means something which may rightly be judged valuable from the specific point of view of the revealed religion.

Next we shall turn to those cases where the word *khayr* is used in opposition to something else. The most usual antithesis of *khayr* is furnished by *sharr* which functions as its direct opposite in any of its various meanings examined above, whether religious or non-religious. Thus, to take a typical example, when *khayr* is used for 'happiness' or prosperity in worldly life, *sharr* is used for 'misfortune'.

Man tires not of praying for good (*khayr*), and if evil (*sharr*) touches him, then he becomes disheartened and desperate. But if we let him taste mercy (*raḥmah*) after distress (*ḍarrā*ᵓ) that has touched him he is sure to say, 'This is my own. I think not that the [Last] Hour is imminent.' (XLI, 49–50)

The precise meaning of the pair, *khayr—sharr*, in verse 49 is disclosed by another pair that immediately follows it in v. 50, i.e. *raḥmah* (happiness or good fortune conceived as God's mercy) and *ḍarrā*ᵓ (ill fortune or distress). It will not be out of place to add here that the Qurᵓān generally considers happiness and misery in this present world a kind of trial by means of which God distinguishes between true believers and Kāfirs.

We test you [first] with evil (*sharr*) and good (*khayr*) as a trial, then unto Us you shall be brought back. (XXI, 36/35)

The next two examples are of particular significance for our purpose in a somewhat different respect; apparently, they simply state that the goodness or badness of a thing has, essentially, nothing to do with man's loving it or disliking it; that one should always judge by the ultimate issue to which it leads. Viewed from the reverse side, however, this would imply that the problem of whether a thing is *khayr* or *sharr* tends to be made dependent on man's natural subjective reaction to it, that is, whether he likes it or hates it. In a word, *khayr* and *sharr* stand for 'likes' and 'dislikes'.



God determines khayr and sharr

> Prescribed for you is fighting [in God's way], though it may be hateful to you. It may be, however, that you hate a thing which is [really] good (*khayr*) for you, and that you love a thing which is bad (*sharr*) for you. God knows, but you know not. (II, 212–213/216)

> Treat them [your wives] well [lit. with *maʿrūf*]. Even if you hate them, it may be that you hate a thing wherein God has placed much good (*khayr*) for you. (IV, 23/19)

It would be almost superfluous to point out that the basic opposition of *khayr* and *sharr* occurs also in the properly religious field, denoting, then, pious deed and *kufr*, respectively.

> Upon that day [i.e. the Day of Judgment] men shall issue forth in separate groups so as to witness their own deeds [in this world]. Whoso has done the weight of an atom of good (*khayr*) shall see it, and whoso has done the weight of an atom of evil (*sharr*) shall see it. (XCIX, 6–8)

Sometimes *sharr* in this sense is replaced by another word *sūʾ* which we shall examine in the next section.

## *ḤSN* and *SWʾ*

These two roots appear in various forms. We shall in what follows examine the most important of them.

1. *Ḥasan*. Like *khayr*, this word has a very wide range of application. It is an adjective which may be applied to almost anything that is felt to be 'pleasing', 'satisfying', 'beautiful', or 'admirable'. And, as in the case of *khayr*, its scope covers both worldly and religious spheres of human life. A few examples will suffice to show this.

> And of the fruits of the date-palm and grapes, you take therefrom intoxicating liquor and good (*ḥasan*) nourishment. Verily, therein is a sign for people who have sense. (XVI, 69/67)

Here, it is clear, the word *ḥasan* is roughly equivalent to 'delicious' or 'agreeable to the taste'. In the next example, the same word refers to something entirely different.

> Her Lord received her [Mary, mother of Jesus] with a good (*ḥasan*) reception and made her grow up with a goodly (*ḥasan*) growth. (III, 32/37)

It should be noted that in this verse, *ḥasan* appears twice in succession. In the first case it means the 'gracious' treatment Mary received at the hands of God; while in the second, it suggests that she grew up in good health to be a graceful woman.

The next passage applies the word to the ideal type of relation between men in social intercourse. More concretely, it enjoins upon men the duty of speaking always peaceably so as to maintain and promote peaceful relations among themselves.

> Tell My servants to speak words that are more peaceable (*aḥsan*, comparative). For verily, Satan is trying to cause discord among them. Verily, Satan is ever for man a manifest enemy. (XVII, 55/53)

*Ḥasan* can also be used in the sense of 'profitable' or 'lucrative' in the domain of business and commerce. The Qurʾān uses it figuratively in reference to pious acts. By doing a pious deed, man lends a very advantageous loan to God.

> Who is there that will lend a good (*ḥasan*) loan to God, so that He may increase it for him manifold? (II, 246/245)

> Verily, those who give in charity, whether men or women, and thus have lent a good loan to God, it shall be multiplied for them, and they shall receive a generous hire. (LVII, 17/18)

God's promise is called a '*ḥasan* promise' because it promises much good to men provided they fulfil its conditions faithfully.

> O my people, has not your Lord promised you a good (*ḥasan*) promise? (XX, 89/86)

> Is he whom We have promised a good (*ḥasan*) promise [meaning the Garden of Heaven] . . . like him to whom We have given the momentary enjoyment of the life of the world, then on the day of Resurrection he shall be of those arraigned? (XXVIII, 61)

Various other things are called *ḥasan* in the Qurʾān, but this much seems to suffice for our present purpose. The job of denoting a 'good work' in the sense of a 'pious' deed within the semantic boundary of the root *ḤSN* is chiefly assigned to the feminine form of *ḥasan*, to which we shall now turn.

2. *Ḥasanah.* This word is the feminine form of the adjective *ḥasan* which we have just dealt with. The feminine form is used as a substantive, and means anything having the quality designated by the adjective. Let us remark at the outset that the word in this sense is, at least in certain contexts, almost perfectly synonymous with *khayr* which we discussed above, in both of its fields of application,

worldly and religious. This point is admirably brought out in the following example:

> Some there are who say, 'Our Lord, give us in this world *ḥasanah* and in the Hereafter, too, *ḥasanah*, and guard us from the chastisement of the Fire.' (II, 197/201)

*Ḥasanah* in this quotation clearly means happiness, prosperity, good luck. The word in this sense occurs constantly in the Qurʾān in close combination with its antithesis *sayyiʾah*. Here I give only two examples.

> If good (*ḥasanah*) befall them, they say, 'This is from God', but if evil befall them, they say, 'This is from thee [Muḥammad].' Say, 'Everything comes from God.' (IV, 80/78)

> If good (*ḥasanah*) touch you [Muslims], it is disagreeable to them [i.e. the Kāfirs], but if evil (*sayyiʾah*) befall you, they rejoice therein. (III, 116/120)

Both *ḥasanah* and *sayyiʾah* sometimes appear in the plural form, thus:

> We have tried them with good things (*ḥasanāt*, pl.) and evil things (*sayyiʾāt*, pl.) that haply they might return. (VII, 167/168)

We might do well to recall in this connection what was said above concerning the divine 'trial' of men by *khayr* and *sharr*.

Just as *khayr* which, as we saw, is in itself an exceedingly comprehensive word, can be used in the narrow, strictly religious sense of 'pious work', *ḥasanah* may be so used with almost exactly the same meaning.

> Verily, God will not treat anyone unjustly even the weight of an ant, and if it is a good work (*ḥasanah*), He will double it, and will give an immense reward. (IV, 44/40)

This is particularly the case when the word is used in explicit contrast to *sayyiʾah*. The meaning of the latter word then changes from evil in general to ungodliness. Examples abound.

> Whoso brings a good work (*ḥasanah*) [on the Day of Judgment] shall be safe from terror that day. But whoso brings an evil deed (*sayyiʾah*), such shall have their faces thrust into the Fire. (XXVII, 91–92/89–90)

In place of the phrase 'to bring a good work', the causative verb *aḥsana* (from the same root) may be used. This verb itself will be analyzed in detail in the following section. Here I am only concerned to show that the phrase 'he who *aḥsana*' is equivalent to 'he who does a *ḥasanah*', and that this implicit *ḥasanah* may further be contrasted explicitly with *sayyiʾah*.

> For those who do good (*aḥsanū*, pl.) shall be the best reward. . . . Those shall be the inhabitants of Paradise, to dwell therein for ever. But for those who commit evil deeds (*sayyiʾat*), the recompense of each evil deed (*sayyiʾah*) shall be the like thereof. (X, 27–28/26–27)

3. *Aḥsana.* The verb *aḥsana* (inf. *iḥsān*) is one of the key ethical terms in the Qurʾān. Most generally it means 'to do good', but in the actual Qurʾanic usage this word is applied mainly to two particular classes of 'goodness': profound piety towards God and all human deeds that originate in it, and acts motivated by the spirit of *ḥilm*.

Let us examine first those cases where *iḥsān* is roughly equivalent to piety and devotion, or to use a more characteristic expression, 'the fear of God'.

> Verily, whoso fears God (*yattaqi*, from *taqwá*) and is patient (*yaṣbir*)—surely God wastes not the wage of those who do good (*muḥsinīn*, part. pl.). (XII, 90)

It should be noted that here the semantic content of *iḥsān* is defined in terms of 'fear of God' and 'patience', both of which, as we saw in Chapter X, are among the most characteristic features of the 'believer'. In the next example, the same word *muḥsin* (part. of *aḥsana*) is equated with *muttaqī* 'godfearing', while its concrete denotatum is explicitly described as various acts of pious devotion.

> Verily, the godfearing (*muttaqīn*, pl.) are now [i.e. after Resurrection] in gardens and springs, taking whatever their Lord has given them. Verily, they were before [i.e. in the present world] *muḥsinīn*: but little of the night they slept, at the dawn they would ask forgiveness, and in their wealth even the beggar and the outcast had a share. (LI, 15–19)

That *aḥsana* in contexts of this sort is practically synonymous with 'doing the *ṣāliḥāt*' will be made clearer from examples that follow.

> The *muḥsinīn* who perform the prayer steadfastly, and give alms, and have unswerving faith in the Hereafter. Those are upon the guidance from their Lord; those are sure to prosper. (XXXI, 2–3/3–5)
>
> Verily, those who believe and do good works (*ṣāliḥāt*)—verily, We waste not the wage of him who does good works (*aḥsana ʿamalan*, lit. 'is good as to deed'). (XVIII, 29/30)

We might add that Abraham who, in complete obedience to God's command, attempted to sacrifice his beloved son Isaac, is called, in reference to this very act, a *muḥsin.*

> O Abraham, thou hast already carried out the dream. Verily, thus do We recompense the *muḥsinīn.* This is indeed a manifest trial. (XXXVII, 104–106)

Such being the case, it is hardly surprising that *muḥsin* should sometimes be opposed to *kāfir* or some of its semantic equivalents.

> So God rewards them for these [pious] words with gardens beneath which rivers flow, to dwell therein forever. That is the reward of the *muḥsinīn.* But those who disbelieve (*kafarū*) and cry lies to Our signs, they shall be the inhabitants of Hell. (V, 88/85–86)

> This is a Scripture confirming, in the Arabic language, to warn those who do wrong (*ẓalamū*) and bring good tidings to the *muḥsinīn.* (XLVI, 11/12)

As I have suggested above, *iḥsān* has another important application: it may denote loving deeds towards others, that is, to be more precise, deeds motivated by the fundamental attitude of *ḥilm.* That *iḥsān* is the most immediate manifestation of the spirit of *ḥilm* will be clearly perceived in the following example:

> A Paradise as wide as the heavens and the earth is prepared for those who fear [God], the godfearing who expend [in alms] in prosperity and adversity, and repress their rage, and pardon men, for God loves the *muḥsinīn.* (III, 127–128/133–134)

He who is always willing to help the poor, is slow to anger, forbears from retaliating, and forgives offences—this is the very embodiment of the virtue of *ḥilm* as we saw in Chapter IV. The next verse is another example showing the close connection between *iḥsān* and *ḥilm.* In other words, the thought expressed by the verse is just the contrary of the spirit of Jāhilīyah.

> Thou [Muḥammad] wilt not cease to discover treachery [i.e. the act of breaking the compact] from them [the children of Israel], save a few of them. But pardon them, for God loves the *muḥsinīn.* (V, 16/13)

The Qur'ān never wearies of emphasizing the duty of showing kindness to parents, if only for the reason that 'his mother bore him with pain and with pain did she give birth to him.' (XLVI, 14/15). The attitude of filial piety is called by the name of *iḥsān.*

> Thy Lord has decreed that you should serve none save Him, and that you should be kind (*iḥsān*) to parents. If one or both of them

> attain old age with thee, say not 'Fie!' unto them nor chide them, but speak unto them respectful (*karīm*) words, and lower unto them the wing of humbleness out of mercy (*raḥmah*), and say, 'My Lord, have mercy upon them, just as they raised me up when I was a small child.' (XVII, 24–25/23–24)

The latter half of this passage shows in concrete terms the real nature of the 'kindness' in question.

As is only to be expected in the spiritual climate of the Qurʾān which gives an outstanding emphasis on charity, the meaning of *iḥsān* in this sense shows a strong tendency to become contracted from comprehensive 'loving-kindness' to that of generosity in alms-giving. Here is a good example which brings out most clearly the element of 'generosity' in *iḥsān* by contrasting it with *bukhl* 'stinginess'.

> Be good (*iḥsān*) to your parents, and near kindred, and orphans, and the needy, and the neighbor, whether of kin or not of kin, the companion at your side, the wayfarer, and what your right hands possess [i.e. your slaves]. Verily, God loves not those who are proud and arrogant, who are not only niggardly, but also bid others be niggardly, and hide that which God has bestowed upon them of His bounty. (IV, 40–41/36–37)

4. *Sayyiʾah.* Like the corresponding *ḥasanah*, *sayyiʾah* is properly the feminine form of an adjective, used in the Qurʾān mostly as a substantive. The adjective in question is *sayyiʾ*, which occurs in Sūrah XXXV and discloses remarkably well the Qurʾanic meaning of the root *SWʾ*. It runs as follows:

> They swore by God a solemn oath that if a warner [i.e. Prophet] came to them, they would surely be more rightly guided than any of the nations. Yet, when a warner did come to them, they only became the more averse, behaving the more proudly (*istikbār*) in the land, and plotting more evil. But the evil (*sayyiʾ*) plotting encloses only those who make it. (XXXV, 40–41/42–43)

Here it is clear that the 'evil plotting' (*al-makr al-sayyiʾ*) refers to all the desperate efforts by which the Kāfirs sought to undermine the monotheistic movement of Muḥammad.

Turning now to the feminine form, *sayyiʾah*, used as a substantive, we may recall that it was already partly examined in an earlier section dealing with *ḥasanah*. There we saw that *sayyiʾah* may denote two entirely different things: it may, on the one hand, mean an unfavorable and disagreeable turn of affairs in human life, all adverse circumstances and ill luck that befall a man; it may, on the other hand, be used for an 'evil' work a man does against God's will, that is, *maʿṣiyah* 'disobedience' as it is often called. This is very important from the viewpoint of Islamic thought because this double meaning of *sayyiʾah* was destined to raise a difficult theological question in connection with the central tenet of the Qadarīyah and Muʿtazilah.

The Maturīdī theologian, al-Bayyāḍī, has an interesting thing to report on this subject. 'The Muʿtazilī al-Jubbāʾī', he says, 'asserts: it is an established fact that the word *sayyiʾah* is sometimes used in the sense of "calamity" (*balīyah*) and "trial" (*miḥnah*), and sometimes in the sense of "sin" (*dhanb*) and "disobedience" (*maʿṣiyah*). It is also certain that God attributes *sayyiʾah* to Himself in the verse "Say: everything comes from God", and that in the following verse He attributes it to man: "And every *sayyiʾah* that befalls thee comes from thyself." Obviously something must be done here to establish harmony between the two statements so that they may not contradict each other. In reality, there is no contradiction because when *sayyiʾah* is attributed to God it is to be understood as "adversity" and "misfortune", while the same word means "disobedience" when it is attributed to man.'[10]

As we see, al-Jubbāʾī uses cleverly the double meaning of *sayyiʾah* in order to establish that 'disobedience', i.e. *kufr* cannot conceivably come from God, for He is essentially God of justice. It goes without saying that al-Bayyāḍī himself, being a man of the Hanafite school, denies categorically such distinction. Everything, he asserts, comes from God, *īmān* as well as *kufr*. If *ḥasanah* in the Qurʾān is to be taken in a general sense *sayyiʾah*, too, must always be taken in a general sense.

In any case what is certain is that the Qurʾān itself uses the word *sayyiʾah* in the sense of 'misfortune' and sometimes in the sense of 'evil deed'. Let us examine carefully the latter case.

Most generally, *sayyiʾah* appears to mean the consequences of *kufr*. The examples that follow will make this point abundantly clear.

> If the evil-doers (*alladhīna ẓalamū*, from *ẓulm* = *kufr*)[11] possessed all the wealth on earth, and the like thereof with it, they would ransom themselves therewith from the evil (*sūʾ*, from the same root as *sayyiʾah*, used approximately in the first of the two meanings of *sayyiʾah* as distinguished above) of the chastisement on the Day of Resurrection. But God will disclose to their eyes what they

[10] Kamāl al-Dīn Aḥmad al-Bayyāḍī: *Ishārāt al-Marām min ʿIbārāt al-Imām* (Cairo, 1949), p. 310.

[11] See above, p. 169.

> never expected to see; there shall appear to them the evils (*sayyiʾāt*, pl.) of that they have earned, and they shall find themselves surrounded on all sides by that which they used to mock at. . . . The evil (*sayyiʾāt*) of that they have earned will smite them. And such of these people [i.e. the Meccan Kāfirs] as do wrong (*ẓalamū*), the evils (*sayyiʾāt*) of that they have earned will smite them, nor will they be able to escape this. (XXXIX, 48–49, 52/47–48, 51)

The next one refers to the Golden Calf which the people of Moses made and worshipped in his absence. So it is evident that the 'evil' deeds here spoken of mean, as al-Bayḍāwī notes, nothing other than the works of *kufr* and *maʿāṣī* 'disobedience' to which they gave way.

> Verily, those who took [to themselves] the Calf, wrath shall come upon them from their Lord and abasement [even] in the life of this present world, for such is the reward We confer upon those who forge (*muftarīn*, from *iftirāʾ*). Those, however, who have done evil deeds (*sayyiʾāt*), but repent thereafter and have faith (*āmanū*), verily thy Lord thereafter is Forgiving and Merciful. (VII, 151–152/152–153)

It is significant that *sayyiʾah* is sometimes opposed to *ṣāliḥah* which I examined at the outset of this chapter. An example showing this relation between *sayyiʾah* and *ṣāliḥah* was also given there. Here is one more telling example:

> As for those who believe (*āmanū*) and do good works (*ṣāliḥāt*, pl.), We shall remit them their *sayyiʾāt* and shall recompense them the best of what they used to do. (XXIX, 6/7)

The expression here translated 'remit (*kaffara*) the *sayyiʾāt*' occurs in another very important passage, which happens to be part of the prayer of the believers in Sūrah III.

> Our Lord, We heard a caller calling unto faith, 'Believe in your Lord!' And we believed. Our Lord, forgive us our sins (*dhunūb*, pl. of *dhanb*) and remit (*kaffir*) from us our evil deeds (*sayyiʾāt*). (III, 191/193)

The commentators usually make a distinction between *dhunūb* and *sayyiʾāt* by saying that the former denotes *kabāʾir* (lit. 'big ones', that is, great or grave sins), while the latter is equivalent to *ṣaghāʾir* (lit. 'small ones'). And this view seems to be fully confirmed by another passage:

> If you avoid great sins (*kabāʾir*) that are formally forbidden you We will remit from you your evil deeds (*sayyiʾāt*) and make you enter Paradise with a noble entrance. (IV, 35/31)

No one will deny that this passage recognizes a very serious difference in degree, and even in kind, between 'big' sins and 'small' ones. In reality, however, this distinction stands on a very precarious foothold, for, after all, there is a real uncertainty as to what is actually meant by 'big' sins. One thing would seem certain. Since, a little later on in the same Sūrah, we find an explicit statement that, 'God forgives not that aught should be associated with Him, but He forgives anything short of that to whomsoever He will. He who associates aught with God has surely forged (*iftará*) a great sin (*ithm*).' (IV, 51/48), it would appear that we could justly regard *shirk* 'associating' as constituting the greatest of all unpardonable sins. But, although this is undoubtedly true in this particular case, it does not in any way preclude the other word *sayyiʾah* from denoting 'associating'. As a matter of actual fact, we have seen above that the worshipping of the Golden Calf—this is nothing but a flagrant case of 'associating' —is counted among the *sayyiʾāt*.

In another passage (Sūrah XVII), after giving a list of deeds that God has expressly forbidden, the Qurʾān pronounces the verdict: 'All this—the evilness of it (*sayyiʾuhu*) is in the sight of your Lord abhorred' (v. 40/38). The items enumerated there are: (1) the slaying of one's own children for fear of poverty, (2) fornication, (3) murder without reason, (4) embezzlement of the legal property of the orphan, (5) dishonesty in commerce, (6) insolence and arrogance (vv. 33–39/31–37). Some at least of these are usually counted among the *kabāʾir*. We might add that in Sūrah XI, 80/78, sodomy is called *sayyiʾah*—the sodomy which, as we saw earlier, is often described in the very Qurʾān as 'an act which is more abominable in the sight of God than anything that has ever been committed by any being in the world.'

5. *Asāʾa.* This word is a verbal form derived from the root *SWʾ*. Briefly, it describes *sayyiʾah* in its dynamic, active aspect; that is, it conveys the idea of 'producing some *sayyiʾah*'. And, of course, in the Qurʾān, the *sayyiʾah* meant is here an act of *kufr*, which is, so to speak, the *sayyiʾah* par excellence. This connection is brought out with explicit clarity in the following example which contrasts 'one who *asāʾa*' with 'one who does *ṣāliḥ*'.

> Whoso does right ('*amila ṣāliḥ*), it is for his own soul, and whoso does evil (*asāʾa*), it is against it. (XLV, 14/15)

No less significant is the next example in which *musīʾ* (part. of *asāʾa*) is contrasted with 'those who believe and do *ṣāliḥāt*'. Moreover, *musīʾ* is likened to a 'blind' man, while the latter is compared to a 'seeing' man, the commonest metaphors in the Qur'ān for the Kāfir and the believer, respectively.

> The blind and the seeing man are not equal, nor those who believe and do the pious deeds (*ṣāliḥāt*) and the evildoer (*musī'*). (XL, 60/58)

The next one tells us in more concrete terms what the act of *asā'a* consists in. It sees 'evil' in the act of *takdhīb*, which is another piece of evidence that *asā'a* means 'to act in a *kāfir* way'.

> The ultimate end of those who did evil (*asā'ū*, pl.) was evil (*sū'*) in that they cried lies to the signs of God and mocked at them. (XXX, 9/10)

6. *Saw'* and *Sū'*. After all I have said in the foregoing about various words derived from the root *SW'*, detailed discussion of these two remaining forms, important though they are, would only be repetition. All I want to do in the present context is to sketch some of the arguable points relating to their meaning and form.

*Saw'* is one of the infinitives of the verb *sā'a* that we have seen above, and is characteristically used as an epithet of the analytic type (e.g. 'a man of courage'), while *sū'* is the abstract noun from the same root. As is obvious, they are twin sisters, extremely similar not only in form but also in meaning, and in some contexts the distinction itself becomes highly problematic.

Let us first consider *saw'*, and examine a few of its typical uses. The construction always takes the analytic form to be represented by the pattern: *rajul al-saw'* (or *rajul saw'*, without definite article), meaning literally 'a man of the being-evil', 'a man of evil nature or conduct'.

> 'O Mary [thus say people to Mary who has just given birth to Jesus before getting married to any man], thou hast indeed committed a monstrous (*farī*) thing! . . . And yet, thy father was not a bad man (*imra' saw'*), nor was thy mother a harlot!' (XIX, 28–29/27–28)

Here it is contextually certain that *saw'* implies unchastity or sexual licence. In a similar way, the people of Sodom are called in Sūrah XXI, 74, *qawm saw'* ('people of evil doing', 'an evil people') on account of their abominable custom. On a level which is more properly religious, the same expression *qawm saw'* is used in reference to Noah's folk, the evidence of their evilness being, this time, the *takdhīb*.

> We delivered him [Noah] from the people who cried lies to Our signs. Verily, they were an evil people, so We drowned them all. (XXI, 77)

The next passage alludes to some of the Bedouin tribes who, on some excuse or other, tried—and succeeded in the attempt—to shirk the duty of serving in the Holy War on the occasion of the Ḥudaybīyah expedition.

> Nay, but you thought that the Apostle and the believers would never return again to their families, and that appeared very fine to your minds. You did think an evil thought (*ẓann al-sawʾ* lit. 'thought of evilness') and you were a people of no value (*būr*, a word meaning 'decayed' or 'corrupt'). (XLVIII, 12)

The reading *ẓann al-sawʾ* is not the only possible one in this and other similar instances; according to some authorities, the alternative reading *ẓann al-sū* is just as permissible. In the opinion of others, there is a definite difference in meaning according to whether one reads *sawʾ* or *sūʾ*, when both are possible: the former implies *fasād*, 'corruption', while the latter means *ḍarar*, 'harm' or 'damage', or *hazīmah*, 'defeat', and *sharr*, 'evilness of condition'.[12] All this, however, is in my opinion quite groundless. The distinction between the two phrases, *ẓann al-sawʾ* and *ẓann al-sūʾ* is merely a matter of syntax.

> The hypocrites, men and women, and the idol-worshippers, men and women, who think (*ẓānnīn*, part. pl.) of God evil thoughts (*ẓann al-sawʾ*)—for them shall be an evil turn of fortune (*dāʾ=irat al-sawʾ*), for God is wroth with them and has cursed them. (XLVIII, 6)

Besides the same *ẓann al-sawʾ* (or *sūʾ*), this passage contains another phrase with *al-sawʾ: dāʾirat al-sawʾ* lit. 'turn of evilness'. This, too, allows two alternative readings, *sawʾ* and *sūʾ*. The same applies also to Sūrah XXV, 42/40, where we find: 'the city that was rained on (*umṭirat*, verb, pass.) by an evil rain (*maṭar al-sawʾ*)'. The city referred to is generally said to be Sodom that was utterly destroyed according to tradition by the rain of stones. In this instance, too, *swʾ* is read in two different ways, and some authorities try to establish a distinction in meaning between them, saying that if it is read *sūʾ* it means 'damage' or 'injury', and if read *sawʾ* it means 'destruction'.

Be that as it may, it is certain that the infinitive *sawʾ* as an epithet is semantically of very wide application, being capable of denoting almost anything that can be called *sayyiʾ*. This is no less true of the noun *sūʾ*.

[12] See al-Bustānī, *Muḥīṭ al-Muḥīṭ*, I, 1021.

Most generally *sū'* means anything felt as being displeasing, disagreeable, or abominable, anything that arouses aversion.

When any one of them is given the news of a girl [i.e. the news that a girl has been born—referring to the notorious dislike of the pre-Islamic Arabs for female children, that went often to the length of burying alive female babies], his face grows dark and he burns with wrath, and he hides himself from his folk because of the evil (*sū'*) of the news that has come to him. (XVI, 60–61/58–59)

This example describes the subjective aspect of the experience connected with the name of *sū'*. And this enables us to understand quite naturally why Hell is so often called in the Qur'ān an 'evil' abode (or resort).

The Kāfirs—upon them is the curse, and for them is the evil abode (*sū' al-dār* lit. 'evilness of the house'). (XIII, 25)

Examples are found in plenty in the Qur'ān, showing that *sū'* in this basic sense may be applied to any kind of harm, injury, affliction, and misfortune. But there is no need here to examine them in detail. So we shall turn our attention immediately to the way *sū'* is used in the ethico-religious field. The first example I give is taken from the Chapter of Joseph. The speaker is Joseph himself.

[My innocence has at last been proved]. And yet I do not claim to be perfectly innocent, for the human soul ever incites to evil (*sū'*) save what my Lord has mercy on. (XII, 53)

Here evidently 'evil' means unbridled indulgence in wordly pleasures.

The next quotation is given as good evidence to show that *sū'* in the religious field is perfectly synonymous with the above-discussed *sayyi'āt*.

God is only bound to turn towards [i.e. forgive] those who do evil (*sū'*) in ignorance, then quickly turn again [i.e. repent] . . . But God is not to turn towards those who do evil deeds (*sayyi'āt*), until, when one of them is about to die, he says, 'Now I turn [i.e. repent].' (IV, 21–22/17–18)

Exactly the same kind of *sū'* that is, 'evil done in ignorance', is significantly contrasted in the next example with *aṣlaḥa* (derived from the same root as *ṣāliḥ*).

Whoso of you does evil (*sū'*) in ignorance, and turns again thereafter and does right (*aṣlaḥa*), verily, [for him] God is Forgiving and Merciful. (VI, 54)

*Sū͗* is also used synonymously with *ẓulm al-nafs* 'the wronging of one's own soul' which is, as we saw, a very characteristic Qur͗anic expression for *kufr*.

> The Kāfirs whom the angels seize [i.e. cause to die] while they are busy wronging themselves. Then [only] will they submit [and say], 'We were not doing any evil (*sū͗*).' Nay, but verily God knows well of what you were doing. (XVI, 29–30/27–28)

In the next passage, the referent of *sū͗* is described in the most concrete terms. Here we have an instance showing what kind of act was an 'evil act' in the Qur͗anic view.

> Pharaoh said, 'O Haman, build for me a tower, so that haply I may reach the place of ascent, the place of ascent of the heavens, and look upon the God of Moses, for I think him a liar.' In this way Pharaoh looked upon his evil act (*sū͗ ͑amalihi* lit. 'evil of his act') as something good, and thus was debarred from the right way. (XL, 38–40/36–37)

## *Faḥshā͗* or *Faḥisha*

*Faḥshā͗* or *fāḥishah* signifies anything foul and abominable beyond measure. It is very often used in the Qur͗ān in conjunction with *SW͗* which we have just examined.

> Follow not the footsteps of Satan; he is a manifest foe to you. He enjoins upon you naught but *sū͗* and *faḥshā͗*. (II, 163–164/168–169)

The commentators have tried to distinguish between *sū͗* and *faḥshā͗* in this verse; much ink has flowed, and a variety of opinions have been offered, but none of them is sufficiently reliable. All we can gather from them is that the two words are roughly synonymous.

> She [the wife of the Egyptian Governor] desired him passionately, and he [Joseph] would have desired her too, had it not been that he saw [just then] a proof of his Lord. Thus did We turn away from him *sū͗* and *faḥshā͗*. (XII, 24)

Here it is contextually clear that the expression, *sū͗* and *faḥshā͗*, means fornication. The same reference is made explicit in the next example.

> Draw not near to fornication; verily, it is a *fāḥishah;* it is evil (*sā͗a* a verbal form from *SW͗*) as a way. (XVII, 34/32)

Sodomy is also very frequently called *fāḥishah*. Here I give only one example.

> And Lot, when he said to his people [i.e. the inhabitants of Sodom], 'What, do you commit such *fāḥishah* as no one in all the world has ever committed before you?' (VII, 78/80)

In Sūrah XI, 80/78, the 'abomination' referring to the same evil habit of Sodom is expressed by *sayyiʾāt*, further evidence that *F-Ḥ-SH* and *SWʾ* were felt to be roughly synonymous in cases of this sort.

In another passage concerning the pagan custom of marrying the wife of one's own father after his death (or divorce), a word meaning the utmost degree of hatred, *maqt*, is used in conjunction with *fāḥishah.*

> Marry not women your fathers married, except bygone cases, for it is surely abomination (*fāḥishah*), a hateful thing (*maqt*), and an evil way (*sāʾa sabīlan* lit. 'is evil as a way'). (IV, 26/22)

The word *munkar* which we have considered above also occurs together with *fāḥishah.*

> O believers, follow not the footsteps of Satan, for upon those who follow the footsteps of Satan, verily, he enjoins *faḥshāʾ* and *munkar*. (XXIV, 21)

Here we see the occurrence of *faḥshāʾ* explicitly attributed to Satan's instigation. Sūrah II, 164/169, quoted at the outset of this section is another example. Indeed, it is characteristic of *fāḥishah* and *faḥshāʾ* that they appear in the Qurʾān, very often associated with Satan's name.

> Satan promises you poverty and enjoins upon you *faḥshāʾ*, while God promises you forgiveness from Himself and bounty. (II, 271/268)

> We have made the Satans patrons of those who believe not. And whenever they commit a *fāḥishah*, they say, 'We found our fathers practicing it, and God bade us do it.' Say, 'God does not enjoin upon you *faḥshāʾ*. Do you say against God that which you know not?' (VII, 26–27/27–28)

On the contrary, God forbids strictly all *faḥshāʾ* and enjoins justice and kindness:

> Verily, God enjoins justice (*ʿadl*) and kindness (*iḥsān*) and giving to kinsfolk, and forbids *faḥshāʾ* and *munkar* and insolence (*baghy*). (XVI, 92/90)

## *Ṭayyib* and *Khabīth*

*Ṭayyib* is an adjective, the most basic semantic function of which is to denote any quality that strikes the sense—the senses of taste and odor, in particular—as very delightful, pleasant, and sweet. As would be expected, it is most frequently used to qualify food, water, perfume, and the like. Beyond this proper field of application, it may also be applied to various other things; thus in the Qurʾān we find such combinations as: *rīḥ ṭayyibah* 'a favorable wind' that carries a ship smoothly on the sea, as opposed to *rīḥ ʿāṣifah* 'a stormy wind' (X, 23/22), *balad ṭayyib* 'a land of good and fertile soil' (VII, 56/58), *masākin ṭayyibah* 'delightful dwellings', speaking of the final resort of the believing men and women in Gardens of Eden (IX, 73/72), etc.

It is noteworthy that in the case of food, which, as everybody knows, constitutes an important item among those things that tend to be surrounded by all sorts of taboos, the Qurʾān brings in the specific idea of 'sanctification', by associating *ṭayyib* with *ḥalāl* which means 'lawful' in the sense of 'free from all taboo'. So in this particular case, *ṭayyib* becomes almost a synonym of *ḥalāl* which we shall examine in the next section.

> They will ask thee [Muḥammad] what is made lawful (*uḥilla* verb, pass. meaning 'to be made *ḥalāl*') for them. Answer, 'Lawful to you are all good things (*ṭayyibāt*, noun, pl.).' (V, 6/4)

> Eat of what God has provided you as lawful (*ḥalāl*) and good (*ṭayyib*). (V, 90/88)

The word *ṭayyib* may also—though not so frequently—be used in the properly ethico-religious sense. Here is a good example:

> Gardens of Eden they shall enter, beneath which rivers flow. . . . Thus God recompenses those who fear (*muttaqīn*), whom the angels seize [i.e. cause to die] while they are good (*ṭayyibīn* pl.). They [i.e. the angels] say, 'Peace be upon you! Enter Paradise because of what you used to do.' (XVI, 33–34/31–32)

It is evident that in this context *tayyib* replaces *muttaqī* 'godfearing'. Besides, it is opposed to 'those who wrong themselves', (in verse 30/28) an expression which, as we know, means Kāfirs.

*Ṭayyib* in the phrase *al-kalim al-ṭayyib*, 'the good speech', that occurs in Sūrah XXXV, 11/10, must be of a similar nature. It is generally explained as denoting the formula of *tawḥīd*: 'There is no god but God.' At any rate, it is certain that *ṭayyib* in this expression means 'religiously good' or 'pious', for the phrase itself appears in this verse closely combined with *al-ᶜamal al-ṣāliḥ* 'pious deed'. The verse runs as follows:

> Unto Him ascend good (*ṭayyib*) words, and the good (*ṣāliḥ*) deed He exalts. (XXXV, 11/10)

The exact contrary of *ṭayyib* is *khabīth.* Here it will be unnecessary to examine cases in which this word is applied to ordinary things and events. All we have to do is to consider briefly some of the typical examples showing its use in the ethico-religious domain. Let us begin with one that concerns the problem of the 'sanctification' of food referred to above.

> He [the Prophet] makes lawful (*yuḥillu*) [in the name of God] for them all good things (*ṭayyibāt*) and makes unlawful (*yuḥarrimu*) for them the evil things (*khabāʾith*, noun, pl.). (VII, 156/157)

It is to be noted that the pair *ṭayyib—khabīth* is very significantly made to correspond with another pair *ḥalāl—ḥarām.* As we shall see the latter pair is based on the idea of ritual 'cleanness' properly belonging to the domain of taboo-thinking.

In the next passage, *ṭayyib—khabīth* corresponds to the opposition of the believers and the Kāfirs.

> Those who disbelieve will be gathered into Gehenna, that God may distinguish the wicked (*khabīth*) from the good (*ṭayyib*), and put the wicked one upon another, and, heaping them up all together, put them into Gehenna. (VIII, 37–38/36–37)

> Bad women (*khabīthāt*) [are fit to be mated] with bad men (*khabīthīn*), and bad men with bad women. Good women (*ṭayyibāt*) [are fit to be mated] with good men (*ṭayyibīn*), and good men with good women. (XXIV, 26)

In the next example, *khabīth* is applied to the abominable custom of the people of Sodom, who are themselves described as a people of *sawʾ* and *fāsiq*. All these elements combined, serve to bring out with utmost clarity the concrete meaning content of the word *khabīth.*[13]

> Unto Lot We gave judgment and knowledge, and We delivered him from the city that used to do abominations (*khabāʾith*, pl.). Verily, they were an evil people (*qawm sawʾ*); [they were] all *fāsiqīn*. (XXI, 74)

[13] As an example of its usage in Jāhilīyah as an ethical term, we may give the following verse of ᶜAntarah (*Dīwān*, p. 62, v. 7): *Yaᶜībūna lawnī bi-al-sawād wa-innamā * fiᶜāluhum bi-al-ḥubth aswad min jildī* 'They [i.e. my tribesmen] revile my color saying that it is black. To say the truth, the wicked things they are doing is much more black than my skin.'

## *Ḥarām* and *Ḥalāl*

With this pair of words we step into the world of taboo-thinking. *Ḥarām* and *ḥalāl* belong to a very old layer of language. In fact, they go back to the old Semitic idea of ritual cleanness. Speaking more strictly, *ḥarām* is the taboo, while *ḥalāl* denotes simply anything that is not held under the taboo, anything that 'has been set free' from it. *Ḥarām* is applied to things, places, persons, and actions; and everything that is so designated is definitely separated from the world of the profane and is raised to a peculiar level of being, that of the 'sacred' in the twofold sense of holiness and pollution; it is, at any event, something unapproachable, untouchable.

Thus to give a typical example, drinking wine and the washing of his head were *ḥarām* to a pre-Islamic Arab who had made a vow to take a bloody vengeance on the murderer of one of his near relatives. And the taboo continued as long as he was under the vow. The situation is made clear admirably well by the following verse of Taʾabbaṭah Sharran,[14] which he said after he executed his vengeance upon the murderer of his maternal uncle:

*Ḥallati al-khamr wa-kānat ḥarām* *
*wa-bi-laʾy mā alammat taḥillu*

> Long was wine *ḥarām* to me, but now it is *ḥalāl*. Hard was, indeed, the toil that made it at last *ḥalāl* to me.

It is highly instructive to see that in the law-books by later jurists, *ḥarām* is generally defined in a formal way as 'an action punishable by law' or—which amounts to the same thing—'anything absolutely forbidden'. The Qurʾanic use of the word seems to represent an intermediate stage in the process of development from the original taboo idea to this legal concept. This incorporation of a pagan idea into Islām was made possible by the introduction of God's free decision. With absolute freedom God forbids anything and removes the ban from anything; and anything He has forbidden will be henceforward *ḥarām*, and the contrary *ḥalāl*. Thus age-old ideas of *ḥarām* and *ḥalāl* have become most intimately connected with God as immediate expressions of His Will. This direct consequential connection between God's act of forbidding a thing and the thing's being a *ḥarām* is well brought out in the following passage.

> We [God] covenanted with you [children of Israel], 'You shall not shed your blood [i.e. you shall not kill one another], and you shall not drive yourselves [i.e. one another] out of home.' . . . But now

[14] Abu Tammām, *Dīwān al-Ḥamāsah*, with comm. of al-Khaṭīb al-Tibrīzī, M. A. ʿAzzām, ed. (Cairo, 1955), I, 21.

> you are killing one another, and driving a party of you out of home . . . when their expulsion was made *ḥarām* to you. (II, 78–79/84–85)

It is natural that, with the advent of a new Prophet, as a new mouthpiece of the divine Will, there should occur considerable changes in the existent system of 'lawful' and 'unlawful'. Thus Jesus in the Qurʾān declares among other things:

> I will surely make *ḥalāl* (*uḥilla*, verb,) to you some of the things that were before *ḥarām* (*ḥurrima*, verb. pass.) to you. (III, 44/50)

In like manner, now that Islām has come, all the taboo-laws of Israel, the Qurʾān declares, are completely superseded by the new—and of course, better—enactments. Thus, according to the Qurʾān, the Jewish food-taboos, to take the most conspicuous instance, were originally instituted as a punishment for their insolence (Sūrah VI, 147/146). As to the numerous taboos of paganism, they are mere 'forgery' *iftirāʾ* against God (v. 145/144). But instead of abolishing food-restrictions altogether the Qurʾān draws up a modified list of taboos, and proclaims them in the name of God.

> These only He has forbidden (*ḥarrama*) you: what is dead [i.e. the meat of an animal that has died of itself, not slaughtered], and blood [shed], and the flesh of swine, and whatsoever has been consecrated to other than God. (II, 168/173)

> Made lawful (*uḥilla*) to you is the game of the sea and to eat thereof, a provision for you and for the seafarers. But forbidden (*ḥurrima*) to you is the game of the land so long you are in the state of *ḥarām* [i.e. on the pilgrimage]. (V, 97/96)

It should be observed that those who perform the pilgrimage themselves, after they have laid aside their 'secular' clothes and put on a 'sacred' garment, are definitely in the state of taboo; they should not cut their hair or pare their nails, and sexual intercourse is a strict prohibition.

It is interesting to note that the Qurʾān sometimes uses this taboo vocabulary on a much higher level, in matters that concern more directly the central tenets of Islām. It creates, as it were, a new moral and spiritual conception of taboo, and gives an ethical content to the primitive idea of *ḥarām*, by placing 'under taboo' various manifestations of *kufr*.

> Say, 'My Lord has only tabooed (*ḥarrama*) abominable deeds (*fawāḥish*), whether outwardly visible or concealed within, and sin (*ithm*), and wrongful insolence (*baghī*), and that you associate

(*tushrikū*) with God that for which He sent down no warrant [i.e. idols], and that you say concerning God that which you know not [i.e. the sin of *iftirā*ʾ]. (VII, 31/33)

There is in Arabic another word for 'a tabooed thing' (*ḥarām*), of which the Qurʾān furnishes a few examples: *suḥt* (or *suḥut*). Speaking of the Jews who say: 'We believe', though in fact they have adopted *kufr*, God addresses Muḥammad and says:

> Thus seest many of them vying with one another in sin (*ithm*) and disobedience (*ʿudwān*), and how they devour the tabooed thing (*suḥt*): Verily, evil is the thing they have been doing. (V, 67/62)

And in the same Sūrah, v. 46/42, the same Jews are called *akkālūna lil-suḥt* 'voracious eaters of the tabooed thing'. As to what is exactly meant by the 'tabooed thing' here, nothing certain can be said, though it is highly probable that it refers to usury. We know that the prohibition of lending money at interest was directed primarily against the Jews.[15] The following quotation from the Qurʾān will confirm this view.

> For the wrong-doing (*ẓulm*) of the Jews, We have put under taboo (*ḥarramnā*) certain good things (*ṭayyibāt*) that were before permitted to them. This has occurred also for their debarring many men from the way of God, and for their taking usury in disregard of the strict prohibition [by God]. (IV, 158–159/160–161)

Concerning *ḥalāl* there is semantically very little to say. It denotes anything that is not 'taboo', or rather, anything from which the ban has been removed. A few examples may suffice.

> O men, eat of what is in the earth, things lawful (*ḥalāl*), good (*ṭayyib*) [note again the combination, *ḥalāl—ṭayyib*], and follow not the footsteps of Satan. (II, 163/168)

In the same passage the thought is expressed again in a somewhat different way: this time, it is the word *ṭayyibāt* that appears in place of the combination *ḥalāl—ṭayyib*:

> O believers, eat of the good things (*ṭayyibāt*) wherewith We have provided you, and thank God, if it is Him that you worship. (II, 167/172)

> All food was lawful (*ḥill* = *ḥalāl*) to the children of Israel save what Israel made unlawful (*ḥarrama* 'tabooed') to himself, before the Law was revealed. (III, 87/93)

[15] See W. Montgomery Watt, *Muhammad at Medina* (Oxford, 1956), pp. 296–297.

The next example concerns the relation between husband and his divorced wife. It is contextually implied that violation of a taboo constitutes a 'sin' which is called *junāh*. This latter word will come up for consideration in the next section.

> If he [i.e. the husband] divorces her [the third time, that is, finally], she shall not be *ḥalāl* (*taḥillu*, verb) to him thereafter, until she marries another husband. Then, if he [the new husband] divorces her, then it is no sin (*junāḥ*) for them to come together again. (II, 230)

As I have suggested before, whenever a taboo is placed upon a thing, that thing becomes raised above the level of ordinary existence: it becomes 'sacred' in the original double meaning of purity and pollution; it is 'untouchable'. This latter aspect of tabooed things seems to be expressed in the Qurʾān by the word *rijs*, which is an exceedingly powerful word with the basic meaning of 'filthiness' or 'uncleanness'. It suggests a feeling of intense physical repulsion.

The fundamental semantic connection between *ḥarām* and *rijs* will be best perceived in the following verse, which gives a list of tabooed food for the Muslims. Here the 'filthiness' is given explicitly as the reason for the prohibition of the flesh of swine.

> Say, 'I find in what has been revealed to me naught tabooed except what is dead [of itself, i.e. not slaughtered], and blood outpoured, and the flesh of swine—for that is a *rijs*—and all *fisq*-things that have been consecrated to other than God.' (VI, 146/145)

In another passage, we find wine, *maysir* (a form of gambling practiced by means of arrows), idols, and divining-arrows strictly prohibited as being 'unclean'.

> O believers, wine and *maysir*-gambling, idols and divining-arrows are all *rijs* coming from Satan's work. So avoid them that haply you may prosper. (V, 92/90)

We should further compare this passage with Sūrah II, 216/219, where wine and *maysir* are condemned as involving great 'sin' (*ithm*).

> They will ask thee [Muḥammad] about wine and *maysir*. Say, 'In both of them there is great sin and also some uses for men, but their sin is greater than their usefulness.'

In another place idols are called *rijs*.

> Shun the abomination (*rijs*) of idols. (XXII, 31/30)

And this is extended to the 'disease' which is in the hearts of the Kāfirs.

> As for those in whose hearts is disease, it [i.e. Revelation] only serves to add *rijs* to their *rijs*, and they all die Kāfirs. (IX, 126/125)

And finally, the Kāfirs themselves are called *rijs*.

> Turn aside from them, for they are unclean (*rijs*), and their ultimate abode is Gehenna as the reward for what they have earned. (IX, 96/95)

I should like to end this section by drawing attention to another word, *najas*, which is almost an exact synonym of *rijs*. The only semantic difference between the two is, according to some Arab philologists, that *rijs* is used mostly in reference to things that are 'filthy by nature', while *najas* means mostly things that are 'filthy according to Reason or Law.'[16]

The word *najas* is used in the Qurʾān in reference to the idol-worshippers, who should not be allowed to come near the Holy (*ḥarām*) Mosque, because 'they are unclean'.

> O believers, the polytheists (*mushrikūn*, lit. 'those who associate') are naught but *najas*. So let them not come near the Holy Mosque after this very year. (IX, 28)

It is related that ʿUmar, who was to become the second Khalīfah, once wished to read the manuscript of a certain Sūrah which his sister Fāṭimah was reading with her husband. (This occurred a little before ʿUmar became a Muslim). Fāṭimah, who was already a devout believer at that time, refused to hand the sheet to her brother and said, 'Brother, you are unclean (*najis*, adj.), because of your polytheism (*shirk*). Only the clean (*ṭāhir*, meaning 'ritually clean') may touch it.' Thereupon, we are told, ʿUmar rose and washed himself clean, and then only she gave him the sheet.[17] This anecdote reveals better than anything else the nature of the taboo-consciousness in which these notions of 'cleanness' and 'uncleanness' originate and to which they properly belong.

## Sins

In this last section we shall deal with the key terms of the secondary level of discourse, whose function consists in classifying the religiously evil acts that we have been considering as a violation of the moral and divine law, and consequently, as something punishable by a heavy penalty in both this world and the world to come.

[16] al-Bustānī, *Muḥīṭ al-Muḥīṭ*, I, 755, quoting from *al-Kullīyāt*.
[17] Ibn Isḥāq, I, 226.

1. *Dhanb.* The Qur'ān applies this word most frequently to heinous sins committed against God. Examples will best explain this point.

*Takdhīb* is a *dhanb:*

> They shall be fuel for the Fire, like Pharaoh's people, and those before them; they cried lies to Our signs, and God seized them for their sins (*dhunūb*, pl.). (III, 9/11)

As we know very well, *takdhīb* 'crying lies to God's signs' is the most typical manifestation of *kufr*; as a matter of fact this latter word replaces the former in Sūrah VIII, 54/52, all other elements remaining almost exactly the same.

> Like Pharaoh's people, and those before them; they disbelieved (*kafarū*) in God's signs, and God seized them for their sins (*dhunūb*).

*Kufr* is a *dhanb:*

> God seized them for their sins (*dhunūb*). . . . That was because their Apostles brought them clear signs, but they disbelieved (*kafarū*), so God seized them. (XL, 22–23/21–22)

> They [i.e. the Kāfirs in Gehenna] shall say, 'If only we had listened to [our Apostle] or had sense, we would not have become the fellows of the Blaze!' Thus they confess their sin. (LXVII, 10–11)

In this passage the word *kufr* itself does not appear, but the reference is clear. In the following, *istikbār*, 'becoming big with pride', which we considered earlier in detail, takes the place of *kufr*, and is accused of being a *dhanb:*

> And Korah, Pharaoh, and Haman! Moses came unto them with clear signs, but they grew proud (*istakbarū*) in the land. Yet they could not win the race. So We seized each one for his sin (*dhanb*). (XXIX, 38–39/39–40)

The intimate connection between *kufr* and *dhanb* is shown also by the fact that the latter is regarded as entailing the punishment of the Fire in Gehenna.

> God looks on His servants [i.e. believers] who say, 'Our Lord, we believe. Forgive Thou our sins (*dhunūb*) and keep us from the chastisement of the Fire.' (III, 13–14/15–16)

*Dhanb* comprises *fāḥishah* and *ẓulm:*

> God loves the good-doers (*muḥsinīn* from *aḥsana*) who, when they commit a *fāḥishah* or wrong (*ẓalamū*) themselves (*ẓulm al-nafs*), remember God and ask forgiveness for their sins (*dhunūb*)—and

who forgives sins save God?—and persevere not knowingly in what they did. (III, 128–129/134–135)

*Dhanb* of *fāsiq* people:

If they turn away [from God's signs], then know that God wishes to smite them for a sin of theirs. Verily, many men are *fāsiq*. (V, 54/49)

*Dhanb* and *sayyiʾah:*

Our Lord, we heard a caller calling unto faith, 'Believe in your Lord!' And we believed. Our Lord, forgive us our sins (*dhunūb*) and remit from us our evil deeds (*sayyiʾāt*). (III, 191/193)

According to al-Bayḍāwī, the distinction between *dhunūb* and *sayyiʾāt* is that the former denotes *kabāʾir* 'great sins' while the latter denotes *ṣaghāʾir* 'small sins'. This interpretation fits in admirably with what is suggested by another important passage (IV, 35/31) which I have already quoted. There we saw God Himself declaring emphatically. 'If you avoid *kabāʾir* which are forbidden you, We will remit from you and your evil deeds.' But it is probable that this interpretation was first suggested to the minds of the commentators by this latter passage itself.

*Dhanb* and *Khaṭīʾah:*

Thou, woman, ask forgiveness of thy sin (*dhanb*); verily, thou art of the sinners (*khāṭiʾīn*, part. pl.). (XII, 29)

This is said by the Egyptian Governor to his wife who attempted, and failed, to seduce Joseph from the right path. It is to be noted that here those who commit this kind of *dhanb* are called *khāṭiʾīn* (lit. those who commit *khaṭīʾah*). This seems to suggest that *dhanb* and *khaṭīʾah* are roughly synonymous. The word *khaṭīʾah* will be discussed later.

2. *Ithm*. Concerning the basic meaning of this word different opinions have been offered by different scholars. *Muḥīṭ al-Muḥīṭ*, for instance, defines it as a violation of *ḥarām*, that is, doing what is not lawful. The commentator al-Bayḍāwī says: *ithm* is a *dhanb* that merits punishment (comm. on XLIX, 12). According to others *ithm* is an unlawful deed committed intentionally, while *dhanb* can signify both what is intentional and what is unintentional. The diversity of opinion gives evidence that a precise definition of this word is almost impossible, its meaning being extremely vague and elusive beyond a certain limit. So we cannot hope to do better than examine this word at work in contextual situations.

The first point to note regarding the actual use of the word in the Qur'ān is that it occurs remarkably often in the legislative portions of the Book. Thus, for instance, concerning the right way to take in commercial dealings on credit, it is said:

> Conceal not the testimony, for whoso conceals it, verily his heart is sinful (*āthim*, part.). (II, 283)

The next example concerns the legal regulation on the making of a testament.

> Prescribed for you, when any of you is about to die, leaving behind wealth, he is to make testament. . . .
> Whoso alters it after he has heard it, the sin (*ithm*) thereof is only upon those who alter it. . . . But in case he fears from the testator some declining (*janaf*, meaning 'declining or deviating' from the right course) or sin (*ithm*, meaning here the wrong intention to deviate from the right course), and so makes up the matter between the parties, then it shall be no sin (*ithm*) for him [to alter the will he has heard]. (II, 177–178/180–182)

In a similar way, in a passage dealing with the qualifications of persons permitted to attend bequeathing as legal witnesses, *ithm* is declared to consist in their not bearing testimony equitably. The following is the formula of oath by which the witnesses should swear never to act unjustly.

> We will not sell it for a price, even though it be on behalf of a near kinsman, nor will we hide the testimony of God, for then we would surely be of the sinful (*āthimīn*, part. pl.). (V, 105/106)

In the next example the act of bringing a false accusation against one's own wife for the purpose of taking back the sum of money that one has given her before, is said to constitute an 'open *ithm*'.

> If you wish to exchange a wife for another, and you have given unto one of them [i.e. the one you are going to divorce] a large sum of money, take naught of it. What, will you take it by way of calumny and open sin (*ithm*)? (IV, 24/20)

That 'calumny' itself is also an *ithm* is shown by another verse relating to an entirely different sort of situation.

> Those who hurt the believers, men and women, without their deserving it, such have laid upon themselves the guilt of calumny and open sin (*ithm*). (XXXIII, 58)

In the next example, *ithm* means the act of unjustly appropriating the property of others.

> Consume not your property among yourselves in vanity, nor seek to bribe by it the judges that you may devour knowingly a portion of the property of others with *ithm* [i.e. sinfully]. (II, 184/188)

The second point to note about the word *ithm* is that it is also used in connection with *ḥarām*. In other words, violation of a taboo constitutes an *ithm*. The following verse comes after the enumeration of forbidden foods—carrion, swine-flesh, blood, and what has been consecrated to other than God.

> But whoso is forced [by hunger into eating *ḥarām* food], and not from insolence and not transgressing, it is no sin (*ithm*) for him. Verily, God is Forgiving, Merciful. (II, 168/173)

> They will ask thee about wine and *maysir*. Say, 'In both of them there is great sin (*ithm kabīr*) and also some uses for men, but their sin is greater than their usefulness.' (II, 216/219)

Thirdly, we may observe that the word *ithm* is applied also to various aspects of *kufr*.

> Let not those who disbelieve (*kafarū*) suppose that Our being indulgent towards them for a long time [i.e. the fact that we do not punish them at once for their *kufr*] is something good for them. We only grant them indulgence that they may increase in sin (*ithm*). (III, 172/178)

It is associated with *shirk*, 'polytheism', and with *iftirāʾ al-kadhib*, 'forgery of a lie':

> He who associates aught with God has surely forged (*iftarā*) a great sin (*ithm*). (IV, 51/48)

> Behold how they forge against God a lie, and that is enough for an obvious sin (*ithm*). (IV, 53/50)

It is noteworthy in this connection that the infernal tree of Zaqqūm which, as we know, is the special food of the Kāfirs in Gehenna, is called 'the tree of the sinful (*athīm*)', showing indirectly that *athīm* means nothing other than *kāfir*.

> Verily the tree of Zaqqūm shall be the food of the *athīm*, like molten copper, boiling in their bellies like the boiling of hot water. (XLIV, 43–45)

3. *Khaṭīʾah*. That *khaṭīʾah* has roughly the same meaning as *ithm* is clearly shown by the following example:

> Whoso, having committed a *khaṭīʾah* or an *ithm*, throws it upon the innocent, has burdened himself with calumny and an obvious sin (*ithm*). (IV, 112)

As usual, the commentators have tried to draw a dividing line between the two words. According to al-Bayḍāwī, for instance, *khaṭīʾah* here means 'small' sin or an unintentional offence, and *ithm* means 'great' sin or an intentional crime. The Qurʾanic language itself flatly contradicts such a distinction. For the Qur'ān applies the word *khaṭīʾah* mainly to the most heinous religious sins. The examples that follow will bring out this point.

> Noah said, 'My Lord, they have rebelled against me, and followed one whose wealth and children have increased him only in ruin, and they have plotted a mighty plot, and said, 'Do not forsake your gods. Do not forsake Wadd, nor Suwāʿ, nor Yaghūth, nor Yaʿūq, nor Nasrʾ. And thus they have led many astray. Increase Thou not these wrong-doers (*ẓālimīn*) save in straying.' Because of their sins (*khaṭīʾāt*, pl.) they were drowned and made to enter into a Fire. (LXXI, 20–25/21–25)

Better than anything else this passage discloses the meaning of the word in question. In the next one, *khāṭiʾ* (part. meaning 'one who commits a *khaṭīʾah*') evidently replaces the more usual *kāfir*.

> Take hold of him, fetter him, then roast him in the Hell Fire, and put him in a chain of seventy cubits! Verily, he believed not in the Almighty God, nor did he ever urge the feeding of the destitute. So this day he has here no true friend, nor any food except putrid pus which none but the sinners (*khāṭiʾūn*, pl.) eat. (LXIX, 30–37)

Here is one more example in which *KH-Ṭ-ʾ* evidently refers to the deeds of *kufr*.

> And Pharaoh, and those before him, and the cities overturned, committed *khāṭiʾah*(=*khaṭīʾah*), and they rebelled against the Apostle of their Lord. So He seized them with a vehement grip. (LXIX, 9–10)

In the following passage, the Jāhilī custom of slaying one's own children for fear of poverty is condemned as a great *khaṭʾ* (*khaṭīʾah*).

> Slay not your children for fear of poverty. We will provide for them and for you. Verily, the slaying of them is a great sin (*khaṭʾ*). (XVII, 33/31)

Here instead of *khaṭʾ* words like *dhanb* and *ithm* might as well be used without causing any change in meaning. It is interesting to note in this connection that there is a verse in which *dhanb* and *KH-Ṭ-ʾ* are actually used side by side in reference to one and the same wrong-doing. It is found in the Chapter of Joseph, and the 'sin' referred to is the evil plot which Joseph's brothers framed against him when he was a little child and for which they are now repentant.

> They [Joseph's brothers] said, 'O father, ask forgiveness of our sins (*dhunūb*) for us, for certainly we were sinful (*khāṭiʾīn*, part. pl.). (XII, 98/97)

I shall give one more example showing the close connection that exists between *KH-Ṭ-ʾ* and *sayyiʾah*.

> They [i.e. the 'hypocrites'] say, 'The Fire will not touch us save for a number of days.' . . . Say, 'Nay, but whoso has done evil (*sayyiʾah*) and is surrounded on all sides by his sin (*khaṭīʾah*), such are the Fellows of the Fire; therein they shall dwell for ever.' (II, 74–75/80–81)

4. *Jurm*. This word is admittedly a synonym of *dhanb*. In the Qurʾān, the word appears mostly under the participial form, *mujrim*, meaning 'one who commits, or has committed, a *jurm*' and the ultimate referent is almost invariably *kufr*. A mere inspection of examples will make this point abundantly clear.

*Takdhīb* is a *jurm:*

> If they cry thee lies (*kadhdhabū*), say, 'Your Lord is of all-embracing mercy, but His violence will not be turned back from the sinful (*mujrimīn*) people.' (VI, 148/147)

*Istikbār* is a *jurm:*

> As for those who disbelieved (*kafarū*), [it will be said unto them on the Day of Judgment], 'Were not My signs recited unto you? But you were too haughty (*istakbartum*), and were a sinful (*mujrimī*) people.' (XLV, 30/31)

> Those who cry lies to Our signs and are too haughty (*istakbarū*) to accept them, for them the gates of Heaven shall not be opened. . . . It is thus that We requite the sinners (*mujrimīn*); Gehenna shall be their couch, with coverings [of fire] above them. Thus do We requite the wrong-doers (*ẓālimīn*). (VII, 38–39/40–41)

The following passage describes in vividly concrete terms the characteristic arrogance of the *mujrim* people towards the believers.

> Behold, those who commit *jurm* (*alladhīna ajramū*) used to laugh at those who believed, winking one at another when they passed them by, and when they went back to their own folk, they returned jesting, and when they saw them they used to say, 'Lo, these have indeed gone astray!' (LXXXIII, 29–32)

*Nifāq* is a *jurm:*

> Make no excuse. You [*munāfiqūn* 'hypocrites'] have disbelieved after your faith. If We forgive one sect of you, We will chastise another sect for that they were sinners (*mujrimūn*). (IX, 67/66)

*Iftirāʾ al-kadhib* is a *jurm:*

> Who does greater wrong (*aẓlam*) than he who forges against God a lie or cries lies to His signs? Verily, the sinners (*mujrimūn*) shall not prosper. (X, 18/17; see also XI, 37/35)

Instances could be multiplied indefinitely. But this much suffices for our present purpose.

5. *Junāḥ* and *Ḥaraj*. These terms are roughly synonymous with *ithm*, and are most often used in the legislative portions of the Book. They seem to mean a sin or crime for which one deserves punishment.

> It is no sin (*junāḥ*) chargeable upon you that you seek bounty from your Lord [i.e. that you seek to gain profits by trading during the period of Pilgrimage]. (II, 194/198)

That *junāḥ* here is synonymous with *ithm* may be seen from the fact that a few verses further on we find this very word, *ithm*, used in place of *junāḥ* in a similar contextual situation.

> Remember God during a certain number of days [in the Pilgrimage], but whoso hastens off in two days, there is no sin (*ithm*) chargeable upon him, and who so delays, there is no sin (*ithm*) chargeable upon him, if he fears [God]. (II, 199/203)

The word *junāḥ* occurs very frequently in regulations touching marriage and divorce. One or two examples may suffice.

> It is no sin (*junāḥ*) for you that you offer a proposal of marriage to women or keep it secret. (II, 235)

> Thou [Muḥammad] mayest put off whomsoever thou wilt of them [thy wives], and thou mayest take to thyself whomsoever thou wilt, and if thou seekest any of those whom thou hast divorced, it shall be no sin (*junāḥ*) for thee. (XXXIII, 51)

The next example concerns the curtailing of prayer in case of emergency.

> When you go on your travel in the land, it is no sin (*junāḥ*) for you that you curtail your prayer in case you fear that the Kāfirs may attack you. (IV, 102/101)

It is no sin (*ḥaraj*) for the weak and the sick and those who find naught to spend [that they do not go forth to war in God's way], if they are true to God and His Apostle. (IX, 92/91)

So We gave her [Zaynab the wife of the Prophet's freedman and adopted son] in marriage unto thee [Muḥammad], so that [henceforward] there should be no sin (*ḥaraj*) for the believers [in general] in respect of [marrying] the wives of their own adopted sons.... There is no sin (*ḥaraj*) for the Prophet about what God has ordained for him. (XXXIII, 37–38)

In this chapter we have dealt with the most important of those Qurʾanic terms that correspond more or less in meaning to the English words 'good' and 'bad'. Our consideration of the examples has clearly shown that it is quite wrong to assert that the Qurʾān does not possess any fully developed 'abstract' concepts of 'good' and 'bad'. True, some of the words are, as we saw, descriptive rather than classificatory. Words like *ḥarām*, *ḥalāl*, and *rijs*, for example, are most concretely descriptive. If they evaluate, they do so only indirectly, that is, through description. *Fāḥishah* and *fasād*, too, are essentially descriptive. But it is also undeniable that some of the words that we have considered in this chapter are to be regarded as classificatory rather than descriptive. *Ṣāliḥ* is still descriptive to a great extent; but it is equally classificatory. Words like *sayyiʾah*, *ḥasanah* are more evaluative than descriptive. And the words that have been dealt with in the last section belong definitely to the secondary-level moral discourse. Earlier, in Chapter I, I have made this point clear by comparing *kufr* with *dhanb*. The former, as we saw, has a concrete descriptive content, while the job of the latter consists in classifying this very semantic content of *kufr*—together with others—in the category of reprehensible and punishable acts.

As I said at the outset, the system of the Qurʾanic ethico-religious concepts is linguistically based on the working of the primary-level language. And the development of a well-organized secondary-level language generally known as the 'five legal categories' is largely the work of the later jurists. And yet, we have to admit also that the Qurʾān itself has a super-structure—although still a very simple one —of a network of secondary-level moral concepts.

# CONCLUSION

We may do well to remember that this book, in the original edition, was entitled *The Structure of the Ethical Terms in the Koran.* By the word 'structure' I meant 'semantic constitution'. Not only does each key concept have its own peculiar connotative structure, but also the entire body of key concepts has itself a more or less closed and independent structure—a system which is, in turn, divisible into a number of subsystems.

The whole matter is based on the fundamental idea that each linguistic system—Arabic is one, and Qurʾanic Arabic is another—represents a group of co-ordinated concepts which, together, reflect a particular *Weltanschauung*, commonly shared by, and peculiar to, the speakers of the language in question. Thus Qurʾanic Arabic corresponds, in its connotative aspect, to what we may rightly call the Qurʾanic world-view, which in itself is simply a segment of that wider world-view mirrored by the classical Arabic language. In exactly the same way, the ethical language of the Qurʾān represents only a segment of the whole Qurʾanic world-view. And the ethico-religious terms constitute a small, relatively independent, system within that ethical segment.

It is solely in relation to this ethico-religious system that each of the terms we have examined acquires its peculiar meaning. Once we have begun to understand the 'meaning' of words in this sense, it becomes obvious that we cannot hope to get at it simply by consulting dictionaries. A special method must be devised whereby we may observe the behavior of each key term in all its concrete verbal contexts. There must, in other words, be a method which will let the Qur'anic terms explain themselves.

In the first section, I have discussed in some detail a method by which we can successfully isolate the connotative structure of each key term. The second and third parts purport to give the main results obtained by the practical application of that method.

The second section is the only historical part of this book. It deals with the transition period which, on the one hand, definitely separates the pre-Islamic age from the Islamic, but which, on the other, connects the two in an extremely subtle way. Semantically, it is one of the most interesting periods in the whole history of Islamic thought; not only because it marks the very beginning of Islām itself, but also because, on a more theoretical level, it throws a full light on the dramatic process by which a traditionally fixed system of values comes to be replaced by a new one. The period, in other words, illustrates the semantic phenomenon in which the key terms forming a system are disintegrated, transformed in their connotative structure, modified in their combinations, and, with the addition of a number of new key terms, finally integrated into an entirely different system.

The matter can be formulated in more concrete terms. It is commonly imagined that the birth of Islām had almost nothing to do with pre-Islamic paganism, that Islām meant a complete and definite break with the preceding period of idolatry. This is certainly true to a large extent. In fact the Qur'anic revelation marked the birth of something entirely new, religiously as well as culturally. It was undoubtedly something unprecedented in the history of the Arabs. It was, in short, a spiritual revolution causing remarkable repercussions in many walks of life, both social and personal, so that even the material side of Arab life was gravely affected by it.

And yet in one respect there is a clear and undeniable connection between the Arabian polytheistic paganism and Islamic monotheism. In my recent work, ***God and Man in the Koran*** (Tokyo, 1964), I have shown that many of the key concepts of the Qur'ān relating to the basic relations between God and man were just a subtly transformed continuation of the pre-Islamic, genuinely Arab conception. Even the connotation of the name Allāh is shown to be no new invention of the Qur'anic revelation. And the same is true of the ethical terms in the Qur'ān.

We would be seriously mistaken and do gross injustice to the pre-

Islamic Arabs if we imagined, because of the low standard of their religious conception and the dominant note of hedonism and sensualism in their poetry, that they were devoid of high moral values. On the contrary, their life was in reality regulated by the rigorous moral code of *murūwah*, consisting of a number of important concepts such as 'courage', 'patience', 'generosity', and 'imperturbable mind'. These moral concepts are of such a nature that their eternal and universal values would be recognized in any age and by any people. But, because it was entirely based on narrow tribalism, the moral code of *murūwah* had a peculiar coloring which kept it from being universally valid.

Some of the pre-Islamic values were totally rejected by the Qur'ān. But most of them were accepted, modified, and developed, in accordance with the demands of the new religion. The old values, thus radically transformed and entirely cut off from the traditional tribal mode of life, were reborn as new ethico-religious values and came to form an integral part of the Islamic system. It is this process of inner transformation of the Arab moral concepts, together with various problems that were raised by it, that I have studied from the semantic point of view in the second part of the present study.

In the third section I have tried to analyze the Qur'anic system of ethico-religious concepts against the historical background described in the second part. I have shown how this system, one aspect of the Qur'anic world-view, is based on a very simple, but very strong and vigorous dichotomy of 'good' and 'bad'. The Qur'ān, instead of using the concepts of good and bad in a more or less abstract fashion, judges human conduct and character in a very concrete form: *īmān* and *kufr*, each surrounded by a host of related concepts, constitute the two pillars of Qur'anic ethics. Human conduct and behavior are described and evaluated mostly in the ethical language of the primary level. The elaboration of an ethical metalanguage is left as a task for the jurists of the coming ages.

It goes without saying that, in the Qur'ān, religion is the source and ultimate ground of all things. In this sense, the ethico-religious concepts are the most important and most basic of all that have to do with morality. Moreover, Islamic thought at its Qur'anic stage, makes no real distinction between the religious and the ethical. The ethical language of the Qur'ān, however, has another important field, composed of key concepts relating to social ethics. This field too is essentially of a religious nature, since all rules of conduct are ultimately dependent upon divine commands and prohibitions. But its concepts concern horizontal relations between human beings living in the same religious community, while the ethico-religious concepts concern vertical relations between human beings and God.

In view of the fact that the Qur᾿anic teaching was destined to develop not only as a religion but also as a culture and a civilization, we have to admit the supreme importance of the field of social ethics, which consists of concepts relating to the daily life of the people in society. And the Qur᾿ān, particularly in the Medina period, has much to say about community life. This side of Qur᾿anic ethics has not been systematically explored in the present work. To do so, another book will have to be written.

# INDEX OF QUR'ANIC CITATIONS

10

# INDEX OF ARABIC WORDS[1]



[1] This index lists all Arabic words that are italicized in the text. The Arabic words are listed under their respective roots which are arranged in the order of the Arabic alphabet. The sub-classification of derivative forms from each root is, however, listed in the order of the English alphabet.

akhlaṣnā, 193
khāliṣ, 193
khāliṣah, 193
mukhliṣ, 192, 193
mukhliṣīn lahu al-dīn, 192
kh–l–ā
khalī, 56
kh–w–f
akhāfu, 199
khāfa, 150, 199
khāfū, 199
khawf, 196, 198, 199
khawfan, 199
khawwafa, 198
khīfah, 198
nukhawwifu, 199
takhāf, 198
takhāfū, 199
takhwīf, 198, 199, 201
yakhāfu, 198
alladhīna, yakhāfūn, 199
yukhawwifu, 199
kh–w–n
khāʾin, 94, 95, 96
khāʾinīn, 94, 95
khāna, 95
khawwān, 95, 96
khiyānah, 91, 92, 94, 95, 97
kh–y–r
akhyār, 220
khayr, 21, 38, 39 202, 213, 216, 217, 218, 219, 220, 221, 222, 223
khayrāt, 205, 219
d–n–á
al-dunyā, 108
d–h–r
dahr, 47
d–w–n
dīwān, 49
dh–k–r
dhākir Allāh, 110
dhikr, 193, 194
dhikrá, 128
dh–n–b
dhanb, 21, 22, 24, 38, 227, 228, 242, 243, 246, 247, 249
dhunūb, 207, 228, 242, 243, 247
r–j–s
rijs, 240, 241, 249
r–ḥ–m
irḥam, 19
raḥīm, 19, 110
raḥmah, 19, 219, 220, 226
r–sh–d
rashād, 194, 195
rashad, 194, 195
rashada, 194
rashīd, 194
rushd, 194, 195
r–k–b
murtakib kabīrah, 157
r–k–n
arkān, 109
r–h–b
irhabū, 200
rahbah, 200
rāhib, 157, 200
rahiba, 199, 200
r–y–b
irtabtum, 181
murtāb, 176
r–y–n
rāna, 128
z–k–y
zakāt, 78, 115
z–n–m
zanīm, 57, 115
z–y–gh
tuzigh, 138
zāgha, 137
zaygh, 137, 138, 140
s–j–n
Sijjīn, 163
s–ḥ–t
akkālūna lil-suḥt, 239
suḥut, 239
s–kh–r
istaskhara, 153
ittakhadha sikhrīyan, 153
ittakhadhtumūhum sikhrīyan, 153
sakhira, 153
yaskharūna, 153
yastaskhirūna, 153
s–r–r
sarrāʾ, 38

ṭ–w–ᶜ
ṭāᶜah, 216
–y–b
ṭayyib, 235, 236, 239
al-kalim al-ṭayyib, 235
balad ṭayyib, 235
masākin ṭayyibah, 235
rīḥ ṭayyibah, 235
ṭayyibāt, 235, 236, 239
ṭayyibīn, 235, 236
ẓ–l–m
aẓlam, 40, 248
lā tuẓlamūna, 167
yaẓlim, 165
yaẓlimūn, 172
yuẓlamūna, 165, 209
ẓalama, 146, 166
ẓalamū, 141, 171, 172, 225, 228, 242
alladhīna ẓalamū, 169, 227
ẓālim, 18, 24, 25, 40, 41, 113, 137, 139, 156, 164, 165, 166, 167, 168, 169, 170, 171, 172, 174, 176, 196
ẓālimīn, 25, 33, 139, 141, 171, 196, 246, 247
ẓālimūn, 41, 137, 167, 170, 171, 209
ẓallām, 18, 165
ẓalūm, 122
ẓulimu, 168
ẓulm, 18, 136, 139, 147, 156, 164, 165, 166, 167, 168, 169, 170, 171, 172, 173, 174, 209, 227, 239, 242
ẓulm al-nafs, 166, 167, 233, 242
ẓulman, 169
ẓ–n–n
ẓann, 132, 133, 141
ẓānnīn, 231
ᶜ–b–d
ᶜabd, 65
ᶜ–t–l
ᶜutul, 115
ᶜ–t–ā
ᶜatā, 146, 148, 149
ᶜataw, 149
ᶜatat, 149
ᶜutūwan, 148
ᶜ–d–l
ᶜadl, 91, 210, 211, 234
iᶜdilū, 210
taᶜdilū, 210, 211
ᶜ–d–ā
ᶜadūna, 173
ᶜadw, 147
iᶜtada, 172, 173, 174
iᶜtadaw, 173
iᶜtadaynā, 172
iᶜtidāᵓ, 156, 174
muᶜtadī, 115, 156, 163, 172, 174
muᶜtadīn, 172, 173
taᶜtadū, 172, 173
ᶜudwān, 239
yaᶜdūna, 173
yaᶜtadūna, 174, 217
ᶜ–dh–b
ᶜadhāb, 134, 135
ᶜ–r–f
maᶜrūf, 205, 213, 214, 215, 216, 217, 221
maᶜrūfan, 215
ᶜurf, 216
ᶜ–z–z
ᶜizzah, 70
ᶜ–ṣ–b
ᶜaṣabīyah, 56, 59
ᶜ–ṣ–f
rīḥ ᶜāṣifah, 235
ᶜ–ṣ–á
ᶜaṣá, 137, 174
ᶜaṣaw, 174, 217
ᶜaṣayta, 147
ᶜāṣī, 114, 152
ᶜiṣyān, 188
maᶜṣiyah, 227
maᶜāṣī, 216, 228
ᶜ–q–b
ᶜaqabah, 69
ᶜ–l–m
ᶜilm, 28, 132, 133, 141
rāsikhūn fī al-ᶜilm, 138
ᶜ–l–ā
ᶜālī, 144, 145, 146
ᶜulūw, 144
ᶜulūwan, 144
ᶜ–m–l
ᶜamal, 206
ᶜ–m–h
ᶜamaha, 138, 150

# INDEX OF SUBJECTS